Lady of the Lotus-Born

LADY OF THE LOTUS-BORN

THE LIFE AND ENLIGHTENMENT OF YESHE TSOGYAL

Translated by
THE PADMAKARA TRANSLATION GROUP

A Translation of
The Lute Song of the Gandharvas
A Revelation in Eight Chapters of the Secret History of the Life and Enlightenment of Yeshe Tsogyal, Queen of Tibet

A Treasure text committed to writing by
GYALWA CHANGCHUB *and* NAMKHAI NYINGPO

Discovered by
TERTÖN TAKSHAM SAMTEN LINGPA

Foreword by
JIGME KHYENTSE RINPOCHE

SHAMBHALA
Boston & London
2002

Shambhala Publications, Inc.
Horticultural Hall
300 Massachusetts Avenue
Boston, Massachusetts 02115
www.shambhala.com

9 8 7 6 5 4 3

Printed in the United States of America
♾ This edition is printed on acid-free paper that meets the American National Standards Institute Z39.48 Standard.
♻ This book was printed on 30% postconsumer recycled paper.
For more information please visit us at www.shambhala.com.
Distributed in the United States by Random House, Inc., and in Canada by Random House of Canada Ltd

The Library of Congress catalogs the previous edition of this book as follows:

Nam-mkha 'i-snying -po, 8th/9th cent.
[Bod kyi jo mo Ye-śes Mtsho-rgyal gyi mdzad tshul
rnam par thar pa khab po mṅon buyṅ rgyud maṅs dri za 'i
glu phreṅ. English]
Lady of the lotus-born: the life and enlightenment of
Yeshe-Tsogyal/ Namkhai Nyingpo and Gyalwa Changchub;
discovered by Tertön Taksham Samten Lingpa;
translated by the Padmakara Translation Group.—1st ed.
p. cm.
ISBN 978-1-57062-384-4
ISBN 978-1-57062-544-2 (pbk.)
1. Ye-śes-mtsho-rgyal, 8th century. 2. Yogis—China—Tibet—
Biography—Early works to 1800. 3. Yoga (Tantric Buddhism)—
Early works to 1800.
I. Gyalwa Changchub. II. Tertön Taksham Samten Lingpa.
III. Title.
BQ998.E757N35I3 1998 98-6838
294.3'923'092—dc21 CIP
[b]

Contents

❀

Foreword

THE STORY OF the life of Yeshe Tsogyal is not merely an absorbing historical document. It is, above all, one of the most inspiring examples of how the Buddha's teachings may be put into practice.

In the early days of Buddhism in Tibet, many of the sacred texts were translated several times from Sanskrit, each version complementing the others and contributing to a complete understanding of the original. In the same spirit, although this extraordinarily important text has already been made available to English readers by the skilled efforts both of Tarthang Rinpoche and his students and of our friend Keith Dowman, we feel that in these early days of Buddhism in the West, to produce another translation, as a way of further acquainting ourselves with the life of Yeshe Tsogyal, may be of some benefit. Throughout this undertaking, we have felt an immense gratitude to all the great masters of our tradition, whose compassionate activities have kept Yeshe Tsogyal's teachings a living source of inspiration even today.

The question is sometimes asked whether Buddhism is a system of belief and practice applicable only in a particular social context. This text, however, describes for us a struggle for spiritual freedom in a whole range of existential predicaments: those of princess, renunciate, ascetic, or teacher, to name but a few—a whole spectrum of circumstances on which the teachings shed their light and open up new and fresh opportunities. Again, it might be suggested that the tradition of Tibetan Buddhism, in the development of which Yeshe Tsogyal played such a crucial role, is something suitable only for Tibetans. But here again, we find that for Yeshe Tsogyal herself, the Buddhadharma was far from being a foreign, exotic practice imported from India; it was the means to reach the very essence of human experience. Neither is it possible to dismiss this text as the glorification of arduous trials. For on the contrary, it is clear that Yeshe Tsogyal consciously decided to tell her story as a help to us in our own lives. She simply shares, without asking for pity or admiration— presenting her experience not as "mystical" or superhuman, but as something profoundly natural and human. Her youthful disillusionment with the ways of the world, her introduction to the teachings, and her training in them, step by step, are all told simply and straightforwardly. Not once do we see her reacting to the desperate situations she finds herself in with self-pity or a tortured sense of martyrdom. In fact, it is her ability to make positive and creative use of whatever came her way that is the greatest of all the messages that come to us in her wonderful biography. It is this that makes her life so extraordinary. May all who read it find encouragement and inspiration!

JIGME KHYENTSE RINPOCHE
Padmakara
March 1995

Acknowledgments

THE PRESENT VERSION of the *Yeshe Tsogyal Namthar* grew out of a project to make the work available in French, and it has been a labor of love rather than the expression of any kind of rivalry or the pretension to improve on the already existing translations of Ven. Tarthang Tulku and Keith Dowman. The text is difficult, spectacularly so in many places. Given its subject matter, this is hardly surprising, but in any case the text is ancient and has many old words and expressions. The translation no doubt has many defects, but this has nothing to do with the eminent authorities who were consulted as often as was possible. In particular we wish to express our profound gratitude to the late Kyabje Dilgo Khyentse Rinpoche, who graciously answered questions on difficult points during his last visit to the West in 1991. Likewise, we owe a great debt of gratitude to Khetsun Zangpo Rinpoche, who generously gave of his time to clarify many passages. Very particularly, we wish to thank Alak Zenkar Rinpoche, who had the kindness to go through the entire text with us and who, with his prodigious knowledge of the Tibetan language, was able to shed light on many a mysterious expression. For it turned out that the text contains many words that have wholly disappeared from standard Tibetan in both its colloquial and erudite forms but that have survived in the language of the nomads of the great plains of north and east Tibet—among whom Alak Zenkar was born and with whose dialects he is familiar. Finally, as always, we wish to express our deepest thanks to our teachers, Taklung Tsetrul Pema Wangyal Rinpoche and Jigme Khyentse Rinpoche, who bestowed the transmission of the text and constantly encouraged us in the work of translation.

Lady of the Lotus-Born was translated by the Padmakara Translation Group, which on this occasion consisted of Helena Blankleder and Wulstan Fletcher. The translators would like to thank their readers for their valuable suggestions: Michal Abrams, Barbara Gethin, Ani Ngawang Chödrön, Charles Hastings, Anne Benson, Adrian Gunther, Geoffrey Gunther, Vivian Kurz, Pamela Low, and Jenny Kane.

Translators' Introduction

THE TEXT translated in these pages is the life story of one of the founders of the Tibetan Buddhist tradition and without a doubt one of the most extraordinary women in the history of world religion. She lived during the heroic age of the Tibetan kings whose empire, then at the peak of its strength, extended far to the east into present-day China and to the north and west into the remote regions of Central Asia, and dominated the entire Himalayan region to the south. Her life unfolded at a crucial moment in the history of her country when the rich and fully developed Buddhist tradition of the sutras and the tantras was being introduced from India and propagated under royal patronage. It was a time of great events and powerful personalities.

Lady of the Lotus-Born is by any standards a masterpiece of literature. Its colorful and lively narrative, the lyrical beauty of its poetry, the profundity of its doctrinal teaching, and its absorbing historical and cultural interest are perfectly balanced and arranged with artistry and finesse. As such, it is easily accessible, and even readers who know little of Tibet or the Buddhist path will be intrigued and charmed by it. The storyline indeed is so well handled and the characterization so vivid and convincing that at times it is not difficult to overlook the fact that this is a text of great antiquity. In point of fact, the life of Yeshe Tsogyal has a peculiar modernity of its own, although not in the ordinary sense of the word. The reason for saying this is that, however exotic and remote certain aspects of the text may appear to the majority of modern readers, *Lady of the Lotus-Born* belongs to a spiritual and cultural tradition that is still vibrantly alive. It expresses ideas and values that for practitioners of the Buddhist path remain living issues of great relevance.

In contrast with the history of Europe and America, the pace of political and social change in Tibet was, until the upheavals of the second half of the twentieth century, extremely slow, allowing the study and practice of Buddhism to proceed steadily, undisturbed by extraneous circumstances and in an atmosphere of almost perfect stability. This gave rise to a cultural continuity that the West has never known, and it may be said without exaggeration that in Tibet virtually the entire range of Buddhist doctrines, as they were extant in medieval India, have been completely and perfectly preserved until the present time. The Tibetan Buddhist tradition embodies to this day teachings and practices that were current and assiduously pursued at a time long before the cultures and even the languages of the modern West existed. So seamless is the tradition of Tibetan Buddhism that if one were to take a lama writing or commenting on a scripture at the end of the twentieth century and place him alongside one of his forebears of the tenth, one would discover a similarity of thought, expression, and attitude that renders them virtual contemporaries.

It is thus that *Lady of the Lotus-Born* has a timeless relevance. However mysterious certain parts of it may seem to the unfamiliar reader, the world described in its pages is still instantly recognizable to twentieth-century Tibetans. And to Tibetan Buddhist practitioners, the story of Yeshe Tsogyal's life and the teachings contained therein are still as pertinent and topical as they were in the eighth century. The same instructions given by Guru Rinpoche to Yeshe Tsogyal, and by Yeshe Tsogyal to her own disciples, are imparted by Tibetan lamas to this day.

The same meditation and yogas are still practiced and their extraordinary results are still attained, even now in the twentieth century.

Lady of the Lotus-Born belongs to the class of Tibetan literature known as *namthar*. It is a "tale of liberation," an account of spiritual endeavor and achievement. It is primarily addressed to Buddhist practitioners as an instruction and encouragement for the long and arduous path of inner transformation, holding up to their devotion an image of sublime attainment. Aside from being a good story, therefore, this text has a profoundly doctrinal content. It is a description of the tantric path and contains many references to the key points of the practice. These references are not for the most part explicit and are frequently couched in the allusive language of poetry and song, the sense of which will be clear only to those well versed in tantric doctrine.

That *Lady of the Lotus-Born* should in this way contain a "secret" component is, traditionally speaking, quite normal. For reasons that the text itself will make clear, the full instructions for the practices referred to are necessarily bestowed only in private by qualified masters and to disciples who have given evidence of their commitment to the teachings and are properly prepared for their reception and implementation.

Nevertheless, the presence of esoteric elements does not by any means render the text unintelligible for the general reader. On the contrary, it is in large measure intended for the edification and delight of everyone. With this in mind, it seems appropriate to discuss some of the broader issues apparent in the book and thus introduce a religious and cultural environment that some readers might find unfamiliar.

Prehistory, Birth, and Early Life

Given that the historical existence of Yeshe Tsogyal is beyond question, and in view of the extraordinary realism and humanity with which her character emerges in the course of the text, modern readers are likely to find the "mythological," almost fairy-tale account of her birth and early years rather perplexing. To be sure, the miraculous circumstances seem to parallel the extraordinary events attending the nativities of the heroic figures of other religions and cultures. All the marvelous accompaniments are there: the shooting star, the strange and prophetic dreams, the mysterious messengers, the painless birth, the appearance of celestial beings and other wonderful portents. And when the child is born, she is of supernatural beauty and precocity. The approach of modern scholarship, from its essentially materialistic standpoint, is to dismiss such events as apocryphal and legendary. In the present case, before jumping to such hasty conclusions, it is important to remember that from a doctrinal point of view, the elements described in the early pages of *Lady of the Lotus-Born* are heavy with meaning. And it is worth remembering that, as a matter of fact, in the discovery of tulkus or incarnate lamas, which continues to be a highly important feature of Tibetan culture, miraculous omens are expected and taken seriously.

Yeshe Tsogyal was, as the text makes plain, a key figure in the introduction and consolidation of the Buddhist teachings in Tibet. She was the disciple and assistant of Padmasambhava, the Lotus-Born Guru, the Indian master invited by the king Trisong Detsen to subdue by tantric means the hostile forces that were hindering the propagation of the Doctrine. So closely was she involved in this work that the story of her life is practically coterminous with the foundation of Buddhism in her country, specifically the teachings of the tantras. Her appearance in the world is therefore not presented as something haphazard, the chance birth of an ordinary being; it is an event of great and far-reaching significance. Yeshe Tsogyal is the predestined assistant of Guru Rinpoche (as Padmasambhava is often called); indeed, she is the indispensable condition for the establishment of the Buddhist teachings. It is for this reason that the first figure to appear in *Lady of the Lotus-Born* is not Yeshe Tsogyal herself, but Guru Rinpoche. "That I might propagate the teachings of the Secret Mantra," he reflects, "the time has come for an incarnation of goddess Sarasvati to appear." And it is as if he literally calls Tsogyal into existence. For without her, as he later explains to the king, the results of his labors would be meager and slow.

In the account of Yeshe Tsogyal's preexistence and her descent to earth, two distinct but interpenetrating ideas may be discerned. To begin with, in view of Buddhist teachings on reincarnation, the notion that she should have "preexisted" is not in itself extraordinary. Moreover, it is normal in Buddhist tradition for the biographies of important persons to begin with references to a line of previous and distinguished incarnations. The obvious purpose of this is to inform the readers that they are in the presence of a great and noble being. More important is the fact that such details underline the fundamental doctrine of karma, whereby character, talents, inclinations, and circumstances, as these manifest in the course of a single life, helping or hindering in the spiritual quest, are all attributable to previous causes. The facts of encountering the Dharma, meeting a teacher, and having an inclination to practice his instructions and the possibility of doing so are all regarded as the fruits of merit, the positive "energy" amassed through virtuous deeds in the past. Consequently, as the preliminary to her encounter with the great Guru and the gaining of a life situation in which his teachings would be implemented to great effect, we read that Tsogyal had "accumulated merit and purified defilements for numbered and unnumbered ages, sending forth great waves of goodness for all that lives." From this point of view, Tsogyal's life is to be seen as the final stage in a long karmic sequence. It was the point at which, as Guru Rinpoche himself said,[1] lingering obstacles were exhausted and dispelled, and the vast deposit of meritorious potential burst into flower.

This essentially evolutionary idea is combined with another

fundamental notion of Mahayana Buddhism. Not only is Tsogyal said to have amassed immense reserves of merit, she is referred to as a Nirmanakaya, an already enlightened being who "came down to earth" in order to set forth the path of Dharma by word and example. Her appearance in eighth century Tibet was, according to this perspective, but one example of the "dancing transmutation of her form" so delightful to the Buddhas of the three times. Not only does she teach through the great unfolding of her wisdom, her life itself is seen as a kind of didactic drama, demonstrating the possibility of inner development and the attainment of the final fruit.

An essential feature of the Nirmanakaya, the perceptible form of an enlightened being, is that while issuing from a transmundane source, it appears perfectly according to the needs of beings and within the range and expectancies implicit in their perceptions. The Nirmanakaya is fully accessible at the level at which it manifests; its primary function is to communicate and to teach. If addressed to humans, it will appear in perfectly human terms and within a network of authentic human relationships, thereby enabling ordinary mortals to enter into genuine contact with it and to progress beyond their limitations. Traditionally, therefore, the idea of Tsogyal's being a Nirmanakaya is not understood as in any way attenuating her humanity or the reality of the weaknesses and obstacles that she must struggle against and surmount.

Another important point to bear in mind is that, according to Buddhist teaching, Buddhahood is not a samsaric event. It transcends the world and cannot be located within the spatial and temporal continuum of unenlightened existence. As Guru Rinpoche says to the king, it is "uncaused, unwrought."[2] It is outside time and the chronological sequence of past, present and future. It is therefore highly meaningful to describe Yeshe Tsogyal as being enlightened even before she engages in the practices that "give rise" to her attainment. Moreover, according to the Nyingma, the most ancient school of Tibetan Buddhism, the Tathagatagarbha, or Buddha-nature, is considered not as a mere potential, but as the true nature of the mind endowed with all the qualities of wisdom. Present in every sentient being, though veiled by adventitious defilement, it is already perfect and fully accomplished. From this perspective, the preliminary chapters of *Lady of the Lotus-Born* may be read as a description of Tsogyal's essential dignity. Her progress towards enlightenment is not so much the "gaining" of something not yet possessed but the disclosure of an already innate perfection. What at the end of the book shines forth in the person of Tsogyal is, however obscured, equally present and equally perfect in every living being.

Teacher and Disciple

Buddhism in general, and Tibetan Buddhism in particular, is well known for placing great emphasis on the importance of finding an authentic teacher and following his or her instructions. The tradition moreover provides extensive criteria whereby the qualities of a possible teacher should be assessed and a judgment made between an authentic master and a charlatan.[3] Buddhism is not a proselytizing faith and Buddhist masters do not advertise themselves or go out in search of followers. It is always for the disciples to make the first move, and they should do so with eyes wide open. Once the teacher has been chosen and the disciple accepted, the resulting relationship must likewise unfold according to certain important principles. This is the central theme of *Lady of the Lotus-Born* and Tsogyal herself exemplifies both terms of the relationship, first as disciple and later as the Guru herself. In chapter four, she describes at length the samaya, or sacred bond, that such a relationship implies.

At the most fundamental level, the importance of the spiritual master derives from the simple fact of our own humanity. Our ability to encounter and assimilate the knowledge that will activate the full potential of the human state depends upon the doctrine appearing to us in ways that are humanly intelligible. Thus the transmission of Dharma requires language, encounter, and human relationships. This may seem a very obvious point, but in practice, a fruitful meeting with the Dharma is far from being a universal fact of experience and is closely tied up with karma and merit, as mentioned earlier. Some people find the Dharma easily and progress swiftly; others find it only rarely and with great difficulty; some encounter it and fail to recognize its worth. And there are some who never find it.

In this connection, it is interesting to consider the general Buddhist view according to which the mind-stream, as it occurs in every sentient being, is something endless and beginningless. It has no assignable origin whether synchronously, in terms of a single moment of analysis, or chronologically, in the sense of being an endless continuum stretching back to infinity through countless eons of time. Grounded in the deluded notion of self, sentient beings seek to achieve their aims, to find happiness and avoid suffering, according to the dualistic interplay of "I" and "other," self and external phenomena. But because phenomena are impermanent, this situation is intrinsically unstable. Beings therefore pass through an unending sequence of states, more or less protracted, cognized as pleasure or pain, all transient and all incapable of bringing lasting satisfaction. This process is not only unlimited, it is uncontrolled and unpredictable even though, within certain broad parameters, it is endlessly repetitive and devoid of purpose. This is the definition of samsara. As the experience of unenlightened beings, it has always been the case and, left to itself, it will continue forever. But since, according to Buddhism, samsara is grounded in the deluded way in which the mind apprehends reality, it is itself illusory and contingent. Samsaric experience reflects not the essential nature of the mind but only its ignorance. It arises adventitiously to the mind's true nature, which is said to be primordially perfect and unsullied by the veils of karma and emotion that cover it. It is neither damaged by the condition of samsara nor improved by the freedom of nirvana. For the vast majority of beings, this nature is utterly concealed, an unsuspected treasure lying long buried in oblivion. And yet it is not remote; it is intimately present in the heart of everyone, so much so that it is sometimes said that its very closeness is what renders it so invisible. Neither is it something inert and lifeless. It responds to stimuli and, in the continuum of a given mindstream, begins to open and manifest in proportion as actions are accumulated that are positive and unselfish and that tend away from the egocentricity that is samsara's root. Such actions produce the wholesome energy that, for want of a better word, we have referred to as "merit"—although when using this word in a Buddhist context, it is important to abstract from it the notion of rewards and punishments.

As "merit" increases, the Buddha-nature begins very gradually to stir. Within the mind, a certain interest in spiritual values will begin to constellate, and at the same time, like an answering echo, signs of the doctrine will slowly start to appear in outer experience. Metaphorically speaking, these could be seen as the externalization or projection of the Buddha-nature manifesting from within. A person in whom such a process begins to unfold will imperceptibly gravitate towards spiritual teaching, finding himself in situations where instruction and the practice become possible. He will come into contact with teachers who can lead him on the path, and finally he will meet a master who is able to place him in the ultimate state of freedom, introducing him, in a way that far exceeds a merely intellectual comprehension, to his own true and primordially perfect nature. This final encounter is the most crucial meeting in the person's entire samsaric existence. For it is here that the interdependent process just described reaches its completion and fulfillment. It might be said that the appearance of such a master is the last manifestation of the person's Buddha-nature on the dualistic level—his function being to bring the disciple to the direct experience of that nature, the discovery of the so-called inner Guru, the Guru within.

With this in mind, we are better able to appreciate the significance of the meeting between Yeshe Tsogyal and Guru Padmasambhava, the end point of a process on the relative level stretching back to beginningless time. When the perfect master and the perfect disciple meet, complete transmission is possible. As Tsogyal herself says: "All the teachings of the Buddha were present in the precious Master Padmasambhava. He was like a vessel filled to overflowing. And after I had served him in the three ways pleasing to a teacher, all that he possessed he gave to me, the woman Yeshe Tsogyal. He poured it out as from one vase into another." It was with Guru Rinpoche that Tsogyal traversed the final stages of her spiritual quest; it was he who revealed in her the enlightenment of her true nature. The climax of this process is described midway through chapter seven at the point where Guru Rinpoche takes his final leave from Tibet.[4] It is a moment of intense anguish for Tsogyal when we are afforded a glimpse of what the relationship with Guru Rinpoche meant for her in human terms. In reply to her impassioned pleas, the Guru sings to her his final teaching, in the course of which he says:

> In the supreme body of a woman you have gained
> accomplishment;
> Your mind itself is Lord; request him for empowerment
> and blessing.
> There is no other regent of the Lotus Guru. . . .

He then goes on to give an exposition of Guru yoga, the meditative practice of union with the Guru, the single most powerful and important practice in the entire range of Buddhist teaching, specifically designed to bring about the culmination of the process that we have just been describing. In conclusion he exclaims:

Nothing will surpass this, Mistress Tsogyal!
Padmasambhava's compassion neither ebbs nor flows;
The rays of my compassion for Tibet cannot be severed.
There I am in front of anyone who prays to me—
Never will I separate from those with faith. . . .

So he departs; and for Tsogyal there is nothing but darkness. "It was," she said, "like waking in the morning from a dream." And yet, in the midst of utmost desolation, realization occurred. "I gained a fearless confidence; the nest of hopes and fears fell to nothing and the torment of defiled emotion was cleared away. I experienced directly that the Teacher was inseparable from myself, and with much devotion I opened the mandala of the *Lama Sangwa Düpa*." Thus she describes in simple, understated terms what must have been one of the most important experiences of her life. The "Lady" and the "Lotus-Born" were joined henceforth in inseparable union.

From then on, Tsogyal becomes the Guru's representative or rather the Guru herself, entrusted with the work of completion. She instructs the king, guides the country, builds up the monastic and lay communities, and conceals the Dharma Treasures. She labors for many years, becoming the focus of an immense concourse of disciples. When the time comes for her own departure, the heartbreaking scene so poignantly described in chapter seven is repeated, although this time it is described at greater length and is accompanied by many teachings and prophecies. The same lamentations are heard, the same admonitions given. Thus, in her advice to Ma Rinchen Chok, Lady Tsogyal advises him to practice Guru yoga and follows this injunction with an astonishingly explicit statement of her true identity as a fully enlightened Buddha, the personification of the wisdom nature.

Meditate upon the Teacher as the glow of your awareness.
When you melt and mingle mutually together,

Taste that vast expanse of nonduality.
There remain.

And if you know me, Yeshe Tsogyal,
Mistress of samsara and nirvana,
You will find me dwelling in the heart of every being.
The elements and senses are my emanations,
And emanated thence, I am the twelvefold chain of co-production:
Thus primordially we never separate.
I seem a separate entity
Because you do not know me.

Later on, before a large and less intimate audience, the same point is made although in a more forthright, lighthearted manner:

Listen to me! Stop your wailing!
My love for you is totally unchanging.
You're acting just like those who cling to permanence!
I have not died. I have not left you, nor departed anywhere.
Pray to me and you will truly see my face.

It is evident from these few remarks that the bond between an authentic teacher and a true disciple is qualitatively different from any ordinary relationship. Paradoxically, for reasons that have been explained and as *Lady of the Lotus-Born* abundantly shows, it is a profoundly human contact and in fact cannot be otherwise. Furthermore, since the teacher must appear in human form, it follows that "he" must be either male or female, and this has obvious implications for the teacher-disciple relationship, which must be played out accordingly. Experience shows that this can involve difficulties for the disciples. It is a delicate area and a fertile field for potential obstacles. In the nature of things, the teacher very often appears as someone profoundly attractive and this can easily trigger the natural emotional responses of samsaric beings who crave exclusive and reciprocal relationships.

This last point, in which the question of devotion is involved, is an important point for disciples of both sexes. As *Lady of the Lotus-Born* makes clear, the authenticity of Tsogyal's devotion and the purity of her approach to the teacher was at all times unshakable and unimpaired. Never for a moment was Guru Rinpoche for her anything other than the perfect embodiment of enlightenment: "Buddha in human form whom I revere!" And never for a moment was Tsogyal's life anything but the perfect example of discipleship. Later however, to her own disciples, she spells out in explicit terms the peculiar nature of the guru-disciple relationship and the correct attitude that should be cultivated. At one point she says:

> Therefore give your ears to my teaching.
> Supplicate and pray to your root guru
> With pure vision, faith and strong devotion,
> Never for an instant thinking
> She's a friend on equal terms.
> Request her blessing and the four empowerments.
> Meditate upon her vivid presence,
> Never parted from you in the center of your heart.

And later, in her song to Gyalwa Changchub, who in his previous life had been her spiritual companion Arya Salé, Tsogyal celebrates the excellent fortune of their association, but then goes on to chide him gently for times when his view of her, his teacher, had been impaired by "ordinariness" and wrong thoughts. From what has been seen in the preceding paragraphs, the profound reason for devotion to the Guru will be evident. It is the means whereby the mind is opened to the transmission of the teachings, the sole environment in which introduction to the inner Guru can take place.

Tantra

The beginning of the fourth chapter informs us that having become the consort of Guru Rinpoche, Yeshe Tsogyal begins her study of the teachings, and it is briefly specified that she received the complete transmission of the Hinayana and Mahayana doctrines together with the instructions connected with the three classes of the outer tantras. This was a preliminary and foundation to the main practice described in *Lady of the Lotus-Born,* which centers around the three inner tantras of Maha-, Anu-, and Atiyoga.

The tantras, which are the almost exclusive preserve of Tibetan Buddhism, form part of the teachings of the Mahayana, the Buddhism of the Great Vehicle. Like the Mahayana sutras, they are animated by the attitude of bodhichitta, the determination to attain supreme Buddhahood for the sake of all beings. A number of features distinguish the tantric teachings, or Vajrayana, from those of the sutra. One of these is the great variety of skillful means whereby the process of attainment is vastly accelerated. According to the sutra teachings, the two accumulations of wisdom and merit required to produce the state of enlightenment are expected to require continuous practice over a period of three countless eons. By contrast, through the implementation of the most advanced tantric yogas, and given favorable karmic circumstances, the fruit of Buddhahood may be actualized within the course of a single human life. Of these teachings, which in India had been secret and rare, Guru Padmasambhava was a supreme master, and it was due to his activity and blessing that they later came to be widely practiced and profoundly understood in Tibet.

The reason for the esoteric character of the tantric teachings is given by Guru Rinpoche to the king.[5] He says that they are kept secret not because they are in some way shameful or defective, but because their power renders them proportionately precious and perilous. Being profound, they are easily misunderstood and are to be transmitted only to appropriate persons at the right time. They are likened to the milk of the snow lion, an elixir of such potency that it will shatter a vessel of anything but the purest gold. Given the secret nature of tantric doctrine and practice, it may seem strange that *Lady of the Lotus-Born* refers so openly to it, and stranger still that such a book should be translated and published in English. In fact, the references in this text to the key points of the practice are, as we have already suggested, concealed in allusive and poetic language. They are powerfully evocative but do not in themselves constitute a method that the casual reader could hope to understand, let alone implement. A genuinely interested person should request instruction from a qualified teacher. Nevertheless, the fact that tantric teachings and practices are referred to in these pages means that *Lady of the Lotus-Born* also partakes of the precious and perilous nature of the tantras themselves. This being so, we feel strongly that it is important, and very much in the interest of those into whose possession it might come, that this book be treated with the respect normally given to sacred scriptures.

In contrast with the ascetic approach of the Hinayana teachings, and unlike the meditative antidotes used on the Mahayana sutra path to counteract emotional defilement, the Vajrayana is characterized by its direct utilization of emotion, as well as the psychophysical energies of the mind and body. The external supports of ritual, visualization, mantra recitation, and yoga are all of great importance. It is convenient to speak of the tantric path[6] in terms of four initiations or four levels of empowerment that introduce the disciple to the different aspects of the fully enlightened state. In the simplest terms, the first of the four initiations empowers the disciple to undertake the yogas of the Generation Stage. These aim at the realization of the true nature of all phenomena and mainly involve the practice of visualization and recitation. The second initiation introduces the disciple to the practices of the Perfection Stage, in which the subtle channels, energies and essences of his or her own body are meditated upon and brought under control. When this has been perfectly accomplished, the disciple is ready to receive the third initiation, which empowers him or her to practice a similar type of yoga but this time taking support of the body of another person, in other words a consort. Finally, the fourth initiation is directly concerned with the introduction to the nature of the mind itself. Yeshe Tsogyal successively implemented the practices of all four initiations. It will be seen how her reception of empowerment and transmission was usually accompanied by extraordinary signs and experiences of profound insight. Subsequently she practiced intensively in order to stabilize this experience and ripen it into full and indelible realization.

The most striking aspect of the yoga related with the third initiation, and one that many readers will find intriguing and perhaps troubling, is that it specifically involves the use of sexual energy. Given that the Vajrayana works directly with the emotions and utilizes various physical and psychic yogas, it would be surprising if it neglected what is after all a driving impulse in human existence. Even so, for many people, the idea of using the sexual act as a spiritual path may seem strange if not actually contradictory. Perhaps this is due to the fact that in Western religions (present mores notwithstanding) the morally correct environment for sexual activity is considered to be marriage, and the spiritual dimension of sex is intimately associated with the begetting of children. At the other end of the spectrum, it is evident in secular life that sex is often trivialized and debased in exploitative and degrading ways. These two contrasting attitudes are apt to complicate our approach to this aspect of the tantra, and in the task of translation it is hard to find a vocabulary able to express the notions of both physical intercourse and spiritual purity in ways that are not either unduly diffident or else tainted by prurience and vulgarity. In Tibetan Buddhism, the instructions associated with the third initiation are regarded as extremely high teachings and are the object of profound respect. They are not widely disseminated and, for reasons that will soon become obvious, are well beyond the reach of the majority of practitioners.

The ability to feel but not to crave, to experience and yet not hanker for more, or indeed for anything at all, is the mark of long training and a sign of great spiritual stature. The practice of the third initiation can only be implemented by people who are able to feel and yet remain without attachment, even in a situation of physical climax. It stands to reason that individuals who are genuinely able to practice in this way (as distinct from those who merely think they are) are few and far between. On the other hand, for those who can implement it, the yoga of the third initiation is said to be of immense power and swiftness. As is evident in the life of Yeshe Tsogyal, it is quick to engender high accomplishment. At the same time, it is a profoundly dangerous path, involving an area in which people are particularly fragile and prone to self-deceit. It is hazardous even for advanced and sincere practitioners because the arising of attachment can be extremely subtle, with the result that they may go astray and fall from the path. It is no doubt for this reason that few people are encouraged to attempt these practices. Active discouragement is much more likely to be encountered. In his commentary on the *Treasury of Precious Qualities*, Khenpo Yönten Gyatso says:

> The teachings say that those who take and practice explicitly the third initiation must have previously trained their own bodies by the path of skillful means, so that their subtle channels are perfectly straight, the wind-energy is purified and the essence-drops brought under control. Trained in the view of the two previous empowerments, they must be able to tread the path with the help of the extraordinary view and meditation, without any craving for pleasure. . . . If a beginner, who lacks this capacity,

> goes around claiming to be a practitioner of Mantra and becomes enmeshed in ordinary desire, he is destined for the lower realms. . . . It is better to practice according to one's true capacity and to the limit of one's ability, believing confidently in the principle of karma and with faith in the Three Jewels.[7]

As we have said, in this yoga, sexual energy is used in a way entirely cleansed of the impurities of ordinary passion and lust. As far as the characters in *Lady of the Lotus-Born* are concerned, it is hardly an exaggeration to say that what took place between them was not sex at all in the ordinary sense of the word, and that the practice evolved in the context of associations quite different from those of ordinary life. The relations between the protagonists were rooted entirely in the practice of Dharma and the commitments of samaya.

"I, The Woman Yeshe Tsogyal"

The life of Yeshe Tsogyal is a tale of supreme human achievement. That it is the story of a woman, and that it is told from a pointedly feminine point of view, makes it a uniquely interesting document. Nevertheless, although the book is naturally of particular significance for women, in that it vividly refers to many of the difficulties and frustrations that have beset religious women down through the centuries, it is important to realize that it is of wider import and embodies a universal message far beyond considerations of gender. It is not our intention here to get involved in controversy arising from the complex and sensitive issues raised by the current feminist debate. And yet within the context of Buddhism as a whole, it is impossible to overlook the fact that *Lady of the Lotus-Born* is unusually outspoken. And this is remarkable for its being such an ancient and traditional document.

Along with a number of other religious traditions, Buddhism

has been criticized for its failure, on the institutional level, to grant parity of status and opportunity to women, and its seemingly implied refusal to admit perfect equality between the sexes in terms of spiritual potential. It is an undeniable fact that, for instance, the Bhikshuni Sangha, or order of nuns, was founded later than that of the monks and apparently with some reluctance on the part of the Buddha. It is also a fact that on the level of Vinaya discipline, the nuns take vows that specifically subordinate them, administratively, to the male branch of the order. And in Tibet, for instance, it is noticeable that while womanhood is not a disqualification (as it is in some religions) from public positions of respect and influence in the religious hierarchy, the incidence of acknowledged female lamas (although high attainment among women has on all accounts been very considerable) is rare. How does all this tally with the fact that Buddhist teaching aims at states of liberation and enlightenment in which the physical and emotional distinctions that separate the sexes have no meaning?

To begin with, it is worth making the obvious but important point that institutional religion, regardless of its spiritual content, is in significant measure a purely human creation. It is conditioned by, and its administrative structures reflect, the societies in which it takes shape. Thus in the management of religious affairs, the relationship between the sexes has usually followed secular imperatives according to which human society traditionally presupposes the private domesticity of women encircled by the external, civic activities of men. While social considerations seem to have been decisive in the formation of institutional structures, this has of course not meant that women have been denied the possibility of engaging in spiritual practice. But though almost all traditions admit in theory that the ability to gain high levels of insight and sanctity is equal in both sexes, the fact remains that the practical possibilities open to women have in many societies often been defined and curtailed by essentially nonreligious considerations. In Buddhism, as we have said, the first disciples who followed the Buddha's call to embrace the life of homelessness were exclusively men. It was not long before women signaled their own intentions to do the same. In view of what has just been said, however, the Buddha's initial hesitation to ordain women and his subsequent insistence that the Bhikshuni Sangha should be subject to the administration of the monks, may be regarded as a reflection of the social patterns just outlined. And the apparent anxiety that it was necessary somehow to locate a group of unattached women within an outer masculine framework may well have been a measure necessary to ensure that the order of nuns would be intelligible and acceptable to the society at that time.[8] The arrangement was in other words dictated by historical and cultural considerations and need not be regarded as immutable in situations where such considerations no longer obtain.

Turning to *Lady of the Lotus-Born*, we find that practically the first picture we have of Tsogyal is of a young woman struggling desperately against the social pressures of her time. Despite her supplications, and forgetful of his wondering assessment of her as a young child, her father insists on her marriage. And she, in her bid for freedom, is subjected to cruelty and outrage. Later, she is obliged, and prepared, to follow a lonely path and is never spared the physical disadvantages of womanhood in a harsh and uncomprehending world. Witness the resentment seething behind the criticism of the royal ministers: "This girl of Kharchen has destroyed her reputation and is the ruin of her family. Will she now be left to bring disaster on the entire kingdom?" Tsogyal is routinely singled out for particular blame and as an object of spite.[9] At one point, she herself speaks her mind to Guru Rinpoche with extraordinary frankness. The circumstances were a request for a specific teaching, but in her outburst we can easily sense the years of struggle and frustration that lay behind it.

> . . . For I am a timid woman and of scant ability; of lowly condition, the butt of everyone. If I go for alms, I am set

upon by dogs; if food and riches come my way, I am the prey of thieves; since beautiful, I am the quarry of every lecherous knave; if I am busy with much to do, the country folk accuse me; if I don't do what they think I should, the people criticize; if I put a foot wrong, everyone detests me. I have to worry about everything I do. That is what it is like to be a woman! How can a woman possibly gain accomplishment in Dharma? Just managing to survive is already hard enough!

All this of course only serves to throw Yeshe Tsogyal's achievement into even sharper relief. Beset by physical weakness that makes her the easy victim of bullies, thieves, and rapists, she succeeds nevertheless, and the great inner confidence deriving from the relationship with Guru Rinpoche, together with the fruits of her meditative experience, allow her to ignore the clamorous disapproval of mere society over which in the end her triumph is absolute. At the conclusion of the book, in an amazing song of victory, the bitter recriminations just quoted are replaced by gentle humor, in which she repeats with irony the kind of things that people used to say about her.

Your "Lady," wild and fit for any deed,
To whom so many things befell, is now no more!
The wench who could not even keep her man
Is now the queen of Dharmakaya Kuntuzangpo!
That sluttish creature, brazen with conceit,
Pretension takes her now away to the southwest!
That whining vixen, fit for any intrigue,
Has tricked her way to dissolution in the Dharmadhatu!
That dejected widow no Tibetan wanted
Inherits now the endless sovereignty of Buddhahood!

With words such as these, *Lady of the Lotus-Born* permanently confounds any notion that womanhood constitutes, in any sense, an obstacle to spiritual attainment. It is true that

Tsogyal is occasionally worsted, as any woman would be, when confronted by male aggression, but in terms of moral strength, physical courage, and perseverance, she is unquestionably victorious. When in retreat in a cave in the high mountains of Tibet, her asceticism brings her near to death, but she remains faithful to her vow and triumphs—in marked contrast to her male companion who "could stand it no longer and went off to find the Guru. . . ." When she is raped by a gang of thugs, the strength of her bodhichitta and accomplishment are such that she is able to utilize the occasion to place her attackers on the Path, transforming a situation of sordid violence into one of the most astonishing and beautiful encounters of the book. On another occasion, when she is blamed for a series of natural disasters and made the object of a veritable witch hunt, the strength of her resolve and the power of her meditation render her totally immune to everything that stupidity and cruelty could devise—"but nothing and nobody could harm the Lady's body." Finally, although *Lady of the Lotus-Born* is dominated by the figure of Yeshe Tsogyal, she is far from being the only example of feminine accomplishment. In the course of the story, she encounters other great yoginis: Mandarava and Shakyadema, who are also supreme adepts. There are also Tsogyal's own extraordinary disciples, Trashi Chidren, Kalasiddhi, and Shelkar Dorje Tso, not to mention Lodrö Kyi and the innumerable nuns of the monasteries that Tsogyal founded and supported.

Such stories of heroic perseverance, of obstacles surmounted, of fear and weakness overcome, are found in the lives of all the great monks and yogis of the Buddhist tradition. The effect of such stories here is to show that Tsogyal is in every sense their equal, fulfilling her womanhood just as they fulfilled their manhood. A categorical statement of this equality of the sexes on the spiritual path is given by no less than Guru Rinpoche himself, who unmistakably countermands traditional prejudice. After Tsogyal has endured the intense hardships involved in her solitary practice of tantric yoga and has won through to accomplishment, he greets her with the following words:

> Yogini seasoned in the Secret Mantra!
> The ground of Liberation
> Is this human frame, this lowly human form.
> And here distinctions, male or female,
> Have no consequence.
> And yet if bodhichitta graces it,
> A woman's form indeed will be supreme!

On the level of sexual identity, there is no need to aspire to be anything other than what one is. Female and male are of perfectly equal standing. The only criterion for preeminence is the presence of bodhichitta, the resolve to attain Buddhahood for the sake of all beings. Any claim to superiority simply on the basis of sexual difference is a fiction and a prejudice.

All the same, this prejudice is deeply rooted and difficult to dislodge, a fact of which Tsogyal herself is perfectly aware. At moments of particular significance, such as the reception of teaching and empowerment, her commitment to the tantras, the difficult journey to Nepal, the attainment of accomplishment, and so forth, she pointedly refers to her womanhood as if to force it on the attention of readers liable to overlook it. Her expression "I the woman, Yeshe Tsogyal," repeated over a dozen times in the course of the book, embodies a teaching of particular importance.

Despite all that has just been said on the subject of heroic womanhood, it is nevertheless true that Yeshe Tsogyal's life and teaching are of universal import. It would be a mistake and an impoverishment to read *Lady of the Lotus-Born* as if it were merely a feminist tract. A vindication no doubt of the potential of womanhood, it is nevertheless a magisterial portrayal of *human* achievement upon the tantric path, the fruit of which lies far beyond the dualistic level at which sexual distinction obtains. The final result of Buddhahood is a completion beyond duality. It is symbolized in Tibetan iconography by the consorts Kuntuzangpo and Kuntuzangmo in union, the perfect coalescence of wisdom and compassion, awareness and emptiness, bliss and voidness, a state beyond words and beyond imagining. Thus while the "Nirmanakaya, universally renowned as Yeshe Tsogyal" is perceptible in human and feminine form, her final reality is utterly transcendent, beyond both male and female. Indeed on the ultimate level, as the text makes clear, Yeshe Tsogyal and Guru Rinpoche, the Lady and the Lotus-Born, are at one in perfect union. "In the absolute space, their name is *Kunzang Pema Yabyum*—the 'All-Good Guru-Consort Lotus-Born.' Their Body, Speech, Mind, Qualities and Activities are present everywhere, wherever space pervades."

Dharma Treasure

Lady of the Lotus-Born is a "Terma" or Treasure-text and thus belongs to a remarkable and very important class of Tibetan Buddhist literature. As such, moreover, it is a text of unusual significance in that it describes the inauguration of the Terma tradition and reveals the importance of the role that Yeshe Tsogyal played in it.

Although the concealing of teachings in order to preserve them till a later time, when they might be disseminated and implemented to greater effect, is to be found elsewhere in the Buddhist tradition, the system of Dharma Treasures, as it is most commonly understood now, is especially associated with Guru Rinpoche and is to all intents and purposes a particularity of the Nyingma school. Moreover, while the Terma tradition is perfectly in harmony with Buddhist teachings on the nature of the mind and external phenomena in general, the manner in which the Treasures are concealed, preserved, and discovered is very mysterious and wonderful. Indeed it is so astonishing that were it not for the fact that great tertöns (Treasure revealers) of unquestioned authority and integrity have lived in our own day, have spoken in detail on the subject and have disseminated teachings drawn from the Treasures that they had themselves discovered, the very existence of Termas would certainly be difficult to believe. The subject of the hidden Dharma Treasures is very extensive and its underlying theory is subtle and intricate. Fortunately, an exhaustive discussion of the phenomenon was composed last century by Jigme Tenpai Nyima, the third Dodrupchen Rinpoche, and has been translated and presented by Tulku Thondup Rinpoche. Interested readers will find an abundance of information in this invaluable text.[10]

For the purposes of this introduction, it may be said in the most general terms that when Guru Padmasambhava went to Tibet, he was aware of the future development of the world and the declining possibilities for spiritual progress. He foresaw the coarsening of the human mind and ethical conduct, and the concomitant pollution of the elemental constituents of the outer universe. He prophesied the dwindling of human strength plagued by disaster, strife, and terrible new diseases, and above all the reduced inclination to engage in spiritual endeavor. He therefore transmitted many teachings to his closest disciples, not with a view to their immediate dissemination, but in order to preserve them for later generations, when they would appear as though fresh from himself, laden with blessings, "still warm with the breath of the dakinis." It is of interest that the vast majority of sadhanas and yogas practiced today by the Nyingma school are drawn from Terma texts. The concealment of the Treasures is not at all to be understood in the normal sense of, for example, hiding a hoard of coins in a field or a cache of manuscripts in a cave as in the case of the Dead Sea Scrolls. When Guru Rinpoche concealed his teachings, he hid them in the deepest recesses of the minds of his realized disciples, prophesying that at some future moment, the disciples in question would take rebirth and bring forth the teaching from the depth of their awareness. As a support for the recollection of these teachings, "Treasure substances" were often concealed in specific locations. These might comprise, for instance, an image of the Guru or, most often, small scrolls of yellow paper containing a text, usually very short and written in symbolic script. The effect of the Treasure substance on the tertön is to stimulate and bring forth from the deepest layers of his mind the complete teaching bestowed by the Guru long before. Once again, the manner in which these substances were "placed" and hidden was extraordinary. Guru Rinpoche and Yeshe Tsogyal concealed them not inside "objects" in the normal sense of the word but within the "essential nature" of the elements, within the "netlike" fabric of phenomena. They may be found inside stones or in the pillars of ancient buildings, in cliff faces, in lakes, even in the air. Moreover, their discovery is only possible for the predicted tertön and even then only at certain moments and in very precise situations of what might be called interdependent coincidence.[11] The Treasure teachings may range from brief instructions and prayers to long cycles of doctrinal material extending over many volumes. In certain circumstances, it is possible for Treasures suddenly to manifest in the mind of the tertön without the stimulus of an external substance.

This, however, was not the case with *Lady of the Lotus-Born*. The entire text was encoded in symbolic script (*dayig*) and was entrusted, as we see recorded at the beginning of the book, to spirit protectors. The latter kept and at length presented it to the discoverer, the tertön Taksham Samten Lingpa (fl. c. 1650), who, thus prompted, recalled the Treasure and committed it to writing. As he exclaims in the colophon to the text, "Here is marvelous wonder, I wrote it as it sprang into my mind!" The symbolic script is usually intelligible only to the predicted tertön, and he alone is able to unfold its meaning. Nevertheless the secret script is sometimes recorded in the decoded Tibetan text, and it has been reproduced in this translation in the positions where it appears in the original.[12]

Although Guru Rinpoche was the prime mover of the Terma tradition, the main work of encoding, writing, and concealing the Treasures was entrusted to Yeshe Tsogyal, and this indeed was one of her greatest responsibilities and gifts to later generations of Buddhist practitioners. Chapter seven concludes with a long but abbreviated list of the places in Tibet where Termas were concealed, and in the preceding chapter Tsogyal summarizes her labors in the following terms:

> Not a single clod of earth that hands may grasp
> Is now without my blessing.
> And time the truth of this will show—
> The proof will be the taking out of Treasures . . .
> The fivefold elements I brought beneath my sway,
> And everywhere, I filled the earth with Treasures.

Whereas the great majority of Terma texts are directly associated with Guru Rinpoche, it is true also that Treasure teachings were concealed by other great masters who had attained the supreme level. These include, for instance, the Indian pandita Vimalamitra, one of the patriarchs of the Dzogchen tradition, and Vairotsana, the Tibetan translator and disciple of Guru Rinpoche. This point is of some importance since internal evidence suggests that *Lady of the Lotus-Born* was a Treasure created and concealed by Yeshe Tsogyal herself. Taksham Samten Lingpa is believed to be an incarnation of Tsogyal's disciple Gyalwa Changchub, who, as we have seen, was the incarnation of her former companion Arya Salé. As Dodrup Tenpai Nyima makes clear, beings able to reveal Termas must have at least the realization of the Perfection Stage practices. On the other hand, the one who originates the Treasures must have the supreme attainment of Buddhahood.[13] *Lady of the Lotus-Born* is thus a testimony of Yeshe Tsogyal's enlightenment.

Lady of the Lotus-Born

NAMO GURU DEVA DAKINIBHYA!

Homage to the host of Guru Dakinis!

O Buddha Light Unbounded,[14] O Sovereign Lord who Sees,[15]
O Lotus Guru,[16] their compassion manifest;
Teacher in the Triple Kaya, Triple Gem, and shield of wanderers,
To you and all the masters of the lineage,
I make offerings.

I bow to Dechen Karmo, Mother of all Buddhas
Of past and present and all future time:
Samantabhadri of great bliss, the Dharmakaya dakini,
And Vajrayogini, Sambhogakaya,
And Lady Tsogyal, the Nirmanakaya.

The dancing transmutation of her form
Delights the hearts of Buddhas in the threefold time.
The Lord of Orgyen made her keeper of his teachings.

Never-failing memory she gained,
She the fertile mother of deep Treasures.

Supreme accomplishment is hers:
The rainbow diamond body.

Guru Dakini who treads the sky!
Her name is Yeshe Tsogyal,
"Victorious Sea of Wisdom."

For the sake of future generations,
this story of her life and liberation,
together with some fragments of her teaching,
the very heart-blood[17] of the dakinis,
has been set forth here and hidden.

Nyongkha Nakpo, fiery lord of demons,
Lion-faced Dugon, guard this Treasure!

SAMAYA GYA GYA GYA[18]

Prologue

Emaho!

PADMA THÖDRENGTSEL, master of mantra, whose nature is that of all the Buddhas, past, present, and to come, is indeed a mighty siddha, born within a lotus blossom, undefiled by human birth. Surpassing even Shakyamuni, he accomplishes the enlightened activity of the Buddhas of the three times. He taught and long preserved the teachings of the Mantrayana—all so difficult to spread. Merely by the power of his thought, he subdued the wild folk of Tibet, the orcs and ogres of the southwest, and heathens, demons, gods, and spirits—all so hard to tame. In his power, he displayed incompatible miraculous appearances—all so hard to demonstrate. And the siddhi of immortal life, so hard to reach, he did indeed achieve.

Now, as a means to propagate the Secret Mantra, he took to himself consorts endowed with special qualities, from the highest heaven down to charnel grounds and sacred places, in divine and human realms, and in domains of nagas and gandharvas. They were more numerous than the sesame seeds with which a vast granary might be filled. Especially in this world, the continent of rose apples,[19] from India, China, Tibet, Gen, Jang, Li, and Hor, he took no less than seventy thousand maidens all endowed with perfect qualities. Yet in reality, he was never separate from the five emanations of Vajravarahi: the Body-emanation, Mandarava; the Speech-emanation, Yeshe Tsogyal; the Mind-emanation, Shakyadema; the Qualities-emanation, Kalasiddhi; and the Activity-emanation, Trashi Chidren. Finally there was the dakini Prabhadhara, the emanation of the Suchness aspect, who makes a sixth. Now of these, Indian Mandarava and Tibetan Yeshe Tsogyal were supreme. The life of Mandarava is told elsewhere;[20] here in brief is the tale of Yeshe Tsogyal.

❁

One
Emanation

SHE WHO IS the mother of Buddhas, past, present, and to come, the nirmanakaya everywhere renowned as Yeshe Tsogyal, accumulated merit and purified defilements for numbered and unnumbered[21] ages, sending forth great waves of goodness for all that lives. In the days of noble Sadaprarudita, when born the daughter of a tradesman, she met the Buddha Dharmodgata, and in the company of five hundred maidens resolved steadfastly never more to be reborn in samsara.[22] Later, when she died, she wandered far and wide through many Sambhogakaya Buddha-fields, and at length, when the Buddha Shakyamuni was present here on earth, she took birth as a woman known as Gangadevi and made a collection of his teachings. Afterward, she lingered again in the Sambhogakaya Buddha-fields, being known as Sarasvati, and there brought forth the weal and benefit of many.

Now, at that time, the Buddhist king Trisong Detsen, a manifestation of the noble Mañjushri, wished to bring the Sacred Doctrine to our country of Tibet. He therefore called upon the mighty teacher Padmasambhava, free from birth and death, who was none other than the Buddha Amitabha appearing in this human world. The king indeed invited him, and built Samye the Glorious, the delight of his heart. He established also innumerable temples near and far, and thereby caused the teachings of the Sacred Dharma to rise and shine like the sun.

It was then that the Great Master Padmasambhava took counsel with himself. "That I may propagate the teachings of the Secret Mantra," he pondered, "the time has come for an incarnation of goddess Sarasvati to appear." And in that very instant, like the moon casting its reflection on the sea, he was far away in the emanated land of Orgyen. Rumors arose as to his whereabouts. It was said by the Tibetan ministers that the Guru had been punished and exiled to the wild marches of Thokar. The pious king, for his part, declared that he was residing in the three Lion Fortresses of Mön, engaged in spiritual practice. As for the common folk, they were gossiping that he had made off back to India with the queen! But the truth was that the Guru was ranging through hundreds of Nirmanakaya Buddha-fields, remaining there for seven years in human reckoning. He summoned to him Vajrayogini, goddess Sarasvati, Wrathful-Frowning Tara, the dakinis of the four classes and those of the sacred lands and places, and elsewhere—all without exception. He took his pleasure with each and every one and roused them with this song of joy.

Hri!
In the secret sky of great desire, desireless,
And through the rays and beams of deep passion,
passionless,
Of the blissful vajra of desire beyond desire,
The time is now at hand to play the Great Bliss,
deep and secret.

Then Sarasvati rose up in the midst of the assembled deities and made this answer:

Ho!
Heruka, Hero, Lord of bliss,
Great dancer that you are!
Dance here if you can!

This sacred lotus holds
The greatest of Great Bliss.
For in this secret space,
There is no grief or pain.
And time is now at hand
To go down to a wild and savage land.

"Samaya Ho!" cried the Lord;
"Samayastvam!" cried the Lady;
"Samaya Hri!" he said; and she, "Samaya Tishta."
"Raho Ham!" he said; and she, "Ragayami."

With these words the vajra of the Lord and the lotus of the Lady were joined, and thus they remained in meditation. Lochana and the four other female Buddhas made offerings and praise. The lord herukas banished forces of obstruction. The Bodhisattvas made prayers for good fortune. The great sentinels held back hindrances, and the four female keepers of the gates raised a circle of protection. The vajra goddesses[23] danced, while the protectors of the ten directions, the mamos and the dharmapalas, pledged themselves to guard the Doctrine. At that moment, the great bliss of the Lord and Lady caused all the worlds to tremble and shake. And in that very instant, from the point of their union a great light burst forth: a red letter *É,* encircled by a garland of white vowels, and a white letter *Wam*, encircled by a garland of red consonants, which dropped—dropped like a shooting star, down to the land of Tibet, down to the valley of Drak Seu.

SAMAYA GYA GYA GYA

Two
Birth

DURING THE PERIOD of the earliest dynasty, from the first king, Nyatri Tsenpo, down to Namri Songtsen, Tibet was divided into seven fiefdoms. But when the great religious king Songtsen Gampo succeeded to the throne, he took the whole of Tibet as his dominion, as did his successors after him. Measureless were the fruits of his prowess. To administer the seven fiefdoms, he established vassal princes by royal decree. Their names were Kharchenpa, Surkharpa, Kharchupa, Gongthangpa, Tsepa, Drakpa, and Rongpa.

The son of Kharchenpa, the founder of a large community of Bön, was Kharchen Zhönupa, whose son was Kharchen Dorje Gön, whose son, in turn, was Kharchen Pelgyi Wangchuk. At the age of fifteen years, Kharchen Pelgyi Wangchuk took to wife Getso of the clan of Nub, and assumed the burden of the chieftainship, for his father died. His heart inclined to Buddhadharma, and following the word of the king, he introduced the Doctrine to his subjects.

Ten years went by, and it came to pass that once, when he and his wife were at play in the delights of love, they both beheld a vision. It seemed to Getso that a golden bee, whose humming was sweeter than the sound of viols,[24] came from the west and melted into the crown of her husband's head. To the prince of Kharchen it seemed that his wife had three eyes, and he saw a girl, eight years old, holding a viol and singing, "*a ah, i ih, u uh, ri rih, li lih, é eh, o oh, am ah*" and "*hri hri hri hri hri.*" She came towards him and vanished. At once the earth shook. There was a burst of light and a roar of thunder, followed by a long, low rumbling. A little spring by the castle swelled into a lake and there were many other signs. That night, Kharchenpa dreamed another dream, this time that he was holding in his hand an eight-petaled lotus that shone with light all around. He heard a voice proclaim that the light filled the universe of a billion worlds. And he dreamed that from the crown of his head there sprang a stupa made of coral. People were drawn to it from China, Jang, Hor, Tibet, Mongolia, Mön, Nepal, and other lands. Some said that they had come just to see it, others that they wished to take it away with them. Some said that they wanted to steal it, others that they wanted to carry it off. In that same dream, it seemed to Kharchenpa that in his hand he held a viol that, though unplayed, filled the three-thousand-fold universe[25] with its melody. And from all these worlds, inconceivable multitudes of people came and listened as though they would never be satisfied.

Getso, for her part, dreamed that she was holding in her hand a necklace of conches and corals. From the corals there came large quantities of blood, while from the conches milk flowed in great abundance. She gave these substances to multitudes of people, but no matter how deeply they drank, they could not exhaust the flow, which filled the world with amrita, red and white. And she heard a voice proclaim that the amrita would not run dry until the end of the age.

At sunrise on the following morning, there appeared a white-skinned maiden whom they had never seen before. She was lovely like a daughter of the gods. "In the household of this princely father," she said, "the Buddha has arisen, the Dharma and the Sangha. *Alala*, this is a marvelous wonder!" And with that she vanished.

For nine whole months, vowel sounds and the words *Hri Guru Padma Vajra Ah,* as well as the tantras of the Secret Mantra, could be heard clearly and continuously resounding, mostly in the Sanskrit tongue. And at length, as the sun was rising on the tenth day of the monkey month in the bird year, Getso gave birth without travail. In that very instant, the earth trembled and there was the sound of rumbling thunder. A rain of flowers fell and the lake increased greatly in volume; and all around its shores there appeared a marvelous array of red and white blossoms, sparkling and in full bloom. The palace was enfolded in a tent of rainbows, a web of crisscrossed rays of iridescent light, visible for all to see. Music filled the sky, and for a long time the sweet sound of a viol could be heard. Many goddesses were seen among the clouds, singing this auspicious song:

> *Hri!*
> Nature of the Dharmakaya, Samantabhadri of great bliss,
> Vajrayogini, Sambhogakaya dakini,
> Nirmanakaya, supreme mother of all Buddhas,
> To you all happiness and fortune!
>
> Dharmakaya dakini, abyss of Voidness,
> Sambhogakaya, Sarasvati, mother of Buddhas in the triple
> time,
> Nirmanakaya, supreme and perfectly endowed,
> To you the victory!
>
> Dharmakaya, expanse of Primal Wisdom,
> Sambhogakaya, mother of exalted ones, white Tara of the
> seven eyes,
> Nirmanakaya, supreme among the living,
> To you we bow!

And letting fall a rain of flowers, they melted into empty space.

At the very moment of her birth, the child recited the vowels and consonants and exclaimed, "Great Lord of Orgyen, think of me!" And kneeling, or sitting with her legs crossed, she would stay staring with wide-open eyes. Unsullied by the impurities of the womb, the flesh of her body glowed white and rosy, her teeth were like rows of tiny conch shells, and her blue-black hair fell to her waist. When her mother brought her butter of the *dri* to eat, she said to her:

I, your child, a yogini nirmanakaya,
Am nourished by the food of pure essences
And unclean foods I now have long forgotten.
But, mother, I will eat—that you may gain in merit.

Essential teachings will be what I eat.
And all samsara will be what I swallow.
Awareness, pristine wisdom, will be now my fill.
Ah Ye!

And with these words, she ate the butter. Her father, lord of Kharchen, exclaimed: "This daughter of mine is far superior to other children. Either she will become a great Buddhist or Bönpo meditator, or she will be a consort for the great king! And since our lake[26] grew so much in size when she was born, she shall have the name of Tsogyal, 'Sea of Victory.' "

After only a month, the baby had the appearance of an eight-year-old child, and, thinking that no good would come of it if people found out, her parents kept her hidden until she was ten. By that time, Tsogyal had grown into a lovely girl, whose beauty, nonetheless, was now well known to everyone. Crowds would come from Tibet, China, Mongolia, Jang, Gen, and Nepal, simply to see her.

SAMAYA ITHI

❀

Three
Disciple of the Guru

NOW IT HAPPENED that the lord of Kharchen and Getso, his wife, took counsel with their household, and all agreed that Tsogyal should be married to no one but the king. For they reasoned that if she were bestowed on an ordinary suitor, the others would certainly be offended and disputes would break out. She was therefore given to none of the young men who had come to seek her hand, and they were all sent home. But then, unexpectedly, the lord of Kharchu, Pelgyi Zhönnu, arrived, and also Dorje Wangchuk, the lord of Surkhar. Each had brought with him a caravan of three hundred horses and mules, laden with gifts. Of course, they both demanded Tsogyal in marriage. And so, because to give her to one would upset the other, it was finally decided that Tsogyal herself should be consulted.

"I will go with neither of them!" she cried. "For then I will sink into the woeful prison of samsara and it will be hard indeed to escape from it! What misfortune! Mother, Father, I beg you, think of this!" But though she begged and begged, they were deaf to her pleas.

"I believe," declared her father, "that there is no one better than either of these suitors. Therefore, do not be an insolent and ungrateful girl. I cannot bring myself to send you far away to China or to Hor. Come now, I will give you to one of these."

To the two rivals he said, "My daughter says that she does

not wish to go with either of you. On the other hand, if I give her to one, the other will be displeased and will cause me trouble. But the girl is my daughter and you are rivals for her hand. Therefore I will drive her out of the house and the one who catches her may keep her. The loser, though, must cause no trouble. If he does, I shall hand him over to the king for punishment!"

Robed in rich silk, and with a caravan of a hundred mules and horses loaded with provisions, the defenseless Tsogyal was brought outside. No sooner was she there than the two rivals were after her, vying with each other in speed. Shantipa, the minister of the lord of Kharchu, was the quickest; and seizing Tsogyal by the hair, he tried to take her with him. Tsogyal dug her feet into a boulder, tearing at it as if it were clay. No one could move her; she was as unshakable as a mountain. Tearing off her finery, the wicked minister whipped her with metal scourges on her naked flesh. "Shameless girl!" he cried, "Your parents were unable to command you! Come! Come with me or I will kill you!" And he beat her.

But Tsogyal sang:

If this human body I have gained,
Once only in the space of many kalpas,
Is not to be a means
To win enlightenment,
Why should I make of it a source
Of sorrow in samsara?

Glorious Kharchu,
High and mighty though he be,
Has not the chances of a single day
To win enlightenment.

So kill me if you wish,
I do not care!

The minister Shantipa retorted:

Woman!
Outwardly your form is fair,
Inside all is rotten!
Because your skin is lovely
You are trouble for our rulers!
Soft outside but inside hard as grit,
Kharchu's wife, my girl, you will become!

And Tsogyal said:

Graced with freedom and endowment,[27]
This human form so difficult to find!
But is it hard to find a body such as yours,
Doing only evil,
Scarcely even man?
Kharchu's wife why should I be?

Again the minister beat her with scourges until her body was mangled and bloody. Finally Tsogyal could bear it no longer; and standing up, she went away with him.

That evening, the minister and his men arrived at Drakda, where they made merry with dancing and song. Tsogyal was in despair. Down her tears fell, mingling with her blood. She thought hard how she might escape, but all to no avail. Then, overwhelmed with sadness, she sang this lamentation to the Buddhas of the ten directions.

Kyema Hu!
Protectors of all beings,
Buddhas of the ten directions, and all Bodhisattvas!
Guardians mighty and compassionate,
With eyes of wisdom and miraculous power,
The time has come to honor
Your great vows of bodhichitta!

My pure white wish
Was whiter than the snow.
But through the deeds of demon foes,
It clouds and darkens,
Blacker than the rust.
O look on me with eyes of great compassion!

My wish was excellent
Like precious gold.
But through the deeds of demon foes,
It is debased,
And worse than alloy.
Turn to me your eyes of wisdom!

My wish to be enlightened
Was perfect like a jewel.
But through the deeds of demon foes,
It falls to crassness,
Cheaper than a stone.
Mighty ones, display your strength!

I wished to practice Dharma,
In this life and form.
But through the deeds of demon foes,
I'm tripped and fall
Into the marshes of samsara.

O you who have compassion
Turn me swiftly from this path!

As soon as the song was over, all the men fell asleep as if besotted by their beer. And swifter than the wind, over hill and dale, Tsogyal fled far away to the south. Next morning there was uproar in the camp. The men ransacked the whole of Kharchen but Tsogyal was nowhere to be found. They looked everywhere but in the end they had to return to Kharchu emptyhanded.

* * *

Now it was at that time that the Master Padmasambhava himself had made his way, in the twinkling of an eye, to Samye Chimphu. The evil ministers discovered this and went there in a body, intending to put him to death. But what they found there was a blazing mass of fire, and they were filled with fear. Returning to the king, they said:

> *Kyeho*!
> Great King, Son of gods and Lord of men,
> That foreign vagabond we brought to justice
> And drove away to Thokar,[28]
> Has gone instead to Chimphu
> And is living there!
> Shall we slay him
> Or once more drive him into exile?

In his heart the pious king rejoiced. And thinking that he would request the Master for instructions on how to attain enlightenment without first having to abandon the defilements, he sent three translators to invite him to return, entrusting each with an offering of three golden ingots.

Later, when the Master was coming down from Chimphu, the evil ministers lay in wait for him in a narrow gorge, armed to the teeth. The Master knew of this and, sending the three translators on ahead, he came on afterwards alone. Making the mudra of threatening, he cried "*Hung Hung Hung!*" and in a mountain of fire that blazed up to the peak of existence,[29] he appeared in the wrathful form of Guru Drakpo and the ministers all fell senseless to the ground.[30] He then appeared in the royal palace where the king was so overcome with fright that he fainted away, although his courtiers could see nothing. The Master then withdrew the manifestation and resumed his peaceful form. When the king recovered his senses, he made many prostrations and circumambulations. He prepared an immense ganachakra feast offering and made the request that he had planned earlier.

But the Master said to him: "The time for revealing the Secret Mantra has not yet come. Train your mind in the practices of the other vehicles, and this time next year I will teach you."

Meanwhile, Yeshe Tsogyal was in hiding in the ravine of Onphu Taktsang where she sustained herself with fruit and clothed herself with the lichen of the trees.[31] But the lord of Surkhar learned where Tsogyal had gone and sent a force of three hundred men to search for her. Discovered once again, Tsogyal was carried helplessly away. Kharchupa heard of this and sent word to the lord of Kharchen, Tsogyal's father:

> High prince, Pelgyi Wangchuk!
> Your daughter, though bestowed on me, has fled
> And, I hear, was found by Surkhar in a distant land.
> What has happened? Is this truth or lies?
> If this was with your knowledge, I will fight you;
> If not, I will make war on Surkhar.

So saying, he gathered a great army.

Kharchen Pel sent this answer:

> This is my reply to Kharchu Dorje Pel.
> Your bride has run away,
> But I will not reproach you.
> I did not know indeed
> That she had left your house.
> How would war be to your gain?

And he massed his troops.

A message then arrived from Surkharpa:

High prince, Pelgyi Wangchuk!
I sought your daughter in far-distant lands
And, finding her, have brought her to my house.
If I offer jewels and wealth untold,
Will you give your lovely child to me?'

But this was the reply he received:

The agreement that we made was binding:
The quicker of the two could have her.
If now I take an offering for my daughter,
There will have to be a fight.
And so for sake of peace, for others and yourself,
Allow my child to wander where she will,
In those far-distant lands.

Surkharpa, however, declared that regardless of the consequences, he would not release Tsogyal. He put the girl in chains and, gathering a large army, prepared for battle. But the news reached the ears of the king, and he dispatched seven ministers to Kharchen carrying this message:

Kharchen Pelgyi Wangchuk, listen!
If you pay no heed to me, your king,
My strength will crush you speedily!
Your daughter is sublime and beautiful,
A worthy queen for me.

Should any of my subjects cause unrest,
His life is forfeit, as the law decrees!

Kharchen Pelgyi Wangchuk then recounted the events in detail to the king and offered his daughter with this message:

Ho!
Lord of the world, and strong among men!
My daughter is the cream and pick of many.

If the king will take her for his queen,
How could this not be a joy to me?
Wars and disputes I already dread
But fear much more the armies of the king!

The king was well pleased, and with a force of nine hundred horsemen he proceeded to Surkhar and frightened its lord into submission.

Now if truth be told, Kharchen Pelgyi Wangchuk had all together three daughters. The eldest one, Dechen Tso, he bestowed on Kharchu Dorje Pel, who was very pleased. The second, whose name was Nyima Tso, he gave to Surkhar Zhönnu Pel, who was likewise satisfied. And the youngest, Tsogyal, was received in marriage by the king himself. Thus, though the original hopes of the two suitors were dashed, the disturbance subsided naturally and peace prevailed. And Tsogyal, bedecked with jewels of every kind, and clothed in garments of the richest silk, made her way to Samye accompanied by the king's welcoming envoys. There the king feasted for three months in celebration of his marriage.

Because Tsogyal had faith in the Buddhadharma, she was made the steward of religion. Many learned teachers instructed her in the arts of reading and grammar, the five major sciences, and all religious and secular wisdom. And in all of this, a few symbolic indications sufficed for her to understand completely.

It was at that time that the king made his invitation to the great master Padmasambhava. He set up a throne of precious substances and offered an immense ganachakra feast. He poured out a mass of worldly riches as high as a mountain, laying out heaps of gold upon a silver mandala, and heaps of turquoise upon a golden mandala. Most magnificent of all, he offered his whole empire: the four central provinces of Ü and

Tsang to represent Mount Meru;[32] China, Jang and Kham as the eastern continent and subcontinents; Jar, Kongpo, and Mön as the southern continent and subcontinents; the three regions of Ngari as the western continent and subcontinents; and Hor, Mongolia and the northern plains as the northern continent and subcontinents. As an offering of all the pleasures of the senses, the king presented his entire kingdom together with his queen. Then, making nine times nine prostrations, he made his request.

"Great Guru, precious one! All my realm I lay before you as a mandala. Precious Master, behold my offerings! All beings, gods and men—you have always held them in your great compassion. I pray you now, bestow on me that supreme doctrine beyond the karmic law of cause and fruit, the Secret Mantras not to be numbered among ordinary teachings, the particular instructions whereby Buddhahood is instantaneously achieved in this very life and body."

In reply the great Guru sang:

Emaho!
Great and pious king, pay careful heed to me!

From the Lotus-field of Great Felicity,
Devoid of place or bearings, nowhere found,
A globe of light, the vajra Body, Speech, and Mind
Of Amitabha free from birth and death,
Came down upon a lotus cup, uncaused, unwrought,
Floating on an ocean vast, unbounded.
Thence am I.

No father, no mother, no lineage have I.
Wondrous, I have risen of myself.
I was never born, and neither shall I die.
I am the Enlightened, I the Lotus-Born.

I, the sovereign of the host of dakinis,
Am holder of the very secret Secret Mantras

Transcending law of cause and fruit.
Tantra, agama, and upadesha,
Teachings for the practice,
Intimate direct instructions,
All this I hold.
And samayas, vital, not to be forgotten.

The offerings of the mighty king are splendid
But Dharma is not bartered for possessions.
To traffic thus would rot the root samaya.
Destruction then would fall upon us both
And at our death would plunge us down to hell.

The whole wide world I have within my power.
Your kingly gifts, though vast, do not suffice
As reason to reveal the Secret Mantras,
Teachings that require a perfect vessel.
For when the precious snow lion's milk
Is poured in other than a cup of purest gold,
The vessel breaks, the milk is lost.

And so I keep these teachings hidden,
Sealed within my heart.

As he sang, he miraculously extended his body, the upper part filling the world of desire, the lower part reaching down to the abysses of hell. Then, in the aspect of a human teacher, he took his seat upon the throne. The king prostrated, throwing himself to the ground like a collapsing wall. "Great Master," he begged. "Am I the king and yet lack fortune? Am I unsuitable as a vessel for the Secret Mantra teachings?" And he struck his body against the ground, weeping. Guru Rinpoche replied: "Great King, listen to me."

Emaho!
The Secret Mantra is called "secret"
Not because it harbors any defect.
But rather it is hid
From narrow minds upon the lower paths.

But you, O King, are fortunate indeed!
With wisdom, breadth of mind, and understanding,
Your samaya and your faith are irreversible;
And with devotion you rely upon your Teacher.

By sensual desire I am utterly unstained,
The fault of carnal longing is unknown to me.
But in the practice of the Secret Mantra
The presence of a woman is required.
She must be faithful, of good lineage,
And pure in her samaya.
She must be fair and excellently wise,
Skilled, and graced with qualities of mercy,
Unreserved in open-handed giving,
A perfect wisdom dakini indeed.

If such a one is lacking,
There will lack the elements that bring about
The ripening and freedom of the mind.
The fruit of practice of the Secret Mantra
Will be slow to come.

Now in Tibet, this land beneath the sun,
Widespread are the devotees of tantric practice.
But those who gain the fruit
Are rare as daystars.
Therefore will I open, Mighty King,
The door of Secret Mantra!

And with these words, the Guru appeared in the form of Vajradhara. Forthwith the king prostrated, striking his head on the ground. And he offered the Lady Tsogyal together with the five substances of samaya. The Master was well pleased and made Tsogyal his consort. He bestowed empowerment upon her, and they went to Chimphu Geu, where they practiced in secret.

SAMAYA ITHI GYA GYA GYA

Four
Teaching and Instruction

IT WAS FIRST in Chimphu Gegong and in Yamalung that, through the true and certain precepts of the Four Noble Truths,[33] the Master urged the Lady Tsogyal to the practice of virtue. He explained to her the Sutras, the Vinaya, and the Abhidharma, which are teachings on the level of the relative truth. He instructed her in the infallible principle of karma, the law of cause and fruit, teaching her the behavior that she should embrace and the actions that she should forsake. And he placed her in the envowed state of purity and virtue. She received and took to heart all the doctrines of the first six vehicles of Dharma. She was able to stabilize her meditation; and grasping the full meaning of all that was explained, she attained a perfect understanding. Goddess Sarasvati appeared to her unsummoned, and she obtained the siddhi of unfailing memory. She beheld the entire world with the eye of flesh,[34] acquiring both ordinary and transcendent clairvoyance, and gained the power of displaying incompatible miraculous appearances.

I shall not enumerate all the teachings the Lady Tsogyal received for fear of the length of such a list. But in brief, as she herself said:

"All the teachings of the Buddha were present in the precious Master Padmasambhava. He was like a vessel filled to overflowing. And after I had served him long in the three ways pleasing to a teacher,[35] all that he possessed he gave to me, the woman Yeshe Tsogyal. He poured it out as from one vase to another. My mind at ease in Dharma, I understood the differences between the nine vehicles, and was able to distinguish true doctrine from false. Knowing the secret of the karmic law of cause and fruit, I conceived a desire for that truly unsurpassable teaching that totally transcends karma. And so I begged the Precious Guru:

Kyema!
In the land of Oddiyana you were born,
And reigned supreme in India among the sages.
In Tibet the regent of the Conqueror,
O Buddha in human form whom I revere!

Though young, I have experienced much.
I was a girl of twelve when sorrows burst upon me.
My parents paid no heed and gave me as a bride:
Such are the customs of this human world.

My heart was not inclined to worldly ways;
I fled for safety to the gorge of Onphu Taktsang.
A suitor's lustful yearning sought me out
And, chained and helpless, I was dragged away to grief.

Lord and Guru, great is your compassion!
The great religious king was my deliverance:
I came to Samye chosen as his queen.
To you he offered me, his bride of sixteen years,
As basis for the third initiation.

I see the secret, now, of karmic cause and fruit,
Bestow on me, I pray, the lofty teaching
That transcends this law.

"His face radiant with smiles, Guru Rinpoche answered me with this melodious song:

Well said, Mistress, Maid of Kharchen!
You are a girl of only sixteen years
And yet have seen the long-drawn sufferings
Of a woman of fourscore!
It was your karma, know this well.
What remains of it has now been purified,
And henceforth only happiness will be your lot:
Rebirth in evil karmic forms is now impossible.

You see the secret of the law of cause and fruit,
And earnestly desire the supreme doctrine of the
Mahayana.
That is excellent indeed.

"With these words of the Master, I crossed the threshold of the teachings of the Secret Mantra, assuming the root and branch samayas. And the Master said:

Kyema!
Listen, mistress, maid of Kharchen,
Queen Samantabhadri, heed me well!
The root of Mahayana, Secret Mantra, is samaya.
Should you let it rot,
The earth beneath will crumble to our ruin!
So be faithful to your vow.

"I first received the four sections of the samaya. These are the root samayas of Body, Speech, and Mind, and their twenty five branches. The fundamental samaya, however, is that of bodhichitta, wherein the relative is sealed by the absolute. From the very beginning, the body is the deity, speech is the spontaneous sound of mantra, and the mind is nothing but suchness, the Dharmata.

"The samaya of the Body has three aspects: that of the master, that of the disciples, and that of the methods of keeping the samaya. The category of teacher has in turn six aspects: the teacher in general, the teacher as guide, the teacher as giver of samaya, the teacher as repairer of samaya, the teacher as liberator of one's mind-stream, and the teacher transmitting the essential instructions. Likewise, there are four categories of spiritual kinship: general, distant, close, and that of sharing the same mandala.

"The means to preserve the samaya of Body is as follows. Outwardly, the teacher and our spiritual brothers and sisters should be for us like our lord, our father and mother and close family. Inwardly, we treat them like our eyes, our heart, our life itself. Secretly, we behave towards them in thought, word, and deed without deceit or guile, as if they were our yidam deities. In short, with our body we make prostrations both to the teacher and to our spiritual sisters and brothers, and we circumambulate them. We prepare their seats, and honor them as though we were their man- or maidservants. We offer them everything that pleases them: our food, wealth, body, and enjoyments. Most especially, the same respect we have for the teacher we show to his wife, sons, daughters, brothers, his father and mother, his sisters and so on, even his servants. This is how the sacred samaya is preserved. In the same way, we give up any sense of disdain towards the disciples, monks, and benefactors, who obey the teacher's instructions and are his servants. In short, just as we respect the teacher, we honor all who are dear to him, as well as his servants, horse, and watchdog. Indeed, without the permission of our teacher or our spiritual brothers and sisters, we would not use, or even covet, a single sesame seed of their provisions, wealth, or belongings. It is said in the scriptures that to step over, tread, or sit on the teacher's hat, clothes, shoes, cushion, bed, seat, even his shadow, is the same as destroying a stupa or statue of the Buddha. What need is there to say that we should refrain, in the presence of the teacher, from striking or killing, theft or robbery? The scriptures say that we should not even joke about such things. And it is quite certain that to repeat to others any faults that the teacher may have, to ascribe to him faults that he does not have, and to respond insolently to his rebukes will cause us to be reborn in the hell of Torment Unsurpassed. There will be no reprieve even though we worship the Buddhas of a thousand million universes. Speaking for myself, I did not transgress even for an instant, or in the tiniest degree, the samaya of Body with regard to my teacher or my spiritual kindred. I did not deceive them, I harbored no grudge against them, I never humiliated them, I had no wrong views about them, I never wished them harm or slighted them.

"The samayas of Speech, related to the yidam deity, have two aspects: the manner in which they are classified, and the means whereby they are kept. As regards classification, there are three types of mantra and four types of mudra. In the case of the mantras, there is the root mantra of unerring cause, the circumstantial mantra of the generation stage, and the action mantra of the recitation. As for the mudras, there is the samayamudra related to the mind, the karmamudra related to the primordial wisdom, the Dharmamudra, and the Mahamudra.

"In order to preserve the Speech samaya, body, speech, and mind must be at one with the mandalas of the guru, deity and dakini, and this is done according to three modes of practice, 'excellent,' 'moderate,' and 'basic.' In these three ways, I myself practiced the seven hundred thousand mandalas of the unsurpassable Secret Mantras introduced to me by the Teacher. In the manner of one possessed of superior faculties, I never relinquished the samadhi of Great Bliss, free from thoughts—the excellent level. I forsook neither the samadhi that views phenomenal existence as male and female deities (the moderate level) nor the samadhi that is uninterrupted like a flowing river (the basic level). At the excellent level of a superior, I practiced the mandalas of Hayagriva and Vajravarahi continually, like a running stream. At the moderate level of a superior, I observed the samaya of practicing Vajrakila in six sessions uninterruptedly, three by day and three by night. On the basic level of a superior, I celebrated once a day the entire cycle of sadhanas of the *Eight Great Herukas*, complete with recitation of the appropriate mantras, ganachakra feast offerings and so forth. I practiced without counting the cost. In the same way, with regard to the other deities, I never neglected any of the mandalas to which I had been introduced, never thinking for an instant that the mere introduction was sufficient. As for those performed on the excellent level, I undertook their approach and accomplishment stages regularly every month, as well as offerings on auspicious days. Regarding the practices carried out on the moderate level, I performed their rituals once every new and full moon, on the eighth and tenth days of the month and so on. As for what was practiced on the basic level, I never failed to perform the rituals once a month. And even on the fundamental level of practice, I performed the rituals once a year.[36]

"The samaya of the Mind concerns the View, Meditation and Action. Again it may be considered from the point of view of classification. This means that when the profound view is experienced in meditation, the outer, inner, and secret practices of union and liberation are implemented. Similarly, as the means to preserve the samaya, there are four classes of secret: four 'general' secrets, four 'intermediary' secrets, 'appropriate' secrets, and 'entrusted' secrets. The four general secrets are the name of the yidam deity, the mantra, the mantra of activity, and the signs of accomplishment. The four intermediary secrets are the places and times of practice, the assistants in the practice, and the ritual substances. The "appropriate" secrets are the offering materials, such as the inner and secret oblations: amrita, torma and so on, as well as implements such as kapala, phurba, khatanga, vajra, bell, mala, and all the elements and supports for the practice of the unsurpassable Secret Mantra. These are, for example, material mandalas, the eight garments of the charnel ground, bone ornaments and the rest, especially the skull drum, the skull cup, and the thighbone trumpet. The four entrusted secrets include the private activities of our spiritual brothers and sisters, such as their secret practice, as well as the evil behavior of ordinary men and women. In brief, we do not speak to others about any actions that would be unfitting to reveal, whether concerning our guru, our vajra kindred, or anyone else.

"These then are the samayas of Body, Speech, and Mind together with the ten secrets: the samayas of Body connected with the teacher and the four categories of disciples; samayas of Speech referring to the three types of mantra and the four mudras; finally, the four outer secrets, the four inner secrets, the appropriate and the entrusted secrets. All these I received from the Teacher, and I kept them purely without letting them spoil for a fraction of a second, even down to the tiniest imaginable particle.

"The Precious Teacher also taught me the twenty-five branch samayas. First, the samayas of the five actions to be performed: union, liberation, stealing, lying, and harsh speech; then, the five samayas of substances to be eagerly accepted: excrement, bodhichitta, flesh, blood, and urine; the five samayas of objects to be meditated upon: the five Buddha Families, the five wisdoms, the five Buddhas, their five Consorts, and the five Bodies; then the five samayas of emotions not to be rejected: desire, hatred, stupidity, pride, and envy; finally, the five samayas of knowledge objects: the five aggregates, five elements, five sense powers, five sense objects, and five colors. As for the detailed samayas explained in other texts, I received those also. Not even for a single second did I fail to uphold the slightest samaya. Therefore, the Master of Orgyen held me continuously in his compassion, and I entered the mandala of the unsurpassable Secret Mantra. The door of the Secret Mantra is empowerment; and of empowerment, samayas are the root. This is why I have explained them."

While they were staying in Samye Yamalung, the Guru unfolded the mandala of the Secret Mantra and introduced Tsogyal to the *Kadü Chökyi Gyamtso*.[37]

At that time, the people were gathering to celebrate the Tibetan New Year, and the ministers, noticing Tsogyal's absence, were asking where she was and whether there had been some misfortune. Nobody knew, and so they approached the king himself. Unable to keep the secret, he told them how he had offered her as consort to the Precious Master. At that, the ministers of Zhang, the great minister Lugung Tsenpo, as well as Takra Lutsen, Zhangton Pön, Gyugyu Ringmo, Mama Zhang, Jarok Gyu, Shentra Go and others, all of them hostile to Dharma, cried out to the king in one voice:

> *Kyé!*
> Great King, Lord of the Tibetan people!
> Has your heart been nourished by a devil?
> Do not skim away the cream of kingly power!
> Do not soak in blood the head of the Tibetan people!
> Do not throw its tail out on the wind!
> Do not treat its ministers like dogs!
> Do not be the bane of this Tibetan realm!

"The tradition of your forefathers," they cried, "the yoke of gold, the lineage descended from the gods, has fallen into the grip of a foreigner, that so-called Padmasambhava, that Indian vagabond, that evil spellmaster! Oh, how easily this calamity has befallen us! The people are oppressed with sorrow. This girl of Kharchen has destroyed her reputation and is the ruin of her family. Will she now be left to bring disaster down upon the entire kingdom?

"Now, great ministers," they continued furiously among themselves, "think well on it, while you still have the breath in your mouths! Even if the king's heart has been torn from his breast, there is still a way to put it back, so the saying goes, provided that the ministers' sack of power has not been ripped asunder. Therefore let us ponder well!"

But before the king or any of the ministers could speak, Goe the Elder raised his voice: "Sire, alas! The counseling of ministers knows no end, and it is said that in the presence of the king, advice should be briefly spoken. Therefore, let the ministers meet together elsewhere." Everyone agreed to this, and the ministers went off to hold their council.

The king was downcast and secretly sent a message to the Guru at Red Rock Yamalung. The Guru received it and replied:

Kyema!
God-like lord of men!
Hardships still arise,
Yet I, the Lotus-Born,
Dread neither birth nor death.

The eight great fears![38]
What evils could they do
Against this form of mine,
Which is supreme, like diamond?
Though all the world be hostile,
What terror could this give to me, the Lotus-Born?

If parents are so easily alarmed,
What safety is there for the children?
If I who am the refuge of all wandering beings
Cannot guard the ones who look to me,
How shall I be guide for boundless multitudes?
Therefore, Great King!
Away with this faintheartedness, and pray!

The king was cheered by these words, and he spoke this counsel in the presence of the people:

Hear me, people of Tibet,
White or black or somewhere in between!
I observe and propagate the Dharma,
Planting thus the Doctrine of the Buddha.

On the light of my belief
No shadow of the Bön shall fall.

Your king protects the Dharma,
Listen to his word!
In Tibet, this land beneath the sun,
I shall nurture places where
The Dharma may be learned and practiced,
That Dharma that unites the sutras and the tantras.

Receive the order of the king and ministers!
Punishment for him who does not heed it!
Invite, therefore, the holy Lord of Orgyen,
Make him offerings, and confess your faults:
Benefits to him who does so!

The ministers Takra and Lugong answered the king:

God-like lord of men, you alone are king!

Give us worthy counsel, Lord,
Advice well thought, well pondered!
Do not be the ruin of your fathers' ways!
Do not cast the laws of the Tibetan land away!
Do not pierce the people's hearts and minds!
The joy and plenty of Tibet derive from Bön;
Who will guard Tibet if not the Bönpo gods?
We beg you, be the shield and guardian of Tibet!

First among the royal queens
Is Yeshe Tsogyal.
Truly she resembles Brahma's daughter.
What has happened? Where is she?
Has that foreign Hindu beggar murdered her?
And you, O King,
Are you so senseless and deranged?
What has happened? Are you not aware?

If this is so, the kingly power will fail
And swiftly come to nothing.

Therefore, bring back Tsogyal.
Restore her to your bed;
And justice fall upon that foreigner!

"As the saying goes," they cried to their fellow ministers, 'Evil magic kept within and no end of mischief; chronic illness in the body and no end of pain.' So let us seize the foreigner and bring him to trial. If he escapes judgment, let us kill him! Fellow ministers, are you with us? We must stand firm. If we are undecided and fail to act vigorously, our noble rank will be destroyed. Shall we let this pig's head of a king destroy his ministers, who are like a pride of lions? True, the word of the king is powerful, therefore let him say what he wants. But the ministers' counsel also carries influence, therefore let us be decided." And most of the Bönpo ministers pledged themselves in agreement.

But Shupu Pelseng, Drugu Ube, Kawa Peltsek, Chokro Lui Gyaltsen, Namkhai Nyingpo, Langdro, Dre, Yung, Nub, and the other Buddhist councillors consulted with each other and said: "Evil times and bitter tribulation for the Dharma! They are plotting boundless, nameless evils against our Lord, the second Buddha. Our great religious king, sky-jewel though he be, is held in no regard. The Dharma will not spread; the Doctrine will not take root; and now they will perpetrate the five sins of immediate perdition. Could death itself be more fearful than this? Even if Tibet were to become a desert, it would be as nothing. Come what may, we must protect our Guru and his Consort." And with these words, they fell silent.

Then the great religious king spoke. "The Master is like Vajradhara in person," he said. "If instead of showing him reverence, you plot against him boundless sins, know and understand, O ministers, that you will suffer evils nine times greater than what you have prepared for him. For it is I who hold dominion upon this earth!" And he was silent.

Even one of the queens, the Lady of Tsepong, spoke to the evil ministers. But there was no agreement. Tumult prevailed. And so Goe the Elder spoke and offered this counsel:

"Majesty! Surely it is better to be in harmony with your ministers than that this realm of Tibet should be broken and disunited."

The king agreed and said to the evil ministers: "Listen, mighty ministers of Tibet, my friends! Power in this world depends upon the king and, if the king is mighty, the ministers likewise have great strength. But without their sovereign, what are the doings of mere ministers? Therefore, do not furrow your king's brow with frowns, but offer him respectful counsel."

The ministers submitted, whereupon the king turned to address the Buddhists.

"Alas!" he sighed. "Even though I strongly hold to the Dharma, yet I am hedged about by selfish demands. Crimes committed in the name of religion can never be justified, and in any case, who could ever harm the vajra body of our Teacher? It is clear that we should all agree among ourselves."

The Buddhists also consented, and so all the ministers gathered in the presence of the king and deliberated carefully. After some time, the king promised that, provided the Teacher was not harmed, he would be given gold and sent back to India, while the Lady Tsogyal would be banished to Lhodrak. All agreed to this. And so, for the sake of the ministers, Guru Rinpoche and Yeshe Tsogyal appeared to comply with the decision. In reality, however, they went to the crag of Zhoto Tidro, to the Great Trysting Place of the Dakinis, the abode of the Green Lady of the Deadly Bell, a place invulnerable to every kind of obstacle. And there they engaged in secret practice.

This was the manner of their departure. The king made an offering to the Guru and his Consort, including three measures of gold powder and seven golden ingots, and requested blessings and prophecies. Thereupon, the Guru and his Consort descended from Yamalung, and in the neck of a raven-shaped rock they concealed a Dharma Treasure, uttering predictions concerning its future discovery. All of a sudden, the twelve Tenma goddesses appeared, bearing a palanquin of white light encircled by a halo of sparkling radiance. The Guru and his Consort stepped into it. The palanquin rose into the air and they departed. The king and ministers of Tibet, and all those in attendance, were filled with faith. And from that time, the place has been known simply as Ökar, "White Light," or Ökardrak, "The Cliff of White Light."

Instantly the Guru and his Consort arrived at their destination.

"At first," the Lady recalled, "we stayed at Tidro, in the Great Trysting Place of the Dakinis, where I, the woman Tsogyal, prepared the customary outer mandala, and with nine prostrations made the following request:

Kyema!
Holy Lord of Orgyen!
Yours is a Vajra Body:
　You do not dread the Demon Lord of Death;[39]
Yours an Illusory Body:
　You vanquish the Demon Child of Gods;
Yours a Vajra Rainbow Body:
　You crush the Demon of the Aggregates.
Yours is a Body displayed through concentration:
　The Demon of Afflictions is transformed into
　your friend.

Immortal Guru, Lotus-Born!
Now in the very center of my heart
I who am called Tsogyal have conceived
Unchanging faith.
My wish, in Yamalung,

For Secret Mantra unsurpassed
Was hindered by the wicked ministers.
But through your mercy, Holy Lord,
We came here riding through the sky!
Look upon me now with knowledge and compassion,
Unfold, I pray, the mandala that
Liberates and ripens.
And till enlightenment should come to me,
I pray you, in your kindness, banish hindrances.

"The Great Master replied to me:

Lovely maiden, girl of Kharchen,
Like the Udumbara is the mandala
Of Secret Mantra unsurpassed.
Rarely does it spring;
It does not linger long.
Except for beings highly favored,
It is hard to find.
Be glad therefore and offer me
The secret mandala.

"And I, without shame or hesitation, nor in the profane way of the world, but with joy and deep respect, displayed and offered the secret mandala.

"From the radiance of the Master's compassionate smile, shimmering rays of rainbow light broke forth and, pervading a thousand million universes, returned and were reabsorbed into his face. Summoned by the syllables *Dza* and *Hung*, they passed through his body, causing the secret vajra to rise in fury, entering the perfect quiet of the lotus.

"By the movements of the dance of bliss, the mandalas of the sun and moon within the eight root chakras of the Guru and his Consort were gradually set ablaze with light, and to the deities residing in each of the eight chakras, the offering was made of the Four Joys. And in that fiery experience of the accomplishment of the bliss of perfect luminosity, difficult to bear, the mandala of the *Heart Essence of the Dakinis,* the *Khandro Nyingtik*, was opened. Within the mandala of the Guru's Body, the ten male and female Buddhas of the five Families, together with the great Vajradhara, became visible and bestowed the empowerment of the Guru's Body. The five aggregates, which are pure in their intrinsic nature, clearly became the five Buddhas. The five elements, also intrinsically pure, clearly became the five Consorts. It was thus that the empowerments and sadhanas of the five Buddha Families of the Guru were bestowed on me.

"Then Guru Rinpoche said: 'The outer vase empowerment has been conferred, together with the means to accomplish the five families of peaceful deities. This presents the external world as a celestial palace and the beings who dwell within it as deities. Practice this for seven days.'

"And so, in accordance with the instructions of the Teacher, I practiced for seven days, considering the outer world as the celestial palace, and the world's inhabitants as male and female deities. Effortlessly, the whole of the inanimate universe clearly appeared as the palace of the deity, and all animate beings, manifested within it, could be clearly perceived as the Buddhas of the five families in union with their Consorts. Constantly, night and day, everything appeared as having the nature of the five families.

"Then the Guru said: 'The time has come to confer the inner aspect of the outer empowerment. Lay out the mandala seven times as before.'

"So, seven times I laid out the mandala with joy and devotion and offered it, saying:

> *Emaho!*
> My body is Mount Meru, king of mountains,
> My limbs the four surrounding continents.
> The lotus of Great Bliss is ground

Of both samsara and nirvana equally.
For sake of beings, lovingly accept
This peerless mandala of Great Felicity.

"The Guru was pleased, and his great peals of laughter, echoing and reechoing around, rocked the three levels of the world, causing them to tremble and shake. He arose in the form of the Padma Heruka, ferocious and strong, and the heruka of the secret sign, stimulated through the furious sound of the syllables *Ha Ha! Hi Hi!*, penetrated the lotus, the Consort's womb. I assumed the countenance of Varahi and the Guru's Body arose as the mandala of heruka Hayagriva, the lord of countless wrathful Buddhas. Thus it was that the mandala called the *Heart Essence of Hayagriva,* the *Tamdrin Nyingtik*, was opened, and empowerment bestowed.

"In the five chakras of the body of the Guru, transformed into glorious Hayagriva, five dakas in union with their consorts revealed themselves, their mandalas appearing with great brilliance, and the empowerment of the Guru's Speech was bestowed. And for me, transformed as I was into Varahi, all phenomena became inseparable from Hayagriva and I understood the nature of the subtle channels, the wind-energies, and the essence-drops. The five emotions were transformed and became in truth the Five Wisdoms. Absorbed in the concentration of the unsullied union of bliss and emptiness, I received the secret empowerment. I attained the eighth Bodhisattva ground, and the method of accomplishing the Guru and Consort as Hayagriva was instantly and totally conferred on me.

"Whereupon the Guru spoke: 'I have conferred on you the secret inner empowerment, with the method of accomplishing the Guru inwardly as the yidam; and I have introduced you to your body as the mandala of the deity, and to the channels, energies, and essence as the deity, mantra and Mahamudra. Practice accordingly from three to seven days.'

"Placing the seal of the butter lamp upon my body,[40] I endeavored until the wisdom, the substance of the empowerment, became stable. To begin with, I was oppressed by pain and discomfort, but eventually the letters residing in the channels resounded spontaneously. Bringing the energies under my control, I understood the meaning of the essence-drop, which is the Mahamudra, and brought to perfection the potential of the spotless blissful warmth. Thereafter the movements of the karmic wind-energy[41] ceased, the wisdom energy entered into the central channel and I displayed various signs of accomplishment. But the Guru said: 'The empowerments have not yet been completed. The corn should not be eaten while it is yet unripe!' And so once more, with faith to see him as greater than all the Buddhas, I requested the Precious Guru:

> *Kyema Ho!*
> Venerable, Precious One of Orgyen,
> Greater than the Buddhas past, present, and to come!
> On lowly beings, like myself and others,
> Bestow, I pray, supreme empowerment!

"The Guru arose in the form of the Red Heruka. From the syllable *Hung* in his heart, rays of light were violently projected and then reabsorbed in the mandala of the Guru. And brandishing the absolute heruka in his hand, he spoke these words:

> *Ra Ham!*
> Sky-dancing Tsogyal, listen undistractedly.
> Queen Samantabhadri, hear me well!
> If you wish to enter
> The mandala of inner essence,
> Offer now the secret mandala of bliss.
> If this method is disclosed,
> Samaya will be overthrown!

"For me, the woman Tsogyal, profane appearances ceased. I stripped myself in the nakedness of Great Felicity, sprinkled the secret mandala of bliss with the five samaya substances, and said:

> Hero, lord of bliss, consider me.
> Guru, lord of Great Felicity!
> The mandala of inner essences I yearn to enter
> With true and certain joy.
> The samaya of this practice,
> With my life I will preserve.

"Stirring the pistils of the lotus with my fingers, in a rhythmic dance, I offered the mandala to the mandala of the Guru. The great Padma Heruka, with the gesture of the hook, drew the mandala of space towards him and, in an overwhelming outburst of tremendous laughter and an expression of ferocious wrath, he placed the great and blazing vajra, the absolute heruka, upon the lotus throne. All appearances were engulfed by the long, slow, resounding roar of Great Bliss. The mandala of the *Glowing Sun of Radiant Space* was opened and the empowerment conferred. In the Guru's mandala of wisdom and method were to be found the sublime Buddha-fields of the four herukas, sovereigns of the four chakras, expressed as myriads of deities, disks of light, and seed syllables. And in that mandala, the empowerment of the Four Joys was given.

"The Guru and I remained in union and, through the blessing power of the chakra in his forehead, a piercingly intense experience of the Primordial Wisdom of Joy came upon me. In the thirty-two subsidiary Buddha-fields, which are the white mandala, there were thirty-two white herukas in union with their consorts, surrounded by hundreds of thousands of herukas similar to them. In their midst, the sovereign heruka of them all, in union with his consort, bestowed on me an introduction to the Primordial Wisdom of Joy. The affliction of anger was purified, likewise the habitual tendencies and obscurations of the body. I realized the aspects of the Path of Joining and, having now the power to work for the benefit of seven universes of the ten directions, I received the secret name of Dechen Karmo Tsogyalma: White Tsogyal, Lady of Great Bliss.

"In the same way, in the sixteen subsidiary Buddha-fields of the yellow mandala in the throat, there were sixteen yellow herukas in union with their consorts, surrounded as before by hundreds of thousands of herukas similar to them. And again in their midst, the sovereign of them all, the heruka of the Jewel Family, united with his consort, bestowed on me an introduction to the boundless qualities of Perfect Joy. The emotion of desire was purified, likewise the habitual tendencies and obscurations of speech. I realized the aspects of the Path of Accumulation and, having now the ability to work for the benefit of twenty universes in the ten directions, I received the secret name of Yönten Gyeché Sermo Tsogyalma: Yellow Tsogyal, Increaser of Qualities.

"Again in the same way, in the eight subsidiary Buddha-fields in the blue-black mandala of the heart, eight blue-black herukas, in union with their consorts, were surrounded as before by hundreds of thousands of herukas. And in their midst, their sovereign, the heruka of the Buddha Family, in union with his consort, bestowed on me an introduction to the Mahamudra, Supreme Joy. The affliction of confusion and the habitual tendencies of the mind were purified. I realized the aspects of the Path of Liberation and, having now the ability to work for the benefit of thirty-six universes in the ten directions, I received the secret name of Drölché Damtsig Tsogyal: Tsogyal, Samaya That Liberates.

"Once again and in the same way, in the sixty-one[42] Buddha-fields of the red mandala that is in the navel, in the midst of the sixty-one herukas in union with their consorts and surrounded by their retinues, their sovereign the red heruka, in union with his consort, bestowed on me an introduction to the Primordial Wisdom of Coemergent Joy, whereby the defiled consciousness with its impure grasping and the habitual tendencies of the body, speech, and mind were purified in equal measure. I realized the aspects of the path of Perfect Purity, and, having the ability to work for the benefit of infinite universes in the ten directions, I received the secret name of Thayé Yeshe Tsogyal: Tsogyal Boundless Wisdom.

"The Guru said: 'For seven days endeavor in the practice of the four Wisdoms in the absolute mandala of the Four Joys, taking the four self-empowerments. Then, in reverse order, meditate on pleasure as Primordial Wisdom.'

"Now, in my practice upon pleasure, which is Primordial Wisdom, essence of empowerment, I continually increased the rhythm of the Four Joys and never allowed it to diminish. Moreover, to allow the bodhichitta to be spilled outside is like slaying the Buddha Amitabha. There is no one left to confess the fault to, and a karma leading to the hell of Torment Unsurpassed is generated. But I was able to reverse the bodhichitta upward, and, by pressing down the vital energy and drawing up the lower energy, I held the pleasure in the 'vase.' I remained attentive to the bliss but did not crave it, and thus I practiced, laying aside all mentally fabricated concentration. Not for an instant did I give way to laziness. When I fixed with mindfulness the bodhichitta in the lotus of the bhaga,[43] ignorance was completely purified and the thousand and eighty wind-energies of the first time period ceased. Arriving on the Path of Seeing the Primordial Wisdom of the two knowledges,[44] I attained the first ground. It was then that I obtained different kinds of clairvoyance. After that, I caused the bodhichitta to rise to the secret center and fixed it there. The interdependent link of conditioning factors was purified, and the wind-energies of the second time period ceased. Thus I attained the second ground. Then I fixed the bodhichitta between the secret and the navel centers. Consciousness was purified and the wind-energies of the third period ceased. Thus I attained the third ground. In the same way, as I held the bodhichitta at the navel, the interdependent link of name and form was purified, the wind-energies of the fourth period ceased, and I attained the fourth ground. Samsara, nirvana, ordinary mind, Primordial Wisdom, and Coemergent Joy were purified and I realized the Svabhavikakaya. After this, I held the bodhichitta between the navel and the heart centers. The six sense faculties were purified, the wind-energies of the fifth period ceased, and I attained the fifth ground. As I held the bodhichitta at the heart, sense contact was purified, the wind-energies of the sixth period ceased, and I attained the sixth ground. The mental state of ordinary sleep was purified, likewise Extraordinary Joy, and as the result, I attained the Dharmakaya. Then I held the bodhichitta between the heart and the throat. Feeling was purified, the wind-energies of the seventh period ceased, and I obtained the seventh ground. The bodhichitta was then held in the throat chakra. Desire was purified, the wind-energies of the eighth period ceased, and I attained the eighth ground. The dream state was purified, likewise Supreme Joy, and as the result I attained the Sambhogakaya. I held the bodhichitta between the throat and the forehead, the interdependent link of craving was purified, the wind-energies of the ninth period ceased, and I attained the ninth ground. Then I held the bodhichitta in the chakra of the forehead. The interdependent link of becoming was purified, the wind-energies of the tenth period ceased, and I attained the tenth ground. The five sense-consciousnesses of the waking state, the body's channels, and also the Primordial Wisdom of Joy were purified. And thus I attained the immaculate Nirmanakaya. Then I held the bodhichitta between the forehead and the ushnisha so that the birth process was purified. The wind-energies of the eleventh period were purified, and I attained the eleventh ground. Afterward, as I reversed the bodhichitta in the ushnisha and held it there, the twelve interdependent links, as far as old age and death, were purified. The twenty-one thousand six hundred wind-energies of the twelfth period ceased, and thus were purified the four impure states: the mental states of sexual climax, deep sleep, dream, and waking. Likewise were purified the channels, wind-energies, and the essence, the mind's support, as well as the Four Joys. Thus I attained the twelfth ground endowed with the Bodies and all the qualities of a Buddha. Becoming one who acts for the benefit of the infinitude of sentient beings, I gained mastery of all the qualities of a Buddha. Thus it was that in six months I realized the purpose of the third empowerment.

"Then Guru Rinpoche said to me:

> *Kyema!* Maiden, Dakini!
> Your form is young and ripened to perfection.
> Maid of sixteen years, it is graced
> With sixfold quality and freedom—
> Diligent, compassionate,
> Lady Sarasvati, great and wise!
> Accomplished in the Secret Mantra,
> Lady, you are Varahi.
> Your mind and body now are all prepared.
> The door of the maturing Secret Mantra
> Now stands open.
> Now, great-hearted being,
> Take a valiant partner!

"Offering to the Precious Guru a ganachakra feast, with my body and all my possessions, I the woman Yeshe Tsogyal requested thus:

> Holy Lord of Orgyen, Thödrengtsel,
> Stem of the Secret Mantra, Holder of the Vajra.
> Vast, beyond repayment, is your loving kindness.
> Whatever is your pleasure, I will do without regard
> For life or limb, though I may die.
> Yet still I beg you to bestow on me,
> The word initiation of the Great Perfection.
> O Teacher, grant the fourth empowerment today!

"But the Master replied: 'The time to enter the vehicle of the effortless Atiyoga has not yet come for you, so practice earnestly the Secret Mantra teachings of the Mahayana.' Thereupon he uttered this prophecy. 'Mistress, without a valiant partner as a skillful means, there is in truth no way for you to undertake the practice of the Secret Mantra. When an earthen vessel has not been fired, it cannot hold anything; when there is no wood, no fire is possible; when there is no fall of rain, no shoots will spring. And so, in the land of Nepal, whither he has found his way from Serling in India, there lives a youth who goes by the name of Atsara Salé, Salé the Indian. He is a hero, a daka, and an emanation of Hayagriva. He is seventeen years old and has on his breast a red birthmark at the level of his heart. Search him out and make him your companion. You will instantly reach the level of Great Bliss.'

"Therefore, taking an ingot of gold and a full measure of gold dust, I set out alone for Nepal—I, the woman Tsogyal."

In the region of Érong, the Lady, our mother, fell among seven thieves who, wanting to steal her gold, pursued her like hounds after deer. But she, recalling the Guru to her mind, considered the thieves as yidam deities and, with the sincere intention of offering all her possessions as a mandala, she sang melodiously:

Kyema!
Seven yidams from the vale of Erong,
Fortune indeed to meet you here today!
May my stock of merit now be filled,
The wishes of all beings satisfied!
Swiftly may my karmic debts be cleansed!

Éma!
Marvelous wonder thus to meet
The Teacher's loving-kindness!

Joyful thoughts arise from deep within.
May beings all be freed by this my gift!

And joining her hands in supplication, she laid out the gold in little heaps.

The seven thieves did not understand her words, but the sound of the Lady's voice touched their hearts. They reached the first level of samadhi and, staring at her with wide open eyes, they said in the language of Nepal: "Ah, Mistress! Where do you come from? Who are your noble parents? Who is your teacher? What is the reason for your coming here? Please, we beg you, sing to us again." Their wild and shaggy hair, which had been fierce and bristling, became smooth, their faces merry with smiles. Their ferocious expressions melted away, and they grinned happily so that you could see their teeth. They gathered in front of the Lady and she, leaning on that three-jointed bamboo staff of hers, sang to them in the language of Nepal.

Emaho!
Seven brigands linked to me by karma from the past!
The mental states of spite and anger
Are Primal Wisdom, mirror-like.
Wrathful anger, fixing on the enemy—
From nowhere else does shining clarity arise.
Simply watch it: that is Vajrasattva.
Do not cling to things as they appear,
But let emptiness arise.

The home of me, this girl, is "Joy-made-manifest,"
The voidness of a pure and peaceful Buddha-field,
World of the Sambhogakaya.
I am not attached to forms and namings of convention,
Therefore, if you want the lovely land
Of me, your mother, I will take you there.

Seven robbers linked to me by karma from the past!
The mental states of pride and self-conceit

Are but the Primal Wisdom of Equality.
"I am first! I want the best for me!":
From nowhere else comes natural equanimity.
Watch this nature—that is Ratnasambhava!
Do not cling to voidness,
Let phenomena arise.

My father is a source that grants me all I need and wish,
An all-providing wishing-jewel is truly my own father.
I am not enthralled by mirages of worldly wealth,
And therefore if you want my father,
I who am your mother will bestow him.

Seven robbers linked to me by karma from the past!
The mental states of lust and hankering
Are but Primal Wisdom All-perceiving.
Wanting to possess, and greed for pleasure:
From nowhere else comes clear perception.
Watch this fresh, unchanging state, for that is Amitabha!
Do not be enthralled by clarity,
Let bliss itself arise.

My mother is unbounded light.
Great Bliss beyond all fathoming is she.
Unattached am I to tastes of joy or sorrow,
Therefore, if you want my mother,
I who am your mother will bestow her.

Seven robbers linked to me by karma from the past!
The mental states of jealousy and dualistic clinging
Are but Primal Wisdom All-accomplishing.
Jealous spite and restless, envious self-pity:
From nowhere else comes fruitful action.
Watch your thoughts,
For there Amoghasiddhi lies.
Do not cling to subtle states or gross;
Allow whatever comes, to come.

My teacher is achievement of the goal,
Completion of activity is my instructor.
Unattached am I to every action,
Therefore, if you want my teacher,
I who am your mother will bestow him.

Seven robbers linked to me by karma from the past!
The mental state of nescience and dullness
Is Primal Wisdom, All-embracing Space.
The clouded mind enwrapped in ignorance:
From nowhere else comes constancy in Dharma.
Watch this ignorance,
For there is Vairochana.
Do not cling to mental sharpness;
Allow whatever comes, to come.

My partner is the artist of appearance.
Because this perfect friend is all my joy,
I am not caught in ordinary duality.
So if you wish to act like me,
I who am your mother will instruct you.

When she said this, the seven robbers experienced irreversible faith,[45] and their minds turned from samsara. They beseeched the Lady for instructions in the Dharma and were liberated. The seven robbers implored her to visit their country, but she declined and instead set off again for Jarung Khashor, the stupa constructed by the three young men of Mön.[46]

When she arrived, she made an offering to the stupa of a handful of gold dust and prayed:

Om Ah Hung!
Here in Nepal, pure land of Conquering Buddhas,
O Offspring of the Dharmakaya, Guardian of beings,
For vast unnumbered periods of time to come,
Remain and turn the wheel
Of teachings unsurpassable,

Saving wandering beings from the ocean of existence.
From this domain of bondage to the land of perfect
freedom,
Protector, may you strongly lead
All human and nonhuman beings.

As she spoke, thousands of rays of light broke forth from the stupa, and within a dense expanse of cloud and mist there appeared the Lotus Guru flanked by the abbot Shantarakshita and the Dharma King Trisong Detsen, with a throng of dakinis all around. The Guru said:

Kyema!
Hear me, mistress, maid of Kharchen!
Your body is now disciplined
And you are patient, cleansed of anger.
May your wisdom be a guide for beings!
Generosity has freed you, and your diligence is perfect.
Proceed through concentration on the grounds and paths.
Do not linger in this place for long,
But find the friend you need and bring him to Tibet.
The door of Mantra, secret and profound,
I once again will open.

And with this instruction, he vanished from her sight.

"And so by stages," the Lady recalled, "I began my search. Not knowing where my future companion would be, I arrived in the city of Kho-khom-hen, at the large market by the southern gate. There, a handsome and attractive youth strolled up to me. There was a gleam of oil on his tanned body. His front teeth were like rows of white shells, and his four canines were like tiny conches curling to the right. His look was open and sincere, and there was a touch of red in the corners of his eyes. His nose was pointed, and in his eyebrows there was a hint of blue. His hair was bound up in a knot turning to the right, and the fingers of his hands were webbed like the feet of a waterbird.[47]

" 'Lady,' he said to me, 'where are you from? Have you come to ransom me?'

"In answer, I sang to him in the language of Zangling:

Emaho!
Listen now, my brave, my lovely boy.
A woman from the center of Tibet,
I am the lady of the holy Lotus-Born.
Where is your home?
What is the name you bear?
What is the reason of your being here?

"The boy replied:

My town was Serling in the noble land of India.
A heathen stole me from my parents' arms
And in this city sold me into bondage.
Arya Salé was the name my parents gave me,
And here I've lived enslaved for seven years."

All the merchants of the town, crowding in the marketplace, were entranced by the Lady's countenance, and for a while they stood there speechless. Then they said, "Mistress, Lady, speak to us a little. For you cheer our hearts, and we will give you great gifts." And so the Lady Tsogyal sang to them this song:

Namo Guru Padma Siddhi Hri!
Samantabhadra, glorious, vastness of the sky—
Within that space the sun of Great Perfection has arisen.
Our mothers wandering in the six realms of samsara
Are no more to languish in the realms of gloom.
Is not Padmasambhava your father?

The adamantine field, unchanging space—
There the Great Compassionate

Is Buddha, free from birth and death,
Knowing neither good nor evil karma.
Is not Padmasambhava your father?

Akanishta is my perfect home, the crag of Tidro—
And I a dákini called forth by the compassion of the Guru.
This bliss-bestowing boy and I are linked together.
Am I not your mother Yeshe Tsogyal?

To Nepal,
A mistress of the Dharma, I have come.
This boy is fortunate, I judge,
And here he should not stay,
For am I not his guardian
Yeshe Tsogyal?

Though the people could not understand its meaning, they listened, enchanted, to the song and exclaimed that the Lady was a sweet-voiced dakini. Later, she made her way to the house where the Indian Salé lived and sat down at the outer gate. It was evening, and when they asked her where she was from and what she was about, she told them various things about herself as they came to mind. Then she said: "My Guru, Padmasambhava, has sent me to buy the Indian slave who is living in your house. It would be good of you to sell him to me."

"Although this Indian is our bondsman," they said, "he is like a son to us. We also paid a great deal of gold for him. We cannot sell him. But if you wish, both of you can live together here and be our servants." The Lady Tsogyal replied:

Where the bright disk of the sun presides,
The shades of darkness have no place.
When the sun sets, only stars appear,
And yet the sun will rise once more tomorrow.

With wishing-jewels to hand,
Who cares for gold and wealth?
But when there is no jewel, we count our costs.
Therefore I will seek this jewel tomorrow.

There, where the perfect Buddha dwelt,
No need was there for skillful means.
The Buddha now has gone, so on such means I must rely.
Tomorrow, means and wisdom will unite.

When the fruit is truly gained,
No need for Salé will there be.
But while I tread towards this goal,
I need him. Therefore sell him.
This is my request.

The whole family—parents, children, and the rest—crowded around, their hearts won by the sweetness of the Lady's voice. They invited her inside and offered her a splendid feast. Then the mistress of the house spoke up.

"When you have bought this Indian boy," she said, "what will you do? Marry him? To be sure, you are a lovely girl and are of good family besides. Therefore, if you seek a husband, stay here with this son of mine."

"My Guru Padma," the Lady Tsogyal replied, "has foretold that this Atsara, this Indian, is someone very necessary to me. I have gold for his ransom and I must have him, come what may."

"Well, how much money do you have?" asked the woman. "When I bought him, I paid five hundred ounces of gold, and I want more than that now."

Lady Tsogyal said: "I will give you all the gold you want, for he is indispensable to me." Then she began to measure her gold dust, but found that she scarcely had one hundred ounces, let alone five.

"Well, now," said the woman, "if you want to buy him, you must have gold. What you have here is hardly enough to pay for the Indian's hand. But you don't have the gold, so what can you do?"

Now, it happened that in that city there lived a merchant called Dhana Ayu, a man of great wealth. His son, Nagani, a youth of twenty years, had been slain in the war that at that time was troubling the country. The parents had brought his body home most tenderly, and so great was their sorrow that they cried out, saying that they would kill themselves at his funeral. The Lady Tsogyal was moved with unbearable pity and went to them. "There is no need for you to grieve," she said. "Give me some gold with which to ransom the young Salé and I will bring your own son back to life."

The man and his wife were beside themselves with joy and exclaimed, "What is gold to us? If you bring our son back to life again, we will give you enough wealth to buy a prince, let alone an Indian boy." So Yeshe Tsogyal promised to raise their son to life again, and they in return promised to give her all the gold and whatever else she needed. And so she placed the body of the youth on a large piece of white silk, folded in four, and sang this song:

Om Ah Hung Guru Sarva Hri!
Samantabhadra is the ground,
Primal purity without delusion.
The path is but the sixfold state
Of beings, mirage-forms, whose
Lives of happiness and sorrow
Are cause and fruit, the karmic law expressed.
What is there to do, then, knowing this is so?

I, yogini, skilled in Secret Mantra,
Held in the compassion of the Lotus-Born, my father,
Have no dread of dying or of being born.

I crush at once the sorrows and adversities of others.
Let us pray for blessings—sure to come.

With these words, she placed her forefinger on the dead boy's heart, and the color of his body slowly began to brighten. She put a drop of spittle into his mouth and into his ears she spoke the words *Ayurjñana Drum*. With her hand she stroked the deep sword cuts, which were healed and made whole. Little by little, the young man came back to life, and at length he completely recovered. The people were struck with amazement and gladness and made prostrations to the Lady. Seeing their son restored to life, the parents took him in their arms, weeping for joy. They showered the Lady with gifts and offered an immense ganachakra feast. Salé the Indian boy was bought for a thousand measures of gold and presented to her. The fame of Lady Tsogyal filled the kingdom and the king himself honored her and invited her to reside there as his spiritual guide. But she declined and made her way to the temple of É in Nepal, taking Salé with her.

There she met the Nepali master Vasudhara, a disciple of the Lotus Guru, and offering him a golden ingot and some gold dust, she requested various teachings and instructions. Knowing that the Lady was the consort of the Precious Teacher, Vasudhara paid her every courtesy, giving her much teaching and advice. At that time, Shakyadema, Jila Jipha, and others were residing at the caves of Asura and Yangleshö. The Lady therefore visited Shakyadema, and with presents of gold, she made this request:

Kyema Ho!
Noble Lady, sister in the Secret Mantra,
I pray you, listen to Tibetan Yeshe Tsogyal.

The Mind, unfailing satisfaction
Of every need and want,

Impartially bestows whatever could be wished:
This is Tsogyal's generosity—
Tibetan Yeshe Tsogyal.

The Mind is stainless,
Free from false samaya.
It dwells in discipline, observant:
This is Tsogyal's discipline—
Tibetan Yeshe Tsogyal.

The Mind is not enslaved by joy or misery,
Nor caught in apathy. But patient,
It withstands both good and ill:
This is Tsogyal's patience—
Tibetan Yeshe Tsogyal.

The Mind, a seamless, flowing stream,
Engenders inexhaustibly
Both nondual bliss and emptiness:
This is Tsogyal's diligence—
Tibetan Yeshe Tsogyal.

The Mind, no matter what arises,
Is Creation and Perfection unified—
And stable resting in the state of Mahamudra:
This is Tsogyal's concentration—
Tibetan Yeshe Tsogyal.

The Mind is Primal Wisdom's blissful dance.
Through skillful means
Is wisdom now perfected:
This is Tsogyal's wisdom—
Tibetan Yeshe Tsogyal.

O you of noble race, bestow
Your teachings on your sister,
Keeping no distinctions.

With great joy Shakyadema sang this reply:

Emaho!

O welcome, sister, consort of our only Teacher!
The doctrines that I hold are few.
But through compassion of the holy Orgyen Sambha,[48]
I have teachings needed at the time of birth and death:
The union of the phases of Creation and Perfection;
The Great Seal, Mahamudra;
Instruction on the Clear Light and the Body of Illusion.
These, whereby the "bardo-womb" is emptied,
Are the teachings of Nepali Shakyadema.

The teachings needed for the transference of
consciousness:
The cultivation of the Avadhuti,
Supported by the subtle veins and energies;
A-shé's[49] inward heat, the blazing up and melting.
These that drive away death's terror and the fears of birth,
Are teachings of Nepali Shakyadema.

My teachings tell of how to bring emotions to the path:
Of how to train in emptiness and bliss,
Relying on the essence of both means and wisdom;
Of how to bring forth Wisdom of the Fourfold Joy,
Through which I am protected from the host of enemy
emotions.
These are teachings of Nepali Shakyadema.

Directions needed for the ignorant and murky state of
sleep:
On how, according to the teachings of the Great
Perfection,
To purify one's dreams and enter Luminosity.
Thus, even in the darkness at the end of time,

I shall not be afraid.
These are teachings of Nepali Shakyadema.

I have teachings needed for the realization of the ultimate:
On how to train in Luminosity,
Relying on the sixfold light,
Perfecting thus the fourfold confidence.
Thus I am dauntless, though the very Buddha should
assail me.
These are teachings of Nepali Shakyadema.

Now no need to count the causal grounds and paths.
For by these teachings Buddhahood is taken in a moment.
How wonderful this fruit, supreme and unsurpassable!
Accomplished mistress, making no distinctions,
Your teachings grant to me, a ready vessel.

With these words, their minds mingled and united, and many teachings were given and received.

Then the Lady Tsogyal and Salé, her companion, made their way to Tibet, to the province of Tsang, where they went to Tidro and dwelt in the Great Trysting Place of the Dakinis. The Lady's benefactors in the region paid her homage, even though an evil rumor had been put about that she had been led astray by demons. Evil mouths were saying that she was engaged no longer in the service of the Lotus Guru, but had got herself an atsara, an Indian vagabond.

When the feast of the tenth day of the month came around, she opened the mandala of the *Lama Sangdü* and just at the moment of the invitation, the Master of Orgyen appeared, riding on a sunbeam.

"And I," the Lady Tsogyal recalled, "smiling through my tears, fell to the ground, prostrating to the Guru. I said to him:

Alas, my Teacher, merciful, compassionate!
Pity me, a woman wrapped in ignorance,

Wandering in evil karma.
Look at me with mercy, Lord,
That I might cleanse my wickedness away,
And never more be parted from you.

The purpose of my journey to Nepal,
To find without mistake the youthful Arya Salé,
Is now achieved. And so I beg you,
Open wide the door of Secret Mantra.
Look on me with pity—
Let the way be free of hindrances.

"Radiant with joy, the Guru smiled and sang:

Kyema!
Mistress, maid of Kharchen,
Listen well, my faithful one!
Should you wish to pass, while in this body,
From this shoreless ocean of samsara,
Rely upon a steersman, an authentic teacher.
Take ship aboard the vessel of the oral teachings!
Hoist the mainsail of profound instructions!
Release the landmark-seeking raven of advice!
Sound the conch! Destroy the sea serpent of hindrances!
Resist the countering gale of karma with a heavy anchor,
And with your faith raise up a fair and following wind.
Stop the leaks with perfect pure samaya,
And ride upon the waves of instant ripening and freedom,
Arriving at the island of the wish-fulfilling jewel.
There you will rejoice, with all desires granted.
A place replete with treasures will delight and please you,
For all unwanted earth and stones will vanish.
The happy moment of perpetual joy has come!

" 'My dear child,' he went on, 'what obstacles did you encounter? Or was it easy and without difficulty? When did you get here?' So I recounted to him in detail the many hardships that I encountered on the way, and all the reversals that I had to deal with in Nepal concerning the gold—about my having to pay the thousand ounces, for which I brought a dead man back to life.

" 'Very good,' the Guru said. 'All these hardships are truly excellent. Innumerable karmic obscurations have been purified. Indeed, you are not a woman who seeks a man with longing. The price you paid was high, but it was good and fitting. You have amassed an immense store of merit and are not at all a woman of rank and lustful passions. The raising of the dead was but an ordinary accomplishment, therefore do not be conceited about it. This young man here is, to be sure, superior to others, and so we will give him the name Arya. And since gold has been paid for him, let us call him Ser-wö, Golden Light.' "

Then the Guru opened the mandala of the *Teacher's Blessings* and brought Indian Salé to spiritual maturity. The Lady Tsogyal herself acted as the support of the empowerment. Thus Indian Salé was truly ripened and established on the path of liberation. He acquired a deep-rooted understanding of the expedient and ultimate teachings, and the Guru appointed him the companion of Tsogyal, saying: "Practice now until you gain accomplishment in the Secret Mantra." The Guru then left for Lhodrak and the Lady and her companion, mistress and disciple, went to a cave that no one had ever found before (indeed it is now known as the Secret Cave of Tsogyal), and there for seven months they devoted themselves to the cultivation of the Four Joys. The Lady Tsogyal could pass through any kind of object, and her body was no longer subject to the phenomena of aging, sickness, and decline. This is to say that she attained mastery of the five elements. The Four Joys became manifest, and she attained the four Bodies.

Then the Guru returned, and together they went and stayed in the great cave of Tidro, where the Guru turned the wheel of Dharma. Now, the Guru had earlier granted to the king of Tibet, protector of the Doctrine, numerous mandalas of the

Secret Mantra: *Shinje É*, for example, *Tamdrin Pawo, Yangdak Marme, Trinle Purba, Dutsi Tö, Mamo Tram,* and others. And the king, while practicing the approach and accomplishment stages, had received certain wondrous signs and omens. Faith arose in his heart and, thinking that he must still request the many very profound teachings of the Secret Mantra, he sent Shupu Pelseng, Gyatsa Lhanang, and Ma Rinchen Chok to invite the Guru and his Consort with gifts of gold.

The three translators arrived at the cave of the Great Trysting Place of Tidro and proclaimed:

> *Kyema!*
> Guru, Lord, and Lady,
> Fleet-foot envoys of the king are we!
> Trisong, god-like master of Tibet,
> Would cross the threshold of
> The lofty vehicle of the Secret Mantra most profound.
> He implores your presence.
> Think of him with kindness and be swift to come!

And so saying, they offered the presents of gold.

The Guru answered:

> *Kyeho!*
> Fleet-foot envoys, faithful, fortunate three sons,
> Your coming is well starred!
> I am Padmasambhava.
> Though living in the human world,
> My mind and all the Buddhas' minds are one,
> For I and Vajradhara are not different.
> The universe I fill with emanations of myself!
> The great and pious king conceives the wish
> To gain enlightenment for beings' sake.
> This is excellent indeed!
> I will come to spread the Secret Mantra now.

The Master and his Consort, Arya Salé, and the three translators set off together for Samye. When they arrived at Zhodrö, the Guru told the three to go on ahead and instruct the great king to prepare a reception; he and the other two would follow. So the three Tibetans went ahead and announced to the king the imminent arrival of the Master, advising him that it was necessary to go and receive him.

Thereupon the ministers of Tibet murmured together. "This so-called Padmasambhava," they said, "is like the sky; nothing can destroy him. He is like a stream of water; no sword can harm him. He is like a mass of flames; his body burns and sparkles. He is like the wind; we cannot seize him. He seems to be really present but it is as if there were nothing there. Let us conspire nothing against him for the moment; let us rather fall in with the decisions of this Buddhist king. But if that wayward queen of ours comes along too and doesn't get what she deserves, the royal power will be undone."

"Now, all this was known to Guru Rinpoche," the Lady recalled, "and he declared: 'Secret Mantra abounds in skillful means, so naturally there is no difficulty.' So saying, he caused me, the woman Tsogyal, to appear to the eyes of others as his three-pronged trident. And so we arrived at Zhodar, where Takra Gungtsen, the representative of the pious king, came to meet us with a company of a hundred great ministers on horseback.

"In due course, the party arrived at Samye, where, before the gate of the great stupa, the king, his ministers, and the court performed an elaborate ceremony of welcome. The king prostrated to the Guru and offered him a golden carafe swathed in a piece of white silk and filled to the brim with fresh rice wine. Then the Guru spoke. 'Now,' he said, 'the Secret Mantra is new and has great power. But though it will spread, in times to come it will be abused and will not be fruitful.' So saying, he entered the central sanctuary. The Tibetan courtiers noticed that Tsogyal was absent and that an Indian servant had been brought along instead. The king reflected that since Tsogyal was not there, his request for the Secret Mantra teachings would be marred by difficulties. Thus he asked the Precious Teacher where she was, for he wanted to see her again. 'Great Guru,' he said, 'where is Tsogyal? Why has she not come, and how might I find her? Is this Indian boy your disciple?'

"A smile played upon the lips of the Great Guru and he sang:

Kyema Ho!
Bodhisattva, Dharma King,
The true condition of this form of mine is space,
And who can count the powers of the master of this
element?
Into space the maiden Tsogyal has withdrawn,
Abiding at the boundary of samsara and nirvana.

This form of mine brings forth appearances,
And nothing is there that it cannot do.
The maiden Tsogyal went into the space of Dharmakaya
And dwells now in Samantabhadri's sphere.

Bliss-voidness is this form of mine,
The magic power of voidness leaves no wishes unfulfilled.
To the sphere of bliss and voidness the maiden Tsogyal
went,
And dwells now in the blissful mansion of the triple Kaya.

So saying, he touched the trident with his hand and, to the wonder of the king, it was transformed back into Tsogyal. Now, some of the common people saw this, including one of the queens, who reported it to the ministers. "That Hindu," she said, "is very crafty. He hid the woman Tsogyal in his trident." Some of the ministers were astonished, but the majority retorted that nobody could trust a word she said. It was impossible for Tsogyal to be inside the trident—there was no way for it to contain even her hand! But they all agreed that something extraordinary—a miracle—must have happened, and they postponed the evil plan that they had previously hatched. But most of the people had faith.

Making his way to the hermitage of Chimphu Gewa, the Guru opened one hundred and twenty mandalas of the Secret Mantras for the twenty-one disciples, the king and his subjects, the thirty-two close followers, the seven noble ladies, and others—in all, a multitude of three hundred and five people. And he brought them to maturity and liberation. He introduced them especially to the sadhanas of the *Drupchen Kabgye, Mamo, Shinje, Phurba, Dutsi, Yangdak, Lama Gongdü, Yidam Gongdü, Gyumtrul Shi-tro, Yangdak Shi-tro, Pema Shi-tro*, and so on. He gave them also sixty-one cycles of *Nyingtik*, seven different *Gongdü*, eleven extensive and abridged cycles of the *Kabgye*, one hundred and two *Thukdrup*, seventy-six pith instructions, one hundred and thirty tantras, and much more.

To the king in particular he gave the seven root sadhanas of *Dutsi Yönten* and twenty pith instructions, telling him to practice them. To Namkhai Nyingpo of Nub he gave the *Yangdak Marme Güpa* and *Gekdül Purnak Nyishu*, and instructed him to practice them in Lhodrak. To both Sangye Yeshe and Dorje Dudjom he gave the root sadhanas of *Jampel Shinjeshe* and the sadhanas of *Chagya Zilnön Lhadruk*, together with twenty main pith instructions and their supplements, telling them to practice at Yangdzong. To Gyalwa Choyang of Kunglung and Gyalwa Lodrö of Dre he gave *Tamdrin Yangsang Rölpa*, the root sadhana of *Yoga Sum* with twenty five supplementary pith instructions, together with twelve tantras and the sadhana of *Tramenma*, telling them to practice in Chimphu itself. To Vairotsana and Denma Tsemang he gave the sadhanas of *Möpa Trangak, Pel Tobden Nagpo*, the root sadhanas of the *Debgye*, and the branch sadhanas of *Drekpa Tobgye*, instructing them to practice in Yamalung. To Kawa Peltsek and Odren Wangchuk he gave, among others, the outer, inner and secret root sadhanas of the

Mamos and the *Newap* and *Legye*, telling them to practice in the caves of Yerpa. To Jñanakumaravajra and Sokpo Lhapel Zhönnu he gave pith instructions for *Yangphur Sangwa*, together with the *Chagya Chenpo Tsedrup Lung*, instructing them to practice in Nyemo Chemai Drak. To Pelgyi Sengé and Chokro Lui Gyaltsen he gave the root sadhana of *Trekpa Trowo Chugyen* and branch sadhanas of *Trekpön Sumchui Kangthab* and pith instructions for activities, telling them to practice in Pel Chuwo Ri. To the translators Rinchen Zangpo and Tingdzin Zangpo he gave the secret sadhana of *Thukje Chenpo*, the sadhana of *Rigdzin Lama* and the *Rigpa Chagya Chenpo Chokgyi Ngödrupkyi Lung*, and told them to practice in the caves of Uru. To Langdro Könchok Jungne and Gyalwa Changchub he gave the *Chinlap Lamai Druplung* and the sadhanas of *Tamdrin Sangwa Kundü* and *Tanak Trekpa*, telling them to practice in the caves of Yeru Shang. To Drenpa Namkha Wangchuk and Khyeuchung Khading, he gave a secret sadhana of *Padma Shi-tro*, the *Dorje Sempa Tsawa Lhadruk* and *Pachik Gompai Thab*, and *Heruka Sumchu Tsadruk Gompai Lung*, telling them to practice in Namtso Do to the north. To Ma Rinchen Chok and Gyalmo Yudra Nyingpo, he gave the sadhana *Chakna Dorje Sangwa Düpa*, twenty transmissions and one hundred pith instructions, especially the sadhanas and instructions for the *Yoga Tsei Druplung*, telling them to practice in the caves of Chimphu itself.

"To me, Tsogyal, he gave the outer, inner, secret, and absolute methods of accomplishing the Mind of the Guru, the root sadhana of *Padma Wang,* and seven different adaptations of it related to the mandala of the Guru. In short, he gave me the sadhana of the Three Roots in one single mandala and told me to practice in the places where images of the Precious Guru had spontaneously arisen, such as Taktsang in Onphu, Taktsang in Mön, and Taktsang in Kham, and especially in Tidro. He also said that, when pains and difficulties arose, I should pray to him and that he would come and give me advice. And he insisted that it would be wrong for me ever to separate from my companion Atsara Salé. These were his directions.

"As a thanksgiving to the Guru for his kindness, the great religious king then offered many perfect and abundant ganachakra feasts, in number equal to that of the mandalas to which the Guru had introduced us. Making a mountainous pile of gold, silk, and all the riches that this world affords, he said:

Kyema!
Mighty Guru, Lord!
The mandala of the Secret Mantra unsurpassed,
So hard to find in many ages, is now found!
Your great compassion is beyond repayment.
From now until enlightenment is gained,
Do not cast us from your lovingkindness, Lord.
A man like me, a king, is lost in inattention,
Caught up in affairs and never free!
Look upon me ever with your eyes of pity!

"And he sprinkled seven handfuls of gold dust over the Guru's body. To each of the chosen translators present, so that they could practice in the places indicated by the Guru, he gave a measure of gold dust, a golden ingot, and brocades of white, red, blue and other colors, as well as clothing, a horse, and a pack animal, and promised that he would supply all that they needed for their practice until they attained enlightenment. The great Guru shone with joy and said to the king:

Kyema!
Great majestic king,
This is the proper way to act!
I am Padmasambhava and have need of nothing.
Yet for samaya of the Secret Mantra,
That you, the king, might gain some merit,
These things I will accept.

The twenty-four disciples
Will attain their goal unhindered.
That the pious king provides for them is excellent.
These are splendid Bodhisattva deeds!

Intrepid practice of the faithful follower,
Padmasambhava's essential teachings,
Sustenance provided by the great religious king:
Endless qualities arise when these three meet!
Pure wish, pure links, and pure activities:
From these will spring
The oceanic qualities of Buddhahood!

"The Master gave oral instruction and advice to the king and each of the disciples, but these are described in their respective biographies and are not listed here. All went to practice in the places indicated by the Guru. I went first to Tidro and entered the mandala of the *Union of the Three Roots*. The general and particular teachings that I received are difficult to count. Simply to hear of them brings liberation. But I have not described them here for I fear the length of such a list."

SAMAYA ITHI GYA GYA GYA

Five
Practice

THE LADY TSOGYAL meditated at Tidro, in the Great Trysting Place of the Dakinis, in "Tsogyal's secret cave" and elsewhere, and all her needs were supplied by the sincere generosity of the local people. At first, she made use of a hermitage set back from the main "Trysting Place," where she persevered in the unelaborate sadhana of Guru Padmasambhava in his peaceful aspect. Her body became the deity, and she beheld the face of the yidam; she recognized the subtle channels and the wind-energy as the mandala of the dakini, and every activity undertaken was accomplished. She was blessed with that extraordinary knowledge wherein the essence-drop, her own mind, arose as the expression of the Teacher. All phenomena became manifest as inseparably united with the Teacher; she experienced a spontaneous devotion towards the Teacher, and at the same time the outer mandala shone iridescent and clear, dakas and dakinis appearing vividly to her senses.

"Within that experience of intense and dazzling luminosity," she recalled, "I came to what is known as the land of Orgyen, the abode of dakinis. The fruit trees there had leaves like razors, and the ground was a mass of corpse-flesh. The hills and cliffs were heaps of bristling skeletons, and for earth and rock there were but scattered fragments of bone. In the middle of this place there was a castle keep, its walls fashioned of three layers of human heads, some freshly cut, some dry, some putrescent, its roof and doors contrived of human skins. All around and at a distance of a thousand leagues, the place was encircled by mountains of fire, a tent of vajras, a rain of weapons, the eight charnel grounds, and a fence of fair lotus flowers.[50] Within this enclosed space I saw flesh-devouring birds and wild, blood-drinking beasts, and I was surrounded by ogres and ogresses and a host of other terrors. They were a fearful sight and yet proved neither hostile nor friendly. And so I entered the stronghold, passing through three successive gates.

"Inside, there were many dakinis, female in appearance and of different colors. They were holding various offerings that they were presenting to the principal dakini. Some of them were slicing off pieces of their own flesh with knives, laying it out and offering it as a ganachakra feast. For the same purpose, some were bleeding themselves, some were giving their eyes, some their noses, some their tongues, some their ears, some their hearts, some their inner organs, some their muscles, some their intestines, some their bone marrow, some their spinal fluid, some their life force, some their breath, some their heads, and some their limbs, cutting them off and arranging them as a ganachakra feast. They offered everything to the principal dakini in union with her consort, dedicating it as a devoted ganachakra.

" 'To what purpose,' I asked, 'are you inflicting all this pain upon yourselves? Is it not enough simply to dedicate your life completely to the Dharma?'

"In answer, they cried:

> *Éma!*
> Slothful woman!
> Only for a fleeting instant
> Does compassion of a true and holy teacher
> Come within our reach!
> Shall we gather in her presence
> And not offer what delights her?
> Put things off till later,
> And we'll never fill our stock of merit.
> Procrastinate, and obstacles increase!

Conviction lasts for just a fleeting instant,
And uncontrived devotion for a passing moment.
Shall Primal Wisdom show itself and we not make
 our offerings?
Put things off till later,
And we'll never fill our stock of merit.
Procrastinate, and obstacles increase!

Only in this moment do we have a human body.
The time to practice Dharma passes swiftly.
Shall we meet a realized teacher
And yet not make her offerings?
Procrastinate, and obstacles increase!

For this moment only does the teacher's presence last.
And entering the Secret Mantra is a thing well nigh
 impossible.
Shall we hear the sacred teachings
And yet not make our offerings?
Procrastinate, and obstacles increase!

"Their words put me to shame. When the moment came for them to make the dedication of their offerings, there appeared in front of each of the dakinis a form of Vajrayogini. She snapped her fingers, and the dakinis were made whole just as before. Then they would request teachings from the principal dakini and go and meditate upon them. This was how they practiced—in all, twelve times a day.

"There was a guardian at each of the gates of the palace, and at the center of the palace stood Vajrayogini, enclosed within a mass of fire difficult to look upon. A detailed description of this Buddha-field is to be found elsewhere and has not been written here for fear of its length.

"Later, when I met Guru Rinpoche again, I recounted my experience to him and, since I also wished to undertake in some measure this practice of austerities, I pledged myself to do so.

But he said: 'These visions are simply meant as an indication; you have no need to perform penances such as the offering of your own flesh as a ganachakra feast. Practice, rather, austerities that are even more difficult!

Éma!
Goddess, Lady Tsogyal, listen!
Listen undistracted, you who are so beautiful to see!
This precious human body is a stem of gold.
If you have gained it and are wise to use it,
You will find continuous subsistence.
Those without this knowledge
Lack provisions for a single day—
Those who do not know will die of hunger!
And therefore it is good to pledge yourself as follows.[51]

Practice the austerity of nourishment
And take as sustenance essential sap
Of stones and healing plants, and let
The air itself be food for you.

Practice the austerity of clothing,
Wearing nothing but a simple cotton cloth,
Then ornaments of bone, and afterwards go naked,
Trusting to the inner heat of tummo.

Practice the austerity of speech:
The stages of approach and of accomplishment
Of sadhanas, your prayers and mantras.
Perform the yoga of the energies
In silence, giving up all useless talk.

Practice the austerity of body:
Prostration, circumambulation, and the cleansing of
    your form.
Sit in vajra posture,
And remain in meditation.

Practice the austerity of mind,
And train in stages of creation and perfection.
Cultivate the essence-drop, both bliss and voidness.
Remain absorbed in these two unified.

Practice the austerity of Doctrine
And be holder of the Buddhadharma.
Perform the sacred task of guarding it
Through teaching, composition, debate, and all the rest.

Practice the austerity of selfless kindness,
Acting for the sake of others.
Help them, pray for them, as Mahayana teaches,
Without a thought for life and limb.

Practice the austerity of compassion,
With equal love for both your child and enemy,
For gold and clods of earth—
Regarding others dearer than yourself.

Thus you will embody all the Buddha's Teaching.
Highest wonder of Great Bliss you will attain.
Acting otherwise, you'll be a false ascetic,
No different from those Indian fanatics.
Understand this well, O girl of Kharchen.

"Thus he spoke, and in response I pledged myself to practice these eight great precepts as the Guru had taught:

Kyema Ho!
The Buddha's law has come into this land of wickedness,
The gleaming fiery crystal lamp[52] into this land of gloom,
The sacred Lord of Orgyen to Tibet, the land of ogres,
Upon unholy beings letting fall a rain of Dharma,
Showing the forlorn the upward path of fortune.
I know of no such actions even at the Diamond Throne
When Buddha was alive and present in this world.

Thus the Guru's kindness is beyond repayment.
The mandala, most secret, of the Secret Mantra
I, the woman Yeshe Tsogyal, have now entered
And will die before I break a jot or tittle
Of the Guru's precepts.
The eight great teachings hard to practice
I have now received. Without a thought
For life, for body, or for worldly power,
I will keep the precepts of my Lord and Teacher,
And will die before I break my sacred pledge.
The three austerities of clothing, food, and nourishment,
The three of body, speech, and mind,
Hardships for the sake of Buddha's Doctrine
And all wandering sentient beings,
The burden of compassion,
Of holding others dearer than myself:
These eight will be my practice
Unalloyed, sincere, and single-minded."

Three times the Lady Tsogyal took this vow of eight austerities. The Guru was well pleased. He gave her advice and predictions and then returned to the king to act as his spiritual guide.

First the Lady Tsogyal practiced the austerity of clothing, relying on the inner heat of tummo. On the heights of the mountain of Tidro, where the high screes give way to snow, she meditated for a year, wearing nothing but a single piece of cotton cloth. At first the warmth of the tummo did not arise and, as the new year gales began to blow, the frost and cold were hard to bear. Her Indian companion could stand it no longer and went off to find the Guru, saying that he would serve him. But because of her vow, the Lady Tsogyal persisted in her meditation. Blisters covered her entire body, and she was racked with anguish, her breath coming in sharp, painful gasps. She was on the point of death when, in invocation to the venerable Teacher, she prayed:

Lord of Orgyen, Lord of Dharma,
Protecting all who wander in samsara.
Sun of loving pity, look on me!
Friendless, I am naked and alone.
The wind howls through this dark and rocky den.
When the blizzards rage,
It is a girl of snow that I become.
My bed is stone, and stone my roof and walls—
They are an icy comfort.
A clod of earth and rock I lie, inert and still.
The Lady of the White Robe[53] is not here,
And I am frozen through and through.
But with the sunshine of your mercy
Bless me! Kindle in me, please, the tummo fire!

"As I said this," the Lady recalled, "the karmic wind-energy moved slightly, and this enabled the warmth of the tummo fire to spring up. I felt ever more strongly a deep and sincere faith towards the Guru, and I sang:

The strong ambrosia of blessings
Of the Secret Mantra, Diamond Vehicle,
Is granted by a true authentic Teacher,
And Vajrasattva, Primal Wisdom,
Brings the Four Joys skipping in my heart.
White Robe has arisen in her proper place;
She offers now her blissful warmth to me.
How great is now my joy.
Yet still I beg your kindness!

"The Master of Orgyen appeared to me in the form of a heruka. He gave me a skull cup filled with beer to drink, and then he disappeared. My experience became continuous and stable: the bliss was truly blissful, the warmth was truly warm, and I was filled with happiness. My body, which beforehand had been completely frozen, was transfigured through and through, like a snake sloughing off its skin. Whereupon I thought that the time had come for the austerity of the bone ornaments. And so, taking off the cotton cloth and donning the ornaments of bone, I practiced for one year the austerity called the *Union of the Three Pith Instructions*. At that time, I had not even a single barley seed left, and so I performed my meditation taking stones and water for my food and drink.[54] After some time, my previous experiences declined, along with my realization. My legs could no longer support the weight of my body. I could not lift my head, and I had difficulty in breathing from my nose and mouth. My mind, too, grew very feeble. Gradually my condition worsened, so that in the end I was on the brink of death.

"And so I prayed to the Teacher. I cried in distress to the yidam and visualized a constant flow of offerings to the dakinis, saying:

From the first I gave my body to the Guru,
Come joy or sorrow, Lord,
I trust myself to you!

From the first my speech was given to the Dharma,
However, Lord, I breathe,
I trust myself to you!

From the first my mind was roused to virtue,
Come virtue, Lord, or vice,
I trust myself to you!

From the first, my form has been the yidam's mansion,
Whatever may befall this dwelling, Lord,
I trust myself to you!

From the first, the winds and channels are the paths of dakinis,

Whatever they may do with them,
I trust myself to you!

From the first, this essence-drop is nature of the
Buddhas Gone to Bliss,
Whether resting in the peace beyond all sorrow,
Or turning in samsara's round.
Look upon all mother sentient beings wandering
in delusion!

Whether I should rest or turn,
Your word for me, your daughter, will decide.

"Then a vision came to me. A woman, red skinned, naked and without the ornaments of bone, appeared and pressed her bhaga to my mouth so that I drank deeply of the blood that flowed from it. My whole being was suffused with bliss, I felt as though my body had become as strong as a lion, and in my meditation I realized the ineffable truth. I thought then that the time had arrived for me to go unclothed and to take the air for my food. And so, for one whole year, relying solely on the air for sustenance, I practiced naked. At first, the movement of my breath came easily and my mind was clear. And different experiences, the display of awareness, dawned without impediment. Later on, a doubt arose in my mind on account of which my breathing was arrested. My throat became entirely dry, and my nose became clogged as if it had been stopped up with wool. My stomach would rumble, and my intestines withered and grew dry. Again I was on the point of death. Summoning up my courage, I appealed to Guru Rinpoche and sang this song:

In the circle of existence
Wandering through countless forms,
Turning in the round of birth and death,
Tortured by the sorrows of the states of misery,

Oh woman! if you bore that heat and cold,
That hunger, thirst, and servitude!—
Can you not sustain this hardship now,
The swift path of the Secret Mantra,
The true potential of a human life?
What else is there to do?
The worst that can befall is death!
Do not retreat from your austerity,
O Tsogyal, courage, persevere!

Kyema Ho!
Sage of Orgyen, self-appearing Teacher,
Enlightened emanation born upon a lotus stem,
miraculous!
Lord of Mercy in a human frame,
Supreme and diamond form
Yet fashioned from the light of rainbows,
Look with pity on us, body-laden beings!
Protect me, left behind in mediocrity.
What am I to do, pressed down and burdened
By this weight of mortal flesh?
Look upon me now, wherever you may be, with eyes
of love and pity!

"No sooner had I finished than the Guru himself appeared in the air before me, enfolded in a globe of light, smiling, and so close that I might have touched him. And he said:

Kyema O!
Listen, noble mistress, maid of Kharchen!
You, the daughter of a princely house,
Still want your beauty and your pleasures!
As before, you cannot bear with hardships!
But now the time has come
To take both joys and sorrows on the path.
Whatever hardships now may fall to you,

Bring them to the path of Great Felicity!
Faithful, gentle lady, do not thirst for happiness!

Kyema!
Listen, mistress, maid of Kharchen,
Youthful consort of the king and ne'er contented!
Tangled, as before, in self-regarding wants!
But now the time has come
To cast aside all needless pastimes.
Meditate on transience, reflect
Upon the states of sorrow.
Faithful, gentle lady, do not thirst for greatness!

Kyema!
Listen, mistress, maid of Kharchen,
Consort of the Guru, conceited and self-satisfied!
As before, you think so highly of yourself!
But now the time has come
To tell your own shortcomings.
Do not hide your hidden faults but lay them bare.
Faithful, gentle lady, do not thirst for reputation!

Kyema!
Listen, mistress, maid of Kharchen,
Your Dharma's just a boast, your pieties all false!
And as before, it's all pretension!
But now the time has come
To cast away deceit and trickery.
Do not waver. Be courageous.
Faithful, gentle lady, do not flaunt yourself!

"When he had finished speaking, he stepped down onto the ground and sat on a rock. 'You are taking things to excess,' he said. 'Extract the essence of medicinal herbs and plants so as to develop the strength of your awareness and restore your body. As for myself, I, Padmasambhava, existing only for the sake of wandering beings, am mindful of the future, until the very emptying of samsara. I will conceal many Treasures of the Sacred Dharma, which shall be forever inexhaustible. Then I must away to Ngayab, realm of dakinis! The care of these profound Treasures, Lady, will be your task. In a short while, I will open many mandalas of the unsurpassable Secret Mantra, and the time will come for you to work for the sake of beings. Therefore prepare yourself.' Giving me this and other more extensive instructions, he departed.

"Then, taking as companions the Indian boy Salé and the girl Dewamo, I, Tsogyal, made my way to the three caves in Mön, each called Sengé Dzong. First I went to Mön-kha Sengé Dzong to practice the extraction of the essence of various medicinal plants. I began, however, by taking the essence of minerals, knowing that the quintessence of all of these is contained in chongzhi, or calcite. My body became like a diamond; no weapon could harm it. My speech took on the qualities of the voice of Brahma, so that even a fierce tigress, when she heard me, became quiet and attentive. My mind passed into the immaculate vajra-like concentration."

Thereupon, the Lady Tsogyal decided that the time had come for her to practice the austerity of speech. To begin with, in order to purify her speech defilements, she performed the stages of approach and accomplishment, and recited prayers and rituals continuously, day and night, no break occurring in the sound of her voice. At first, she recited vidya-mantras and dharani-mantras such as the hundred syllables and many others, thus performing the confessions and purifications according to the three classes of Kriyatantra. Then she undertook the recitation of the mandalas of the dharani-mantras, of the Upatantras and Yogatantras, such as of the five Buddha Families, and of the three classes of Bodhisattva. Finally, she applied herself to the prayers, confessions, and vows of the Sutras, the Vinaya rules, the practice of Amitayus, and to the trainings in Abhidharma, grammar and logic. Her endeavor was unstinting. The first effect of this was that her voice began to falter and an opening appeared in her throat from which blood and pus poured in great abundance. Her larynx became stiff and cramped and agonizingly painful. It became dry and then swollen with blood and pus. Death was only a step away. But she finally succeeded in reciting as much as she wished, without discomfort, and her voice was such that her words came clearly in a melodious and unbroken flow. Loud, medium, or soft; quick, slow, or moderate—she had perfect mastery. In sum, her voice assumed the sixty qualities of melodious speech, and she attained the seven powers of unfailing memory.

Thereupon, she opened the mandalas of the *Eight Great Herukas*, according to the level of Mahayoga, and performed the approach stage until she enjoyed the vision of the deities. Passing then to the stage of accomplishment, she practiced until she became inseparable from them. Seated with her legs in the vajra posture and her hands in the mudra of meditation, she first beheld the whole array of deities. Many signs and abilities arose, such as blazing lights. Then she received the predictions and authorizations of the yidam deities and attained the eight great ordinary accomplishments. The supreme accomplishment came to her as the "vajra-like" concentration and the concentration of "heroic fearlessness," and she received the prediction of her final enlightenment in the expanse of Samantabhadri.[55]

Then she opened the mandala of the *Lama Gongdü* and practiced according to the Anuyoga transmission. Having gained complete mastery of her body through mantra, wind-energy, and meditative concentration, she set the mandala of *Lama Gongdü* in the root chakras of her body and faultlessly applied the key instructions for the subtle channels, wind-energy and essence-drop, making them the object of her meditative experience.

At first, her subtle channels were painful, the wind-energy was reversed and the essence stiff and motionless, but she persevered, refusing to consider as undesirable the sufferings that were almost killing her. And so, in due course, she beheld the vision of the deities and, mastering the subtle channels, wind-energy, and essence-drop, she severed the four streams of birth, old age, sickness, and death.

It was then that she became what is known as an accomplished adept. How impossible it was, she reflected, to repay the Precious Teacher for his kindness! And she sang:

> *Kyema O!*
> To Guru Padmasambha I bow down, my Lord
> and Teacher!
>
> This heap of atoms gathering from time without
> beginning,
> O Lord and Teacher, you have made of it
> The king of mountains, Sumeru.
> And now it seems that I, this mountain,
> Might bring forth the benefit of beings.
>
> Virtuous Indra, come, assist me bounteously!
> Except for those in wild ravines dispersed,
> Who lack perhaps good karma from the past,
> A happiness and joy will fill and satisfy
> The heaven of the Four Great Kings
> and all celestial realms.
>
> This ocean growing drop by drop from time without
> beginning,
> O Lord and Teacher, you have made of it
> The seven seas of blissful play.[56]
> And now it seems that I, this ocean,
> Might bring forth the benefit of beings.
>
> Virtuous Nanda, come, assist me bounteously!
> Except for frogs and fishes of the fens
> Who lack perhaps good karma from the past,
> A happiness and joy will fill and satisfy
> The naga-lands and please the eight great naga
> kings.

A great sage, merits gathering from time without
beginning,
O Lord and Teacher, you imbued
With knowledge inexhaustible.
And now it seems that I, this mighty sage,
Might bring forth benefit for beings.

Chief of men, religious king, assist me
bounteously!
Except for dwellers in the savage outer marches
Who lack perhaps good karma from the past,
A happiness and joy will fill and satisfy
The Shravakas and all who dwell within this
world.

The fruit of merit gathering from time without beginning,
O Lord and Teacher, you have turned
Into a human body full of meaning.
And now it seems that I, this woman,
Might bring forth the benefit of beings.

Children blest with fortune, come, assist me
bounteously!
Except for evil ones, perverted in their thoughts,
Who will perhaps refuse and shun the Dharma,
A happiness will fill the homelands of Tibet
And all its faithful people.

Then she took as food the essence of a hundred and eight different medicinal herbs and plants. The four great divine sages appeared to her surrounded by the four hundred and eight medicine goddesses.[57] Each was holding a vase of nectar containing a specific healing virtue, which they offered to Tsogyal, praising her with these verses:

Kyema Ho!
Now is the greatest of all wonders yours,

O human child—our sister once
When up among the gods you dwelt,
And with pure prayers brought forth the cause
Of such great wisdom!
Guiding the gandharvas with a lute's sweet sound,
O Tsogyal, Sarasvati, you we praise and glorify!

And when the mighty Buddha turned,
In later times, the wheel of Dharma,
With pure intentions you became a Shravaka,
A virtuous nun, who with her eyes of mercy
Was the guide of beings, all without exception.
O Tsogyal, Gangadevi, you we praise!

Now when the exalted Vajradhara
Assumes the form of Master Padmasambhava
And turns the wheel of Dharma,
His teachings you compile, whereby
The door of Secret Mantra is thrown open.
Ascetic for the sake of beings, O Tsogyal, you we praise!

All teachings spring within the vast expanses
Of your mind. You take
The essences of drugs and poisons
To play with them as with a draught of immortality.
Your body of eternal youth is perfect
With the marks of Buddhahood.
Nurse of wanderers through time, we praise you!

You drive away the sicknesses
And lingering ills of beings.
You cure them with immortal nectar,
Essence of all medicines.
Healing-goddess, mother of all remedies:
Is this not you, O Tsogyal, you alone?

And with these words they rose into the sky.

Now, at that time, because the outer and the inner worlds are linked together interdependently, the girl Khyidren came and offered the Lady Tsogyal a large quantity of honey. Tsogyal ate everything and then devoted herself to physical austerity. First she performed circumambulations, then prostrations and so on, all the time, day and night. The skin of her forehead, and the palms of her hands and soles of her feet, cracked open down to the very bone. Out came blood and pus in great abundance. Then she practiced the innumerable different forms of bodily purification, mostly according to the texts of the different pith instructions. She passed through the three levels of physical exhaustion. The essential fluid in the joints of her limbs changed into lymph, boiling and aching, causing them to cramp and swell. Her subtle channels were dislocated. Their ends opened and her body began to weaken. Later, however, the pure essence separated off from that which had degenerated, and her spirits rose. The essence stabilized in the nature of primordial wisdom, the knots on her subtle channels were loosed, her twisted limbs straightened, and all illness was cured. Whatever had been severed was knit together again; whatever had been wrenched and dislocated was restored to its proper place. Thus a firm foundation was established for the accomplishment of Secret Mantra.

Tsogyal then withdrew to the most solitary caves, like that of Sengé Nering. There she sat, vowing never to relinquish her vajra posture, but to remain with unwavering gaze, in silence, and with no relaxation of her bodily position. And so she stayed absorbed in concentration. The malevolent gods and spirits of the region could not tolerate the brilliance of the Lady's concentration and assailed her magically with seductive and wrathful forms, visible and invisible phantoms. At first, they repeatedly appeared to her as different kinds of food, or again they took the form of clothing, horses, elephants, and so on, all the goods and wealth this world affords. But the Lady quelled them all with the intensity of her concentration. Seeing their illusory nature, she felt a profound detachment and distaste for worldly things, and this sufficed to make some of the objects disappear. Others she transformed through concentration into earth, stones, and the like. Others disappeared after becoming, according to her wish, treasures of food and wealth for the benefit of the country in ages to come.

On another occasion, the spirits took the form of a band of handsome youths, their faces beautiful and complexions wholesome, good to smell, well built and sturdy—a joy to look upon. To begin with they spoke to her respectfully, addressing her as "Mistress" and "Lady," but later they called her "girl" and "Tsogyal," and began to speak to her with words of desire. They started by teasing her playfully, but little by little they uncovered their manhood, saying things like, 'Hey, girl, is this what you want? Do you want its milk?' And they put their arms around her waist, fondling her breasts, playing with her sexual parts, kissing her, making love in all sorts of ways. Some of the young men disappeared, subdued by the strength of the Lady's concentration. Others, through the concentration that perceives all things as illusion, faded away, mere phantoms. Still others, through the counteractive meditation of a Bodhisattva,[58] were changed into blackened corpses, hideous old men, lepers, blind men, cripples, and idiots, all of them loathsome. And being thus transformed, they disappeared.

Then fearful visions began to occur. The whole earth trembled and shook, there came a crashing and rumbling, louder than a thousand thunders. Lightning flashed black, white, red, yellow, blue, and many-colored—bright lights almost unbearable. All sorts of sharp weapons appeared, pointed daggers, spears, and knives of fearful blue metal, all bristling and clashing together in front of her. Tsogyal could hardly endure it. But through her unshakable concentration, she remained confident and fearless, even though it seemed she might be sliced in pieces and killed. And once more, everything melted away.

Yet again, some days later, the forms of different wild animals appeared: tigers, leopards, red bears and yellow bears, roaring and growling, blocking the entrance to the cave from above and below, coming into it from all sides, snarling and howling. Some had their mouths wide open, showing their fangs, as if to devour her. They lashed the ground with their tails, tearing at it with their claws, their bodies quivering, their fur standing up, their manes bristling. But with unshakable confidence, Tsogyal abandoned all attachment to her body, feeling a deep compassion for all of them. And they faded away.

Suddenly the place was filled, swarming with all kinds of worms and insects, led by a horde of spiders, scorpions, and snakes. Some got into her ears, eyes, and nose, others were biting and scratching her, climbing on her, jumping onto her. There were insects fighting among themselves. They were tearing each other to pieces and devouring each other. All kinds of things magically appeared. Trembling a little with horror, the Lady Tsogyal felt compassion for them. It became more and more frightening and repulsive, until she thought: "Many times have I vowed to have no attachment in any circumstances for my body, speech, and mind. These living beings that we call insects have arisen due to karma. Why should I be frightened by the magic sleights of wicked spirits? All actions are the issue of thoughts, good or ill; and since all that happens thus is merely thought, I should accept everything equally." And in this spirit of confidence she sang:

What we understand to be phenomena
Are but the magical projections of the mind.
The hollow vastness of the sky
I never saw to be afraid of anything.

All this is but the self-glowing light of clarity.
There is no other cause at all.
All that happens is but my adornment.
Better, then, to stay in silent meditation.

Thereupon she entered into a concentration of perfect equanimity, beyond good and evil, acceptance and rejection. And all the visions disappeared. But again other sights and apparitions arose. Truncated limbs were being hurled about, repugnant forms shooting and whirling around. She saw a huge head to which there was no body, its gaping jaws stretching from the earth to the sky, and in between, its tongue flicking and twitching. It had great fangs, pale and sharp, and it came closer and closer. Or again, in a castle, small like a white mustard seed, she saw many people fighting battles. Or else there would be all-engulfing fires, pouring floods, falling rocks, trees crashing down, howling winds, and more. But she remained immovable in the vajra-like concentration, and finally everything melted away.

Then, from É in Nepal to Ja in Mön, hordes of gods and spirits came. They were of the tribes of Khatra and Kangtra in the land of Lo, and said, "Behold, we are legion." Some were weeping, others screaming, groaning, bellowing in their fury. And they began to work their mischief. From above they hurled their thunders. From below their fires blazed up. In between came water swirling. Choking blizzards of furious weapons raged. But this only served to strengthen the Lady Tsogyal's realization. Pure awareness broke forth, and her wisdom channel opened. An unshakable faith rose up in her and she sang:

Emaho!
The Dharmakaya,
Wisdom of the Great Mother;
Essence of the ten perfections,
Practice of deep wisdom,
These are now fulfilled.
No appearance now will frighten me:
All arises as the play of Dharmakaya.
These phantoms are but the compassion of my Teacher.
I pray that he might send me more and more!

Emaho!
Wisdom of Samantabhadra,
Essence of the View, the Meditation, and the Fruit,
The practice of not meddling with arising thoughts,
These I have perfected.
Thoughts and concepts hold no fear for me:
Whatever comes is but the play of thoughts.
These thoughts are the compassion of my Teacher;
I pray that he might send me more and more!

Emaho!
The Wisdom of the Lotus Guru,
The essence of the all-pervading Ati,
The practice of the stainless Mind,
These I have perfected.
Concepts of defilement do not come to me,
Defilements are the play of ultimate reality.
All that I perceive is merely the compassion
of my Teacher;
I pray that he might send me more and more!

Emaho!
Observance of the woman Tsogyal,
The essence of the Secret Mantra,
The practice of equality of joy and sorrow,
These I have perfected.
I do not choose between the good and bad,
For both bring progress to my meditation.
All appearance is compassion of my Teacher;
I pray that he might send me more and more!

Yet again, the hordes of gods and spirits from the three lands of India, Nepal, and Tibet came upon her with their demon captains, red, black, and blue, trying in all sorts of ways to beset her with obstacles. But they failed, and so they stirred the human inhabitants to hostility against her. For through the agency of the gods, the whole of the land of Mön was convulsed by untold calamities. A darkness came down such that no one could tell day from night. There were floods, thunderstorms, hailstorms, snowstorms, rainstorms, and plague. All sorts of miseries occurred. Everyone was saying, "Who is attacking us? Where is all this coming from?"

Now it happened that a hunter, a native of Mön, had seen Tsogyal.

"Over there," he said, "in the cave of Nering rock, there is a Tibetan woman who seems to be both deaf and dumb. Isn't she the one? Who else could it be?" They all agreed that she must be to blame and they came in a band to put her to death. They reached the cave and cried, "Tibetan beggar woman! Through your witchcraft our land of Mön has been plunged into inky darkness. It has become a land of gloom. Lightning and hail are beating down, and plagues and miseries have come upon us. Drive away your evil magic or we will kill you right away!"

The Lady thought to herself, "They are under the influence of gods and spirits; nothing will help! Whatever happens, I must carry it onto the path. Whatever comes about, I must simply let it be. Whatever I have to go through, I will not give up my vow." And so, without answering, she remained seated, her eyes wide open and staring. Some decided that she was ashamed, others that she was refusing to listen to them. And they threw dust into her eyes and pricked her ears with their knives. But she remained as she was, without a care.

"Atsi!" they cried, "this is a tough little vixen!" And they shot arrows at her, beat her with sticks, pierced her with knives and spears. But nothing and nobody could harm the Lady's body. So they called her "pömo jigméma," the fearless Tibetan woman, and, telling each other that there was no help for it, they went back home.

At that time, the girl was present who had previously offered honey to Lady Tsogyal. She was the daughter of the king of Mön and was therefore very rich and influential. She had great faith in the Lady and made prostration to her. She returned and would offer sometimes buffalo milk, sometimes honey and whatever pleasing service she could. Not long afterwards, all the gods and spirits that had previously displayed the magical illusions came and offered their life force to the Lady Tsogyal. At their head were demons, tsen spirits, and nagas, and these pledged to guard the Lady's teachings and to annihilate her enemies. They said:

> *Eh Ho Ho!*
> Joy of Padma Thödrengtsel,
> Victorious lady, noble Heruka,
> None could overwhelm you!
> We confess our evil wills to you and our misdeeds.
> We who are your servants and familiars
> Offer you our life force and our strength,
> And will be subject to your every word.
> We will not break this pledge of ours!

Each of them made an offering of their life force and then departed. In like manner, Rahula, Vajrasadhu and all the other powerful gods and spirits of Tibet came and offered their life force. And they took their leave after promising that they would protect the teachings of the Buddha. Thereupon all the inhabitants of the country, both men and women, who previously had done the Lady so much mischief, gathered before her and confessed. Indeed, Hamra, the king of Mön himself, began to regard Tsogyal as an object of faith and wonder. It was his daughter who previously had offered the honey—a lovely girl of thirteen years, endowed with all the qualities and bodily signs of a dakini. Her name was Khyidren, "She Who Leads the Hounds." The king, prompted by his faith, offered her to Tsogyal who changed her name to Trashi Chidren, "Propitious Guide of All."

Tsogyal then went off to Paro Taktsang, where she performed a final austerity on her own account, the practice on the essence-drop, the union of bliss and voidness. Nourishing her three companions, Atsara Salé, Mönpu Salé, and Atsara Pelyang, on the essences of medicinal plants, she trained unstintingly, day and night, for seven months. At first the whole of her body was disturbed and lost its strength, and her mind was dull and agitated by turns. The lymph fell sharply from the upper to the lower part of her body. She was oppressed by disease, fever, pains, and shivering, and once again came near to death. But then all the lymph transformed into the essence-drop, and the whole of her body was filled with bliss. This was at first a kind of bliss mingled with emotions, followed by a bliss of immense Primordial Wisdom and finally a stable, flowing bliss of Wisdom. Then, little by little, the white and red essences blended so that the duality of subject and object disappeared. Her body became the mandala of the Victorious Ones. And through the offering of bliss, she attained the state of Great Bliss within a body of Great Bliss. The whiteness of her body became suffused with a rosy glow, and she assumed the form of a heruka-heroine, ever-youthful, endowed with the charm of a girl of sixteen years. It was then that she had a vision of the mandala of Amitayus and obtained the immutable diamond body untouched by death and aging, becoming thus a vidyadhara with power over life. It was prophesied that she would remain in this world for two hundred and twenty-five years.[59] Glorious Hayagriva and Vajravarahi banished hindrances. The five dakas and five dakinis accomplished her enlightened activities, following her like her shadow. Bodhisattvas sang their prayers of good augury. As a life-dominating vidyadhara, she received the name Mistress of Eternal Life, Blue Light Blazing.

Later, Tsogyal made her way, with five disciples, to Onphu Taktsang, where the Precious Teacher was then residing. The Lady went ahead to meet him and made prostrations.

"Is this a valiant heruka that comes to see me?" he said. "How are you? How was your journey?" Then he continued:

Kyema Ho!
Yogini seasoned in the Secret Mantra!
The ground of Liberation
Is this human frame, this common human form—
And here distinctions, male or female,
Have no consequence.
And yet if bodhichitta graces it,
A woman's form indeed will be supreme!

From unoriginated time, the double
Stores of wisdom and of merit you have filled!
Now freed from faults, endowed with qualities,
Highest of all women, Mother of Enlightenment,
Are you not my happy, blissful Lady?

Your own good now you have attained.
Strive for others, benefit all beings!
Could another woman wondrous as you
Exist here in this human world?
None in the past, indeed, nor any now,
And neither will there be in future time.
Ah Yeshe Tsogyal, Victorious Sea of Wisdom!

From now until the end of time to come,
Five emanations you will body forth,
Prolonging Buddha's teachings thirty years.
Especially in the land of Dak, you will appear—
A woman with the name of Drölma.[60]
You will take the essence of the teachings
Of the Prajñaparamita,
Teaching the profundity of Chö, a doctrine
That will be the highest benefit of beings.
At that time, this Indian Salé here
Will be a bhikshu with the name of Thöpa.
My Lady, he will be your consort
Opening the secret door.
Trashi Chidren, here, this girl of Mön,

Will be your only daughter,
And Mönpu Salé, then your son, a crazy yogi.
Atsara Pelyang will appear as Trapa Ngoshé.
My Lady, he will be your secret consort:
Supreme profit for yourselves and others!
And I, who at this time am Padmasambhava,
Bearing then the name of Indian Dampa,[61]
Will begin from Latö to disseminate and spread
The pacifying discipline of Shi-che.
Lady, when we two have met once more,
The links auspicious for the Secret Mantra will be forged.
The pacifying doctrine, Shi-che, deep and skillful,
Will bring into the world a little joy.
It will not linger long.
But in the lofty realm of Lotus Light,
You and I will once more join inseparably
And in Sambhogakaya form will work the benefit of beings.

With this and other predictions, the Precious Teacher cheered and inspired Yeshe Tsogyal. And she, to thank him for his kindness, sang this song:

Emaho!
Stem of the Secret Mantra, Holder of the Vajra,
Deathless, unconditioned, Boundless Life,
Heruka, Lord of strength and power,
All are none but you, O Padmasambhava!
And nowhere shall I find your like again.

Through your kindness, highest guide and mentor,
Now I have attainment in the Secret Mantras.
I have gained the powers of the eight great siddhis
And am mistress of the sutras and the tantras—
Even with the lowly body of a woman.
Thus is my good fortune excellent!

My form has now become the deity:
Ordinary perception now has vanished totally,
Mirage-like absorption now has dawned.
The elements are subject to my power.
My speech to mantra has been turned;
The babbling of useless talk has faded
And the vajra-like absorption has arisen.
Of all the Dharmas of the sutra and the mantra
I have now the mastery.

My mind becoming Buddha,
Common thoughts have vanished into space;
"Heroic fearlessness" has dawned upon me.
My mind is now identical with Vajradhara.

My Lord and Teacher, great is your compassion!
From now and in all future time and place,
Throughout the whole succession of my lives,
And even if your lotus feet were ever to abandon me,
Another teacher I will never seek.
Therefore look upon me kindly, never leaving me.
Great is your compassion, far beyond repayment!
All transgressions of samaya relating to your Body,
Speech, Mind, Qualities, and Action
Were the fruit of ignorance.
I confess them now and promise
To avoid henceforth the slightest faults!
The kindness of the Guru I implore:
Now for every being's sake,
Please turn the Dharma wheel of Secret Mantra!

Then she recounted in detail how she had practiced her austerities and won accomplishment, how there had been deceptive apparitions of gods and spirits and human beings, and especially how she had accomplished the Secret Mantra at Paro Taktsang and beheld the assembled deities of Amitayus.

His face radiant with joy, the Guru placed his right hand on the head of the Lady and said: "The time has come for you to perform, here in this place, the yoga of the vidyadhara of immortality. The events in Paro Taktsang show that if you practice accordingly, and with the blessings of the Teacher, success will surely come to you. I will open the mandala of Amitayus and grant you the empowerment, but you must find a companion as support for your long-life practice. Likewise, Khyidren, this girl from Mön, possesses the character and all the physical marks of a wisdom dakini of vajra activity. Give her, then, to me and I will make her my consort for the mantric practice of Vajrakila. For it is necessary to disseminate many oral instructions on Vajrakumara, otherwise the Secret Mantra will not spread in this foolish land of Tibet, and the yogis who practice it will be unable to protect even their own lives. Indeed the multitude of gods and spirits of Tibet, the enemies of Dharma, will create obstructions, and the spreading of the Secret Mantra will be halted. And even were it not so hindered, it would vanish speedily."

"Then I," the Lady Tsogyal recalled, "made prostrations, and to thank the Guru for his kindness, offered him a mandala of gold and turquoise together with the girl Trashi Khyidren. I said: 'Great Guru! Vast is your kindness in bestowing on me, the woman Tsogyal, the pith instructions for the yoga of long-life. But tell me, what kind of companion will I need as a support for it? Is Atsara Salé unsuitable? Great would be your compassion if you opened for me also the tantric mandala of Vajrakila. I have offered you the girl Khyidren. Now in your kindness, I pray you to open for me the door of the Secret Mantra. For I am a timid woman and of scant ability; of lowly condition, the butt of everyone. If I go for alms, I am set upon by dogs; if food and riches come my way, I am the prey of thieves; since I am beautiful, I am the quarry of every lecherous knave; if I am busy with much to do, the country folk accuse me; if I don't do what they think I should, the people criticize; if I put a foot wrong, everyone detests me. I have to worry about everything I do. That is what it is like to be a woman! How can a woman possibly gain accomplishment in Dharma? Just managing to survive is already hard enough! So I beg you, give to me as well the instructions for Vajrakila that are bound within your heart.'

"The Guru paused, reflecting for a while, and then he said: 'It is as though the long-life practice were the captain, and Kila the protective escort. For this reason, whatever work one does in the Secret Mantra, it is important first to practice Kila so as to dispel obstacles. Moreover, Kila is your yidam deity; consequently you may practice it. But whether you do Kila or the long-life practice, you have need of a companion. Go therefore to Uru in Tibet where there is a boy of fourteen years. His father's name is Lhapel, his mother's Chokroza. He is of the clan of Lang. Make him your companion in the practice and together you will accomplish the yidam.'

"Following these instructions, I discovered the boy and returned to the Guru. The Master said:

> This boy, a knowledge-holder of Kilaya,
> Will attain the vajra-life.
> He will not be defeated easily—
> A hero, demon-taming, predicted by the deity,
> Possessing the great strength and power of lions!
>
> Let his name be Lhalung Pelgyi Sengé,
> Lion of Glory whom the Deity Foretold!

"He then introduced the boy to the mandala of the Secret Mantra and brought him to maturity.

"Afterwards, Lhalung Pelgyi Sengé, Namkhai Nyingpo of Lhodrak, Ma Rinchen Chok, myself Yeshe Tsogyal, and Dudjom Dorje, the five principal spiritual offspring of the Guru, met together, along with others, to practice the sadhana of Kila."

The girl Dewamo, now called Pelgyi Chönema, was appointed vajra cook.[62] Atsara Salé and Atsara Pelyang were appointed vajra dancers with the names Karma Dondrub and Karma Tharché. Mönpu Salé was named Jampa Pelzang and was appointed vajra assistant. To begin with, Yeshe Tsogyal was the main consort, while later Trashi Kyidren was the "liberation" consort. The Guru and his two Consorts opened the mandala of forty-two Étram, which are related to the Vidyottama tantra of Vajrakila, as well as the mandala of the seventy-eight Kilas, and undertook the practice for seven days, whereupon all the signs and marks of realization perfectly appeared. They saw the assembled host of the deities of Vajrakila. The material phurbas flew, laughing and floating in the air, ablaze with fire and scattering a sweet perfume. That same evening, inconceivable signs occurred. The Guru arose as Dorje Drolö (united with Tsogyal in the form of Ekadzati and with Khyidren transformed into the tigress). He subjugated Tibet and its four surrounding regions, along with all the gods and spirits of a million universes. Riding upon the tigress, into which the girl Khyidren had been transformed, the Guru in union with Yeshe Tsogyal remained absorbed in the samadhi of Vajrakila. He was brandishing in his right hand a nine-pointed vajra, and in his left he twirled a metal phurba, projecting countless wrathful and ferocious emanations identical to himself. One of these, named wrathful Blue-Black Vajrakila, went to Paro Taktsang, where he subdued and bound under oath all the gods and mamos, demons and the eight classes of spirits in the lands of Mön, Nepal, India, and other savage regions to the south. Another emanation, with the name of wrathful Blood-Red Vajrakila, went to the second Taktsang in Kham, where he overpowered the gods, demons, and eight classes of spirits in Kham, Jang, China, Hor, and other barbarian countries. Binding them with oaths, he took their life force.

Now, there was at that time an evil naga living in a corner of Lake Manasarovar.[63] He was a shape-shifter and, taking the form of a red ox, he came before the king and begged for protection. His legs were torn and pierced by nails, and his skull was split apart so that blood and brains came seeping through. His tongue was lolling out, and his eyes were starting from their sockets so that it seemed as if they would fall from his head.

"What has befallen you?" asked the king.

"Padmasambhava," came the reply, "that son of heathen savages, is bringing us to ruin, the gods and humans of Tibet! It is thus that he torments the Tibetan gods and spirits, innocent though we be! I have come, Great King, to seek your protection."

The pious king was stirred to deep compassion, but no sooner had he uttered the words, "You may stay," than the ox vanished. "What might this be?" the king wondered, and then the Guru told him:

O Great King, your pity was misplaced!
Now throughout the garland of your future lives,
Attainments will be mixed with hindrances
In an unending stream.
The lives of those who practice Dharma
Will be brief and many-troubled.
From now three generations will elapse
And then this red demonic ox will come again—as king!
And once again he will be known as "Ox."[64]
His elder brother he will slay
And evil laws will frame, whereby
The very names of sutra and of mantra
Will be blotted out.
This is karma,
There is neither help nor remedy.

But at that moment, Pelgyi Dorje made the wish: "May I have the power to overwhelm him," he exclaimed.

"That was well said," the Guru replied, and prophesied that he would indeed subdue him. He bestowed on him empowerment, calling him Pelgyi Dorje (for it was at that time that he received the name), giving him there and then detailed predictions, scrolls, and oral instructions. He introduced him to the extremely powerful sadhanas of the twenty Kilas and so forth, with the injunction that he should practice them.

"I, the woman Tsogyal, performed the practice of Vajrakila with the youth Pelgyi Sengé, and before long we saw the deities of the mandala and gained accomplishment. We were then introduced, by means of empowerment and sadhana, to *Phurba Chindü*, which is related to the root texts of Vajrakumara. Its upper section is a method for attaining enlightenment, a peaceful sadhana related to Vajrasattva, while its lower section, a method for applying the various activities such as 'liberation,' is that of the *Dukphur Nakpo*, the 'liberating' activity of which is linked with the Kila Sons.

"Then our Guru said, 'I, Padmasambhava, possess no teaching on the cycle of Vajrakila more profound than this. Practice it and draw upon its strength! When you have done so, transmit part of it orally and the rest conceal as a Treasure.'

"Afterwards, he introduced us to the mandalas of *Tsepamé Ökyi Trengwa, Dorje Trengwa, Sangwa Kundü, Gyalwa Kundü, Lhachik Pumchik*, and sixty-two long-life deities. And so, Pelgyi Dorje and I, vajra kindred, undertook the practice, without straying into laziness even for a moment. And thus we beheld the vision of all the deities and accomplished with ease the level of the vidyadhara of immortality."

It was at that time that Yeshe Tsogyal brought down the wicked Bönpos, but this, as well as her last austerities, will be recounted later. From Kailash to Jamling, on twenty-five ranges of snow mountains, in eighteen important holy places and in a hundred and eight lesser sites, twelve great hidden lands, seven places of wonder, five secret enclaves, and seven million Treasure grounds, in every corner of Tibet she practiced in a way that surpasses the imagination. Some of this will be spoken of later, but that this book might not become too long, it will not be told in detail.

SAMAYA GYA GYA GYA

Six
Signs of Accomplishment

A DETAILED ACCOUNT of the signs that arose in the course of Yeshe Tsogyal's practice was given in the previous chapter and will not be repeated here. There follows nevertheless an abbreviated version in verse, in the Dakini's own words.

Stirred, in Tidro, by the allegorical display of dakinis,[65]
I undertook the eight austerities,
Extracting certain tokens of attainment.

Residing at a place where snow and moraines meet,
I came upon the heat of tummo fire
And threw away the clothing of the world.
In the Trysting Place of Dakinis
The fourth empowerment's warmth was mine,
And all that I beheld was cleansed,
Becoming thus the presence of the Teacher.

In Nepal I brought a dead man back to life
And by this means my Atsara I ransomed
To gain the essence of the path profound.
My speech was vibrant with the melody of Brahma;
My body journeyed like a rainbow to celestial fields;
My mind became the Wisdom of the triple time.

In Sengé Dzong I took the sap of healing herbs
And saw the vision of the deities of medicine.
In Nering I subdued and quelled the uproar
Of a host of demons, and attained accomplishment.

I beheld the face of all the deities I practiced,
And I attained accomplishment with ease.

At Paro Taktsang, with my three companions,
I trod the path profound and deep;
And I, Heruka of Great Bliss,
Controlled and brought within my power
The subtle veins, the essence-drop and energies,
And likewise the five elements I tamed.
My body, speech, and mind transfigured
As the Triple Kaya,
The prophecies of Amitayus came to me.
From Vajravarahi inseparable,
I then became the mistress of all mandalas.

At Onphu Taktsang I attained Kilaya
And seized the life force of the gods and spirits
Of a thousand million worlds.
The deities of Amitayus' mandala I saw
And reached the level of a deathless vidyadhara,
Diamond-like, invincible and indestructible.

Throughout the far-flung regions of Tibet,
In every hill and dale,
The places where I practiced are uncountable.
And not a single clod of earth that hands may grasp
Is now without my blessing,
And time the truth of this will show—
The proof will be the taking out of Treasures.
In lesser sites, so many that the mind cannot encompass,
The imprints of my hands and feet now fill the rocks.
And mantras, syllables, and images,
I placed and set to be
The stay and basis of the future faithful,
And prayed that, linked with them,
They might derive great profit.

These are signs of my attainment:
Demons and the evil-minded were subdued,
The fivefold elements were brought beneath my sway,
And everywhere I filled the earth with Treasures.

Since unfailing memory I gained,
The whole of Padma's teaching I collated.
Since intrepid confidence is mine,
The future I predict, and shield the fortunate.
Since I am the peer of all the Buddhas,
I bring their labors to completion—
The work of those who in the present, past, and future
time
Are gone to bliss.
And thus I am adorned with all attainments.

In brief, to tell my ordinary accomplishments,
I hold phenomena beneath my sway.
I have the power of fleet-footedness,
The universal remedy and the balm of magic sight,
And entry to the hidden lands
Concealed within the sky and earth and secret zones.

Then to tell of my supreme attainment.
I possess the threefold concentration.
The wisdom mind, Samantabhadri's vastness,
Is not hid from me,
And Ultimate Reality is but my jewel and plaything.
I do not hope for Liberation
And of the pains of hell I have no fear.
Far from the nihilism of nonbelievers,
Such is the calm assurance of profound Dharmata!
The Great Perfection, which no action may accomplish,
Is indeed the fruit that I have won,
The all-pervading presence of the Atiyoga.

Wherever space pervades, my wisdom mind is present;
My compassion now outshines the sun.

Greater are my blessings than the billowing clouds,
And swifter than the rain I bring accomplishments.

My faithful ones, who follow me in future times,
Your prayers to me are thus of highest moment,
For I have forged the links that bind us.

Know that I will guide you even in the states of sorrow,
While those who turn away, forsaking me,
Will turn their backs on all the Buddhas.
Only suffering can be the fruit of such an error.
Yet even then, my love will not forsake them,
And when their karma is exhausted, they will come to me.

SAMAYA GYA GYA GYA

Seven
The Benefit of Beings

THE ONLY GOAL of a Buddha's teaching is the good of those who wander in samsara. There is no other reason for a Buddha's actions. In this chapter we will therefore speak of three things. First we will tell of how the Lady Tsogyal planted firmly the precious teachings of the Buddha, subduing demons and those of evil mind. Then we will speak of how, once the Buddhadharma was established, she propagated it, building up the Sangha by means of both the sutra and the tantra teachings. Finally, the tale is told of how she concealed great and inexhaustible Treasures of Dharma, so that for as long as this world lasts, and until samsara is no more, the Doctrine of the Conqueror might increase unfaltering.

When Nyatri Tsenpo, a scion of the Shakya dynasty of India, took Tibet as his dominion, the religious tradition of Bön was widespread. Then, by gradual degrees, beginning with Lhathothori, the heir of that same dynasty, the Buddhadharma was introduced, so that the name of Shakyamuni came to fill the four provinces, and the doctrine of the ten virtues was proclaimed. Now the religion of the Inner Bön was propagated at the same time, and was found to be in harmony with the Buddhist teachings. It was thought that the Buddha Shakyamuni and Shenrab,[66] the patriarch of the Bön, were but two aspects of the same reality, and many were the images and representations of them both. The Inner Bön was named the New Translation School of Zhang Zhung.

During the lifetime of the great religious king Songtsen Gampo, an emanation of the Arya Avalokiteshvara, two images of the Buddha Shakyamuni were brought to Tibet. Beginning with the two temples of Lhasa and Ramoche, a hundred and eight temples were built to subdue and control the evil forces in the march-lands and the four central provinces.[67] Sacred images and paintings were everywhere to be found, after the styles of both Nepal and China. Moreover, when the image of Tara known as the Jomo Zhelzigma appeared of itself in Trandruk, so great was the wonder of the king that he made for it a temple of surpassing beauty. The name of the Three Jewels, the recitation of the six-syllable mantra, and images of the Great Compassionate One filled the whole of Tibet to the very confines of China.

The Inner Bön and the Buddhadharma both spread at that time, and no shadow of sect or faction lay between them. It was said that circumambulation to the right was a sign of Mahamudra, circumambulation to the left a mark of Dzogchen, while prostrations indicated the great Madhyamika. This was an age when people strove in their practice without quarreling over differences. The king established laws based on the teaching of the ten virtues. Many tantras of the Great Compassionate One, in extensive, medium, and concise form, were translated by Thönmi Sambhota, and the king, his ministers, and his wives strove perfectly in their practice of them.

But Songtsen Gampo died, and within twenty-five years of his passing, the perverse tradition of Gyu Bön began to grow in strength and its darkness overshadowed the Buddhadharma and the Inner Bön. The followers of the Inner Bön were banished to Kham, Kongpo, Tsang, Jar, and other regions on the borders, and even to this day they have remained weak and without a voice. Attempts were made to blight and ruin the Dharma to its very roots, but since the counsels of the kings and their ministers were ever at variance, it was not wholly destroyed. Yet it languished and dwindled. The land was marred by the evil lore of the Gyu Bön, and in later days when the throne was filled by Trisong Detsen, the Pious King, there was much that hindered the spreading of the Teaching.

According to the tenets of their false doctrine, the Gyu Bön denied the existence of pure lands. As their gods, they worshiped eight classes of spirits, such as Gyalpo and Gongpo, as well as place gods and earth lords, and the deities of luck and of prosperity—all of them bound within the circles of the world.[68] It was their custom to banish their daughters when their sons brought home wives into their families. Their traditions contained much ancient lore, and they loved to hold elaborate riddle-games and contests of words. The gods of luck and prosperity, they said, were to be propitiated by dance and song. In autumn, they would offer the blood sacrifice of a thousand stags; in spring they cut off the legs of hinds as their life-ransom; in winter, they made blood offerings to the gods; and in summer they made smoke offerings to the Patriarch of Bön, their founding father. And so it was that they amassed the karmas of the ten nonvirtues and the sins of immediate perdition.

All is insubstantial mind, so they believed, manifesting in the form of gods and spirits, which are nothing but the mind. They held that of three possible goals, the highest was rebirth in the sphere of Nothingness; lower than this was rebirth in the sphere of Infinity; and least of all was rebirth in the sphere of Neither Existence nor Nonexistence.[69] The sign of the accomplishment of these levels, they would say, was that the gods would show themselves. In the best case, they would consume the flesh of the sacrificial victims; less good, they would drink of the blood; or, finally, they would cause rainbows to appear. Most of the people in their ignorance took all this to be true doctrine, and adhering to the ruinous tenets of the Gyu Bön, brought disaster upon themselves. It was a pernicious tradition that filled the land and was upheld and fostered mostly by the ministers of Zhang.

Throughout that period, Buddhist paintings and sculptures

disappeared. The Dharma was neither taught nor studied. The temples of Lhasa and Trandruk fell into disrepair, while those of the provinces were ruined. Now, because the country had fallen into such an abject condition, and in order to reestablish the doctrine of the Buddha, the noble Bodhisattva Mañjushri sent his emanation, and the great religious king Trisong Detsen was born. He invited many learned scholars from India, among them Shantarakshita, the Bodhisattva from Zahor. The temples of Lhasa, Trandruk, and Ramoche, dear to the heart of the religious king Songtsen Gampo, were restored and reconsecrated. But when the preparations were being made to construct the temple of Samye, so many obstacles were created by the gods, the people, and the Bönpo priests of Tibet that for a time the building was delayed. Thereupon, the Abbot Shantarakshita gave this counsel: "No one," he said, "be they humankind or gods or spirits, could ever harm the one who has attained the diamond body, the lotus-born master of Orgyen. Invite him here, else there will be no end to this adversity—for you, the patron, and for me, the teacher!"

The king immediately dispatched three of his courtiers to India. They were adherents of the Dharma and trained as translators, and their mission was to supplicate the Precious Teacher of Orgyen. The three translators came without mishap into the presence of the Guru and, having delivered the invitation, returned with him to Tibet. The Tibetan king, his ministers, his courtiers, and his queens felt an irresistible faith in the Guru. The first reception party went as far as Zhongda to greet him, while a second party, nearer home, met him at Lhasa. And in the grove of Ombu, the king himself, attended by all his court, took the bridle of the Guru's mount. The minds of the Guru and the king mingled into one. The king, his ministers, his courtiers, and his queens gazed with devotion upon the Guru and, overwhelmed by the splendor of his presence, felt irresistibly drawn to obey his every word. Even the Abbot

Shantarakshita made prostration to the Guru and stayed awhile to discuss the Doctrine.

Then the king, with his ministers and court, the Abbot, and Guru Rinpoche, together with the translators, made their way to Samye, where the Guru examined the site and gave predictions.

"During the life of my forefather Songtsen Gampo," said the pious king, "one hundred and eight temples were built. But because they were scattered throughout the land, it was impossible to maintain them, and they fell to ruin. It is my wish, therefore, to build the same number of temples within the confines of a single precinct."

The Guru approved, and through the power of his concentration caused to appear four temples and eight subsidiary shrines as symbols of the four continents with their subcontinents and, in their midst, the main sanctuary to represent Mount Meru.[70] Everything was enclosed by a surrounding wall, and was clearly visible for all to see.

"Great King," the Guru asked, "would a temple thus designed be pleasing to your Majesty?"

The king was beside himself with joy. "This is beyond all I had imagined!" he cried. "Is such a building possible? If we succeed in making it like this, then Samye, or 'Beyond Imagination,' indeed shall be its name!"

"Do not be fainthearted, Great King!" replied the Guru. "Simply act, you cannot but succeed! You are the king. The people of Tibet are subject to your will, while all the gods and spirits I hold beneath my sway. How can we fail?"

So Samye was built. The outer structure of the temples was finished, and they were filled to overflowing with representations of the Body, Speech, and Mind of the Buddhas. The Sangha was established. A college of one hundred and eight great translators was founded, all of them extraordinary beings predicted by the Guru. Likewise, three thousand men were called from the thirteen main divisions of the Tibetan people, and of their number, three hundred embraced the monastic life, ordained by the Abbot Shantarakshita and with the Guru as their tantric master.

The translators began their labors upon the Buddhist scriptures. But the Bönpo ministers, hostile to the Dharma, as well as the Bönpos mentioned above, strove to throw obstacles in their path, and it happened on several occasions that certain of the translators were driven into exile. Finally, after the work had been halted for the third time, the Buddhist Sangha and the Bönpos decided to found their own separate communities, the latter also deciding to establish a burial ground at Yarlung. And for a time, there was peace between the king and his ministers.

Now, it came to pass that an invitation was sent to twenty-one learned men of India, and the hundred and eight translators, who had been scattered in all directions, gathered again at Samye. From the thirteen divisions of the population, a multitude of three thousand men entered the monastic order together. And likewise from Zhang Zhung and other places, seven Bönpo scholars and seven Bönpo wizards were invited to Ombu, the grove of tamarisks.

At that time, the Guru and his Consort were residing at Onphu Taktsang and so the pious king dispatched the great translator Drenpa Namkha[71] and three attendants to invite them. Black Eagle-Flight, the Precious Teacher's great steed, was also sent, while the others in the party were each provided with a mount and a pack animal. Back they sped to Samye. But the Guru said that they should go for a while to Lhasa, and there he performed seven actions propitious for the establishment of the doctrine of the Secret Mantra. It was then also that Shakyamuni[72] spoke to him and gave predictions. They continued on to Samye and at Surkhar, in front of a stone stupa, were met by a reception party. At Samye, on the plain of Yombok, a great throne was set up, and the Precious Teacher took his seat. The twenty-one learned men of India and the

Tibetan translators made obeisance to him, whereupon the great master Vimalamitra and the scholars exclaimed: "How wonderful to have met the Guru of Orgyen, Padmasambhava himself in person! *Alala!* This is indeed through merits gathered over many eons of time!" And they gazed upon the Guru's countenance, their faces wet with tears. Great indeed was the joy of Guru Rinpoche and Vimalamitra at their meeting, like a father reuniting with his son. Hand in hand they went up into the main temple. The pious king, the Abbot, and the court made prostrations to them in the upper hall of the temple before repairing to the topmost chamber, dedicated to Vairochana, where they took their seats.

The Guru declared that for the Dharma to be propagated, a threefold consecration should be performed and also three fire-offerings for the subjugation of demonic forces. The consecration was duly carried out, but, swept away in a moment of distraction, the king failed to request the last fire-offering and therefore the Guru did not perform it. "Thus will it come to pass," the Guru foretold, "that though the Dharma will indeed increase, evil will grow and spread with equal pace."

Now, as the final month of the Tibetan year came around, the people, Buddhists and Bönpos both, gathered at Samye for the rites of homage to the religious king. Five Bön scholars were invited to Samye. They did not recognize or comprehend the representations of the Buddha's Body, Speech, and Mind. The doctrine of the ten virtuous deeds was foreign to their understanding, and they neither made prostrations nor performed circumambulation. They sat down in a row, leaning back against the images. And the king and most of his ministers were grieved.

Early the next day, before taking his refreshment, the king met the Bönpos in the uppermost sanctuary before the image of Buddha Vairochana. The Bönpos said to him: "Lord and Majesty, who is that naked figure supposed to be, up there in the middle, surrounded by the figures of eight naked men? What is their origin? Are they not Indian panditas?"

The pious king replied: "The figure in the middle represents the Buddha Vairochana and he is surrounded by eight Bodhisattvas. These are Buddha-images, and it is by making prostrations and offerings before them that we expiate our evil karma and gather merit."

"And what," they asked again, "are those two hideous figures down there, blocking the door? They are statues of murderers, surely. What are they made of, and what purpose do they serve?"

"The two figures down by the door," answered the king, "are representations of Glorious Legden Nakpo. He is the wrathful and all-powerful destroyer of those who violate their samaya, and friend of those who practice Dharma. The images are made from various precious substances by skilled craftsmen and have been blessed by Padmasambhava, the great sage of India. They are necessary for the spreading of the teachings and the purification of defilements."

"What can come from mere clay modeled by a craftsman?" they retorted. "You have been deceived, O King! Tomorrow, we the Bön will show you marvels and an offering of great merit. We the Bön can show you real signs of accomplishment that will inspire you with faith." Later, as they were walking and taking their ease outside, they saw the stupas and asked, "What are those things over there with the hoods of vultures on their tips, wrinkles in the middle and what looks like heaps of dog filth at the base?"

"They are called 'the offspring of the Sugatas,'" replied the king, "or 'representatives of the Dharmakaya.' These names are deeply meaningful. They are the ripening of the Sambhogakaya and, as nirmanakaya, they provide a basis for the offerings of beings. Thus we call them chörtens, supports for offering. The spire indicates the thirteen stages of the Dharma; it is adorned with the umbrella-canopy and the crown ornament symbols of the eighty physical perfections of a Buddha. The central dome, in the form of a round vase, stands for the palace of the Dharmakaya marked by the character of the four immeasurable qualities. The base is a throne, carried and adorned by lions. It is symbol of the treasure-house of all that could be wished."

"Made with such hard labor and yet completely useless!" snapped the Bönpos. "Useless as a fighting ground for warriors, useless as a hiding place for cowards. This is utterly outlandish! Our king has been the dupe of black-hearted Indians!"

But the king and his ministers let it pass and paid no heed.

Then the Bön gathered in the three temples of the queens to perform the royal ceremony of worship. The Buddhist monks were stationed in the eight subsidiary temples, while the panditas were in the sanctuary of Hayagriva. The Bön declared that since this was to be a ceremony for a great king, they had need of a thousand stags with antlers fully grown. They needed hinds with turquoise halters; yaks, sheep, and goats, male and female, to the number of one thousand apiece; together with a complete set of royal robes. All this was speedily provided by the king. They said further that they needed all kinds of worldly goods, and these they also received. Eight kinds of beer and nine kinds of grain they said they required, and all was duly provided.

"Now, O Great King," they cried. "Come with your court to meet the Bön!"

So the king and his queens, his ministers, and all his court, proceeded to the place. And there, in the center, they saw the nine Bön scholars seated in a line. To right and to left were the ranks of nine great wizards and other Bönpos. There were many Shen Bön, termed Servants of the Sacrifice, each carrying a knife. There were also many so-called Purifiers who carried large quantities of water in golden ladles with which they lustrated the beasts, the stags and so forth. There were Black Bön who scattered grains over them, and Questioners whose task it was to question the gods and spirits, and to receive their answers.

"Here are stags!" the Shen Bön cried. And they cut the throats of the victims and made their offering. In the same way, they immolated the yaks, sheep, and goats, slashing their throats: a hecatomb of three thousand male beasts. Then they sacrificed the female deer, hacking off their legs. "Here are dri and ewes, and here are nanny goats," they shouted as they offered them, flaying the skin off the animals' limbs while they were still alive. Similarly, they sacrificed horses, oxen, dzo, mules, dogs, fowl and pigs, killing them in different ways and offering their flesh. The stench of burning hair filled the whole of Samye. The Butchers dismembered the victims, the Distributors divided the meat and shared it out to those who were present, while Counting Men kept an account. Then the Bloodtakers came, filling their vessels of copper and arranging them on skins, while on other skins they piled up the meat, chanting the spells and incantations of the Bön. Then, before the eyes of the unhappy king, his queens, and his ministers, the blood began to boil and steam. The steam gave off a great shimmering as of rainbows, and the fell voices of disembodied spirits could be heard: *Hushu, Haha*—sounds deranged and shrill.

"These," they shouted, "are the voices of the swastika gods—Cha and Yang, Fortune and Prosperity!" And filled with awe, they offered up the bloody flesh and gore.

"Can such a wretched offering be of any benefit?" asked the king.

"It is for the monarch's good estate that we do these things," the Bönpos replied. "For us the Bön, it is rather to our detriment. Is your faith not kindled, O Great King? Are you not moved to wonderment?"

But the pious king was sick at heart and the others were at a loss, not knowing what to think. And all in a quandary, they returned to the main temple.

Now, the translators and panditas had been watching these

events and said: "One doctrine cannot have two teachers. If the east is low, the west will naturally be high. Fire and water can never keep company. It is nonsense to mix the teachings of the Buddha with the tradition of these heathens. Evildoers should be banished far away! Not for a single moment can we take the part of the black-hearted, nor should we even drink the water in the valleys where samaya-breakers dwell. Let us away to solitude! Let us cultivate samadhi!"

And so they sent word to the king and supplicated him nine times, saying: "Either the Buddhadharma will be established in the land of Tibet, or the doctrine of Bön will prevail. But not for a moment can the two stay side by side."

When the message had been read for the last time, the pious king summoned before him his ministers and his court and spoke thus:

"*Kyema Ho!* Hear me, ministers and all my court. The traditions of the Bön and of the Buddhists are like the palm and the back of a single hand. One must be accepted and the other rejected; one is to be practiced and the other laid aside. No reconciliation can there be between them. These are the counsels of the Indian scholars, the Tibetan translators, and the Sangha of the three thousand, newly ordained. What shall we do?"

The Bön ministers from Zhang replied: "Sire and Majesty! Happy indeed if the river could keep company with its banks! A similar situation arose some time ago, and it was necessary to banish many translators who behaved improperly. Do the same again. Let the Bön keep to their proper place and the Buddhists to theirs. Then there will be peace."

It was Goe the Elder who decided the case. "If Bön prospers, the king is unhappy and fainthearted. If the Buddhadharma prospers, the ministers lack confidence and are ineffective. If the two are placed on an equal footing, they are like fire and water, mortal enemies. Let us uproot anything that menaces the kingdom. A public trial will settle the matter. Truth will be separated from falsehood by disputation and will be decided by the casting of votes. The correct doctrine will be revealed and distinguished from the false, and nothing more need then be done. Tomorrow, therefore, with the king presiding from on high, and the ministers and court seated before him, let the Buddhist monks take their place in a row on the right and let the Bönpos face them on the left. And let the contest begin! Philosophical positions will be distinguished, and then we will drink to the truth, casting falsehood far away! Let miracles be worked as the mark of truth; let each display his powers and skills! Then, if Dharma be proved true, let us hold to it and let the Bön be uprooted. But if Bön be true, let the Dharma be abolished and Bön confirmed. Let us make a law to this effect. Let punishment fall on any who transgress it—king or minister, queen or courtier! All of you, take a pledge!"

The king, his ministers, his queens, and his court agreed and gave their word. Even the Bönpo ministers pronounced themselves in favor of the pledge, for they thought that the Buddhists could in no way vie with the Bön in miraculous displays and wonder-working. Then the pious king spoke to the Buddhist panditas, saying:

Emaho!
Learned sages,
Lofty masters of accomplishment, pay heed to me.
Like executioners are Buddhists and the Bön.
When they meet, they give no quarter!
Confusion fills the king, his queens, and ministers,
And Bön and Buddhism are doubted equally.
Tomorrow, therefore, they will both contend:
Striving with each other in miracles and powers,
With signs of truth and tokens of attainment.

Whichever doctrine is revealed as true,
The king and ministers will believe and follow.
Falsehood will be utterly suppressed and banished,

Driven to the wilderlands along the borders.
Consider this, the judgment of the king and ministers.

All the panditas rejoiced and gave this answer to the king:

Sacred Majesty, powerful among men!
This is the proper way to act,
The way of all religious kings!

That which is not Dharma will be overcome by Dharma.
Demons and the evil-hearted will be cowed by truth!
The sages and accomplished masters gathered here—
None is greater even at the Diamond Throne!

In former times, the heathens were subdued by truth,
Why should we now fear to rout the Bön?
Let penalties be dealt to those who lose,
And let them not remain or linger here!
Right it is to drive them hence with laws!

This reply was pleasing to the king and he spoke about it in detail to the Bön, telling them to prepare themselves. They assured him that if it came to a debate, their nine scholars would win, and their nine wizards, so they said, would also be triumphant. And so, on the fifteenth day of the new year, a high throne was set up for the king at Samye in the middle of the great plain of Yombok. On the right-hand side the translators and panditas took their seats, with the Buddhist scriptures piled up like a wall. To the left sat the Bön with their scriptures arranged in similar fashion. In front were the ranks of ministers and courtiers. And pressing all around was a great multitude of people, the red and the black, the religious and the lay, from all four provinces of Tibet.

The king was the first to raise his voice. "People of Tibet who live beneath my sway!" he cried. "Gods and men, Buddhists and Bön, ministers of state, queens, and all my court, hear your king! The kings of old nurtured Dharma and the Bönpo teaching with an equal hand. And so it is that, since the Bön have grown and spread beyond their measure, I have tried to set a balance between the two traditions, after the manner of Songtsen Gampo, my forefather. But a deadly enmity now lies between the Dharma and the Bön, such that one must be adopted and the other cast aside. The king and ministers are thus assailed by doubt. The differences between the two teachings will now be made plain, and we will take to ourselves the one that gains our confidence. Anyone who rejects this decision will be destroyed by the power of the law. The tradition that is proved to be untrue will be banished to the outer marches of the kingdom, and in the whole of this Tibetan realm its name shall be utterly blotted out. This is our doom and law! The vanquished shall accept defeat, and to the winners we will grant the honor of victory. And all shall follow them."

Nine times this edict was proclaimed, and when the ministers announced it from the law-scrolls, all submitted to it. At that moment, the Great Guru of Orgyen appeared seated in the air at about the height of a palm tree.

"*Kyé!*" he exclaimed. "Good it is to distinguish the tenets of the Dharma from those of Bön! Hold a preliminary trial of wits, for this is the first stage of every debate. Then lay the ground with an explanation of your own tradition, a joy indeed for every lineage! Finally, present your arguments, making clear your premises and conclusions, dividing truth from falsehood. Thus the difference between the doctrines will be revealed. Conclude by giving evidence of your accomplishment, for this will show your strength and will inspire the king and ministers with confidence." So saying, he assumed the form of Buddha Shakyamuni, so that the king, his ministers, and all the Bön were overwhelmed with its splendor. An emanation of his speech appeared as Padmasambhava himself, the master of the assembled panditas, thus giving even greater courage to the scholars and translators. The emanation of his mind arose in the form of Dorje Drolö, demoralizing those whose opinions were perverse, and displaying incompatible miraculous appearances, such that even the Bön praised him with unfeigned devotion.

Then Atsara Pelyang vied with the Bön, measuring himself against them in a verbal tournament. And in this the latter were victorious. The Bön party raised their standard and praised their gods. The king sent them a present of drink, whereat the Bön ministers were greatly pleased and sent generous gifts to the Bön contestant. The king was downcast, but the Precious Master said, "Quick to win and quick to lose! They have done well in the riddle-game, but this has nothing to do with the Dharma. Now the nine Bön scholars and the great panditas will debate on religious matters." Thereupon, the mighty sage Vimalamitra rose from the front row and said:

> Everything arises from a cause.
> That cause the Tathagata has explained.
> The exhaustion of this cause,
> The great Renunciate has set forth:
> Do no wrong of any kind,
> Practice virtue to perfection,
> And your own mind perfectly subdue.

Then he sat in vajra posture, floating in midair. With three snaps of his fingers, the nine Bön wizards fainted away, while the nine Bön scholars were struck dumb and sat there bewildered, unable to answer. In the same way, the twenty-five Indian scholars, and the hundred and eight Tibetan translators, each began with a scriptural exposition and then went on to debate, showing different authentic signs of accomplishment. The Bön were left speechless and were unable to work any true miracles, floundering in confusion and darkness.

The Bön ministers rebuked them. "So!" they cried. "They have won the debate! But now let each of you demonstrate his miracles. These monks have dazzled the entire population of Tibet, gods and men, with their wonders; their disputations are a delight to hear; their demeanor is charming and the people are so happy with them that we, the ministers, feel we have been tricked. Whatever you are capable of, signs of accomplishment, miraculous powers, or evil spells, be quick about it!" And in the fury of their evil hearts they whipped up the Bön with harsh and terrible words: "These Indian barbarians have contaminated the swastika gods of the Bön. We will not contend with the panditas now but will slay them with magic later. We will dispute instead with the translators, for they are Tibetans!"

Meanwhile, the pious king was showering the panditas with praise, presenting each of them with a measure of gold dust, a golden ingot, and brocade robes. The banner of the Dharma was raised aloft; the conch was sounded, and a rain of wonderful flowers actually fell from the sky. Deities appeared in the heavens, with words of poetry on their lips, and the people of Tibet, filled with awe, their faces wet with tears, gave their hearts to the Dharma.

But on the rows of the Bön there fell a deluge of hail and rocks, so that the Bön ministers cried out, "The gods have revealed who is in the right!" And they made prostrations to the Buddhist scriptures, placed the feet of the panditas upon their heads, and confessed their sins to the translators. The pious king beheld a vision of Mañjushri and understood within his heart what was true Dharma and what was falsehood. Most of the people were saying that the Buddhists had the victory, with a doctrine that was great and wondrous. And with that, they began to disperse, giving their word that they would all practice it.

The religious king, however, decreed that the Tibetan translators and the Bönpos should prepare themselves for debate. The great translator Vairotsana measured himself against Thangnak, while Namkhai Nyingpo contended with Tongyu.

And likewise each of the translators debated with one of the Bön, even though not a single one of their opponents could rival them. The king had decided that established truths should be recorded by white pebbles, while falsity should be marked by black. Vairotsana took nine hundred white pebbles for the truth, while to Thangnak fell five thousand pebbles of falsity. With shouts of joy, the translators raised their banner. Namkhai Nyingpo of the clan of Nub gained three thousand white pebbles and Tongyu thirty thousand black, and again the translators held aloft their standard. Tsogyal vied with Yudrung Bönmo Tso of the Chokro clan and worsted her in the contest. As will be told, she performed wonders that left Bönmo Tso speechless. In the same way, the one hundred and twenty translators were successful, and all the Bön, the nine great scholars at their head, were defeated and left dumbfounded. Their tongues shrank in their heads, their lips grew stiff and hard, the sweat stood out upon their brows, their knees trembled and shook, and not a word could they say.

Then the time arrived for the contest in signs of accomplishment. Vairotsana began by holding the three levels of the world in the palm of his hand. Namkhai Nyingpo rode upon the sunbeams, displaying many marvels. Simply by pointing his phurba, Sangye Yeshe subdued harmful forces and with a stroke could destroy his enemies. Striking rocks with it, he could pierce them through. Dorje Dudjom, fleet-footed as the wind, encircled the four continents in a single instant, offering as proof to the king seven treasures from the farthest reaches of the universe. Hayagriva's horse-head sprouted from the crown of Gyalwa Choyang and filled a thousand million worlds three times with the clamor of its neighing. In a trice, he subdued the three levels of the world, the Lord of the Tsangri heaven, and others, and offered in testimony the nine-spoked golden wheel of Brahma. Gyalwa Lodrö walked upon the surface of the water without sinking. Denma Tsemang routed the Bön with his exposition of the Buddha's teaching, explaining the whole of the Kangyur from memory, and causing vowels and consonants to appear in the sky, visible for all to see. Kawa Peltsek made servants of the arrogant spirits. Odren Zhönnu swam like a fish beneath the waters of a lake. Jñana Kumara caused nectar to flow from a rock. Ma Rinchen Chok broke off a boulder and ate it as if it were bread. Pelgyi Dorje passed through hills and cliffs unobstructed. With the mudra of the hook, the mantra of summoning and the power of his concentration, Sogpo Lhapel caused a pregnant tigress to appear from the south, and Drenpa Namkha summoned wild yaks from the north. Chokro Lui Gyaltsen invoked before him in the sky the Bodhisattvas of the three Families. Landro Könchok Jungden brought down thirteen thunderbolts and aimed and shot them as if they were arrows. Kheuchung captured birds, binding them simply by the power of his concentration. Gyalmo Yudra Nyingpo was all-triumphant in grammar and logic, and by the force of his concentration influenced other people's perceptions, causing things to disappear or to change their shape. Gyalwa Changchub rose into the air, seated in vajra posture. Tingdzin Zangpo flew up into the sky and in a single instant could survey the four continents. In the same way, the twenty-five mahasiddhas of Chimphu, the hundred siddhas of Yerpa, the thirty tantrikas of Sheldrak, the fifty-five yogis of Yangdzong and others, each demonstrated a different sign of accomplishment. They changed fire into water, water into fire. They flew in the sky, passed unhindered through rocks and mountains, walked on water, transformed a small quantity into a greater and a great quantity into a smaller, and performed many other marvels. The Tibetans could not but have faith in the Dharma, whereas the Bön had no choice but to surrender. The ministers favorable to the Bön were left speechless. And to be sure, the Lady Tsogyal defeated all the Bön with whom she contended.

And so the Bön began to weave their evil sorceries:

> Power of a weasel's stink,
> Pap that's thrown to maw of hound,

Butter lamp that's drowned in gore,
And a strong beast's pitchy fell,
Mighty Tsen and evil fiend,
And the rest . . . all cast and sent!

Nine evil spells they made, and in the same moment, nine young monks were struck down dead, their faces to the ground. But the Lady put spittle in the mouth of each of them and they were restored to life, their wisdom nine times sharper than before. Thus the Bön were worsted in the contest once again.

Making the threatening gesture of the pointed finger in the direction of the nine wizards, Tsogyal spoke the syllable *P'et* nine times. They collapsed, unconscious, unable to move, reviving only when she uttered the syllable *Hung* nine times. In like manner, she showed her power over the five elements. She sat upon the air in the vajra posture. From the fingertips of her right hand there came a whirling wheel of five-colored fire so that all the Bön were afraid, and from the fingertips of her left hand came five-colored streams of water swirling down to the great ocean at the edge of the world. With her bare hands she broke away the rocks of Chimphu and molded them into different shapes. She projected twenty-five emanations, identical with herself, each of which performed a different sign of accomplishment.

Throughout Tibet, the Bönpos were the object of universal mockery. "Look!" the people sneered, "they cannot even stand up to a woman!" But the Bön retorted, "Tomorrow our nine wizards will bring down thunder and in a single moment will reduce Samye to a heap of ashes!" And they went off to Hepori, and there indeed they drew the thunder down. But Tsogyal wrapped it all around the tip of her forefinger. And, making the mudra of threatening, she hurled it at the Bön settlement of Ombu so that it was blasted and broken to pieces. Thirteen thunderbolts fell upon the Bön, after which they went to Samye, begging for mercy.

And so it was that the Bön were driven away, having been defeated also in the trial of magic strength. Nevertheless, Takra, Lugong, and certain other ministers could not be ousted, for their power was very great. They went again to Ombu, and there, by means of the nine cycles of Pelmo, the greater and lesser deeds, they cast their enchantments into fire, earth, and air, striving mightily to bring the whole of Tibet down into ruin. The king sent word to the panditas and translators, asking for means to avert this disaster. At that moment, Guru Rinpoche uttered a prediction and instructed the Lady Tsogyal to go and protect the king. Thereupon, in the central sanctuary she opened the mandala of Vajrakila and practiced it. Seven days passed, and she beheld the vision of the deities and demonstrated the power she had attained. The malediction turned upon itself and the Bön became their own executioners. Takra and Lugong and the five other ministers hostile to the Dharma were slain instantly; and eight of the nine wizards were destroyed, only one remaining. Thus it was that by the power of magic, the covens of the Bön were vanquished and laid waste.

Straightaway, the great and pious king summoned all the Bönpos to Samye and punished them with moderate severity. The Guru said, "The Inner Bön are in harmony with the Dharma, therefore leave them as they are. As for the depraved Bön, however, they are no different from the fanatical heathens. And yet it would be wrong to kill them. Let them therefore be banished to the borderlands." Following the counsel of the Guru, the pious king caused all the Bön writings to be sorted out and named as "outer" or "inner." All the books of the Outer Bön were burned, while those of the Inner Bön were concealed as Treasures. The Inner Bön were then sent to Zhang Zhung and the outer marches of Tibet, while the Outer Bön were banished to the land of Treulakchan in Mongolia.

And from that day forth, the king, his ministers and court, and all who lived beneath his rule, Tibetan or outlander, were bound by law to shun the Bön and to hold to the Dharma.

Thus the land of Tibet, as far as Trigo in China, was filled with the Buddha's Doctrine, and many were the communities of the monastic Sangha, and groups of students and practitioners. When the pious king promulgated the second religious law, the Dharma-drum was beaten in Samye, the Dharma-conch was blown, the Dharma-banner was hoisted and the Dharma-thrones were set in place. The twenty-one panditas of India sat on seats of nine brocade cushions, while Padmasambhava, the Mighty One of Orgyen, together with the Bodhisattva Abbot from Zahor, and Vimalamitra, the Sage of Kashmir, sat at the front upon great thrones of gold. Vairotsana and Namkhai Nyingpo the translators took their seats on nine cushions of brocade, while all the other translators sat on brocade cushions also, two or three apiece. Then the king presented them with sumptuous gifts of gold and other things. To each of the Indian panditas he gave nine rolls of brocade, three golden ingots, three measures of gold dust, and so on, piling them up as high as mountains. To the three Masters from Orgyen, Zahor, and Kashmir he offered mandalas of gold and turquoise, heaps of silk and satin and numberless other lovely gifts, requesting them to propagate the twofold tradition of sutra and mantra in the land of Tibet. The great panditas smiled with joy and said, "This is excellent indeed." The Abbot, the Master, and Vimalamitra gave their word that they would guard the Teachings of the Buddha until the wishes of the king should be fulfilled.

Within a single year, three twin communities were established. A college was founded at Samye for seven thousand students and at Chimphu a meditation center for nine hundred practitioners. At Trandruk a college was built for one thousand students and a center at Yangdzong for one hundred meditators. Finally, a college for three thousand students was established at Lhasa, with a center at Yerpa for five hundred meditators. In addition to these religious establishments, amazing colleges and houses of meditation were founded at Langthang in Kham, Rawagang in Menyak, Gyaltham in Jang,

Jatsang in Mar, in Rongzhi and Gangdruk, Dongchu in Powo, Ronglam in Barlam, Puchu in Kongpo, and also in Chimyul, Danglung in Dakpo, at Tsuklak—for the four provinces of central Tibet, at Takden Jomonang in Tsang, at Labchi and so on, all over Tsang and Tsangrong, as far as Ngari.

Yeshe Tsogyal protects and cultivates the Sangha

The Buddhist tradition, the monastic houses, the tantric colleges, and the teachings of the Dharma spread unchallenged throughout Tibet. The sages of India, China, and Nepal returned to their homes greatly satisfied, loaded with the gold and wealth offered in appreciation of their kindness. But the Abbot, the Vajra Master, and Vimalamitra remained in Tibet to turn the wheel of the sutras and tantras. Thus were fulfilled the heartfelt wishes of the pious king. His power and the breadth of his dominion had reached their zenith. His enemies on the four frontiers were subjugated and the evil Bön had waned. And so, when he had realized his every aspiration, down to the very last, he laid the kingly power upon his son, Prince Muné Tsenpo. He was fulfilled in every happiness and bliss, untouched by the slightest pain or illness. And it was thus that the eve of his passing arrived. He spoke some words of counsel to the princes and the queens, his ministers and the court. At midnight he cast flowers of consecration in all the temples and bestowed his blessing. Before dawn he recited the text of the generation stage of his yidam deity and, as day was breaking, in a state of radiant clarity, he dissolved into the heart of noble Mañjushri and disappeared.

Now, it came to pass that the crown prince was murdered by one of the queens, who poisoned him with herbs, and in his place the prince Mutri Tsenpo was set upon the throne. It happened also at that time that the queens who were hostile to the Dharma sowed strife and discord between two Dharma communities. But the Lady Tsogyal, with her compassionate skill, brought them together and reconciled them. Such quarrels were then forbidden by the laws.

At that time, the woman Bönmo Tso[73] was living at Hepori. She was of the Inner Bön of the Chokro clan and had known Tsogyal well since childhood. She gave Tsogyal some poisoned nectar to drink. But Tsogyal perceived this and, having drunk it, said:

> *Kyema!*
> Heart-friend, listen well.
> That was powerful and tasty nectar,
> Which my spotless diamond body—
> Wonderful indeed!—has changed
> Into a draught of immortality!
>
> The plan you hatched has gone awry
> And yet has brought to me much merit.
>
> Do not harbor jealousy against me;
> Practice, rather, Buddhism and Bön with equal fervor.
> Supplicate your yidam, and your Dharma kindred
> View with pure perception.
> On the helpless, look with lovingkindness,
> And be devoted to your lord the Guru.

As she said this, her body was transfigured into shimmering rainbow light, and in each of her pores there was a vajra. Bönmo was overcome with shame and moved away to another country. But because of this, the queens were filled with spite and banished Tsogyal to Tsang.

First she stayed at Kharak Gang, gathering around her a community of three hundred meditators, so that in later days the place was known as Jomo Kharak—Kharak of the Lady. Thirty-nine of these three hundred yogis attained accomplishment and gained miraculous powers. Moreover, of these thirty-nine, twenty were able to benefit beings, and seven even reached the level of Tsogyal herself, their work for the sake of others being thus immeasurable.

Afterward, Tsogyal practiced at Jomo Nang. One thousand nuns gathered there, of whom one hundred were able to secure the true benefit of beings. Seven became equal to Tsogyal and three hundred attained accomplishment. That is why this place is known as Jomo Nang, the Lady's Family. She then went on to practice at Sangak Ugpalung, and the whole of Tsang was filled with her renown. A thousand monks and yogis, and one thousand three hundred nuns, gathered there, and by means of the unsurpassable Secret Mantra, Tsogyal brought them all to spiritual maturity and liberation. All of them became Non-returners.[74] Seven of them became known as the Seven Fortunate Ones of Tsang, and eighty were celebrated as great yogis. She bestowed on all of them the teachings of the oral transmission lineage, and in Jomo Nang she propagated the ear-whispered lineage of the essential pith instructions. Thus Ugpalung became a seat of learning in the scriptures, and many siddhas appeared in Kharak and Jomo Nang likewise.

It happened later that the Lady Tsogyal was in Shampo Gang where she was assailed by seven bandits who violated her and robbed her. But she sang this song to them, introducing them to the Four Joys:

Namo Guru Padma Siddhi Hri!
Sons who, meeting me, your mother,
Have but now received the four empowerments,
Through the strength of merits gathered in the past,
Do not be distracted from the rhythm of the Fourfold Joy!

When you saw the mandala of me, your mother,
Powerful lust arose within your minds:
Through this yearning you received the
 Vase Empowerment.

Experience the nature of desire,
Mingle and unite it with the deity
Of the stage of generation.
The so-called yidam deity is nowhere else.
Meditate upon your lust, my sons,
As the very body of the deity.

With space, the mandala of me, your mother,
You were joined. Your subtle channels
Trembled with Great Bliss. The anger of your minds
Was stilled and love was born. And by this strength,
Empowerment of the Secret[75] you have gained.
Experience the nature of your Joy,
And hold it for a moment blended with your subtle winds.
Such is Mahamudra, nothing else.
Experience, O my sons, the bliss of Mahamudra.

Joining with the blissful space of me, your mother,
Roused by the helpless laborings of instinct
To mingle with my mind, your minds, as one—
This blessing gives you the Empowerment of Wisdom.
Hold the nature of this bliss unwavering,
And mingle emptiness therewith.
The spotless state of voidness-bliss is nothing else.
Experience, O my sons, the supreme Joy of Great Felicity!

Joining with the blissful channel of myself, your mother,
If you do not lose, but keep, your bodhichitta,
The dualistic sense of self and others ceases.
Through this Primal Wisdom you obtained
Empowerment of Awareness-Power.
In the midst of your perceptions,
Preserve an uncontrived simplicity of mind.
Your pleasure mix with emptiness—
The Great Perfection—this and nothing else.
Experience, O my sons, the coemergent Joy that
exceeds joy.

How utterly sublime this teaching is, what wonder!
Liberation comes from merely meeting it!
The Four Empowerments are obtained at once;
And by the Fourfold Joy, accomplishment is ripened.

As she spoke these words, the seven thieves, in a single moment, attained spiritual maturity and liberation. They assumed a mastery of the subtle channels and wind-energies and became adept in the rhythms of the Four Joys. And even in their physical bodies, those seven robber-mahasiddhas went to Orgyen and there brought about the limitless welfare of beings.

Later, the Lady journeyed to Nepal, accompanied by six disciples. There, with the help of previous benefactors and the Nepali king, Jila Jipha, she disseminated many of the Guru's essential instructions. It was there, too, that she accepted as one of her disciples a girl of fourteen years, known by the name of Dakini, whose father's name was Bhadanana and whose mother was called Nagini. Because she was indeed a dakini of the "Body lineage," and because she was to attain accomplishment in the Mantrayana, she was named Kalasiddhi.

Then Lady Tsogyal made her way by stages from Khoshö to Mangyul where she opened the tantric mandala related to the Guru. She practiced for one year and, with the help of her instructions, Kalasiddhi, Lodrö Kyi, Dechenmo, and Seltra, among others, gained accomplishment. As many as two hundred of the faithful gathered together there, and whereas previously the Buddha's teaching had not spread much there, the country became a religious land, and its inhabitants, both men and women, grew in understanding of the crucial doctrine of the law of karma.

At that time, the religious king Mutri Tsenpo dispatched three of his courtiers with an invitation for Lady Tsogyal. And she, leaving the nun Lodrö Kyi as her regent in Mangyul, traveled back to Tibet in the company of Kalasiddhi and eleven other disciples. On her way to Samye, the people of Kharak,

Jomo Nang and Ugpalung came to venerate and honor her. A wonderful reception was made for her by the king, and a procession of the yellow-clad monks conducted her to the main temple. Great was the joy of the ministers, courtiers, and translators as they greeted her. It was as if they had thought her dead, only to find that she was alive again.

To the mortal remains of the great Abbot Shantarakshita, the Lady Tsogyal offered a mandala composed of seven handfuls of gold dust and nine pieces of silk. And with her face wet with tears she said:

Kyema Kyehü!
Alas! Supreme and holy teacher!
The sky is vast and wide,
The starry multitudes are many,
But if the seven-steeded sun has gone away,
Who will drive away the gloom of ignorance?
What lamp of light remains for this,
Tibet's dark land?
Where has gone the stainless orb of crystal fire?
If you no longer guard us with the rays of your
  compassion,
Who will guide us now, the sightless staring blind?

The royal treasure-house is filled with wealth,
But since the wishing-gem is here no more,
What hope is there for sorrow's end
In this, a land of pretas?
Where has gone the precious wish-fulfilling jewel?
If you no longer guard us with your all-supplying bounty,
Who will shield the lame who go with limping feet?

Many are the lords and princes in this cosmos of a billion
  worlds,
But if the universal king has gone away,
What protection can there be, what hope of safety,
For Tibet, this wilderland?

Where have you departed, lord and emperor of the world?
If you no longer guard us, teaching us the discipline,
Who will shield the dumb that babble senselessly?

Though learned and accomplished ones are many
In the central land of this, our world.
If you, Great Abbot, are not with us,
Who will be the holder of the teachings?
Where have you departed, peerless regent of the Buddha?
If you do not protect us with the sutras and the tantras,
Who will shield us now, the living dead?

Alas, supremely learned Shantarakshita,
Lord among the lordly Bodhisattvas!
Protector, through your grace,
May I myself and others
Enter, in our every life, the door of Dharma.

May I, through teaching of the sutras and the tantras,
Ripened, freed, and brought to bliss,
Accomplishing the benefit of others
By means of four attracting qualities,[76]
Perform the perfect actions of the Buddha's offspring.

May I become a perfect teacher of the Dharma,
Hoisting high the flag of triumph never to be furled!
Crossing thus the ocean with this boat-like body,
For sake of Doctrine and all wandering beings,
May I become their teacher and their captain.

And from the upper part of the sacred reliquary there came a voice:

Om Ah Hung!
The actions of all Buddhas, past, present, and to come,
You have performed!
Boundless, equal to the confines of the sky,

Such has been the compass of your action!
The doctrine of the Victor, root and branch,
Pervades and fills the ten directions!
All-embracing mother
Of the Buddhas past, present, and to come,
May you prosper!

The voice was heard by all assembled there, and they rejoiced.

Thereafter, Lady Tsogyal became the spiritual guide of the king. She dwelt at Chimphu for eleven years, never parting from the Guru her lord, propagating the Doctrine through teaching and practice. From the secret treasure-house of his heart, Guru Rinpoche drew out all the teachings and essential instructions of the Secret Mantra, holding nothing back. He gave it all to her, like a brimming vessel poured into another.

Then he said: "The time is not far off when I shall go to Ngayab, realm of dakinis. But first I must place, throughout the land of Tibet, inexhaustible teachings, vast and profound. You must take these Treasures in your charge. This girl here has been rightly called Siddhi. She is of the conch family in the Body lineage of dakinis and is accomplished in the Secret Mantra. I will take her as my consort for the purpose of propagating many different pith instructions of the Secret Mantra, unheard of anywhere else. And as Treasures I will then conceal them."

"In accordance with the Guru's wish," the Lady Tsogyal recalled, "I offered him the girl Siddhi as his consort and afterwards opened the mandala of the *Lama Gongpa Düpa*, bringing to spiritual maturity and freedom the king Mutri Tsenpo, who was engaged in furthering the Dharma teachings, after the manner of his father.

"It was then that all the instructions the Precious Master had given, and which were to be concealed as Treasures, were committed to writing. This was done by Namkhai Nyingpo, who was adept in the art of writing with miraculous speed; by

Atsara Pelyang, most exact and careful; by Denma Tsemang, excellent in orthography, speed and accuracy; by Kawa Peltsek, adept in orthography; by Chokro Gyaltsen, a master penman; by Yudra Nyingpo, skilled in grammar and logic; by Vairotsana, accomplished in all these arts; and by myself, Yeshe Tsogyal, who had attained unfailing memory. And there were others too—the twenty-five disciples and many heart sons. Some wrote in Sanskrit, some in the scripts of the dakinis, some in Newari, some in fire script, some in water script, some in air script, some in blood script. Some used Tibetan letters, both *uchen* and *ume,* the *chagkyu* scripts of both long, short and thick black letters. Some wrote with the scripts of *dru* and *drutsa, khong seng* and *khyinyal, kangring,* and *kangthung,* with all the signs of punctuation. We compiled a million cycles of practice upon the Mind of the Guru, ten thousand cycles of *Nyingtik:* tantras, agamas, and upadeshas and so on, all extremely profound. Those that were extensive were nevertheless of crucial importance; those that were short were nonetheless complete; however easy to practice, they were filled with great blessings; profound and swift, they were replete with all that was needful. In order to inspire confidence, lists of location, inner and innermost prophetic guides, and predictions concerning their discovery were added. All was arranged and set in order."

It was thus that the Guru and his consort Yeshe Tsogyal, at one in the wisdom of their Minds, brought about the benefit of beings through their skillful means and wisdom. At one in the enlightened motions of their Speech, they unfolded naturally the teachings of the sutra and the tantra. At one in their miraculous powers of Body, they had the world's appearances beneath their sway. At one in their enlightened Qualities of Knowledge, they contrived the benefit of beings. At one in their Enlightened Action, they had mastery of the four activities. In the absolute sphere, their name is Kunzang Pema Yabyum—the All-Good Guru-Consort Lotus-Born. Their Body,

Speech, Mind, Qualities and Activities are present everywhere, wherever space pervades.

Sometime later, they set out from Chimphu and gradually made their way on foot throughout the whole of Tibet, filling it with blessing. To begin with, they visited the three Taktsang, or tiger caves. In Paro Taktsang of Mön, they placed the Treasures in different places and left a prediction concerning their discovery. Guru Rinpoche said: "This is a place of the Guru's Mind. Whoever practices here will attain the accomplishment of Mahamudra. When I, the Guru, was in Akanishta, these supports of my Body, Speech, and Mind appeared of themselves." And he blessed and prayed over the image of Dorje Drolö, a stupa and a six-syllable mantra—all of them self-arisen.

They then proceeded to Onphu Taktsang in Tibet. There the Guru brought beneath his power all the spirits, appointing them as guardians and Treasure lords, and set in place the innermost prophetic guides.

"This is a sacred place of my Body," he said. "Whoever practices here will attain the accomplishment of immortal life. When I was born upon the lake of Dhanakosha, these supports of my Body, Speech, and Mind appeared by themselves." And as before, he blessed and prayed over the images, the three-syllable mantra, the nine-syllable Rulu mantra, a stupa, and a vajra.

Then they went to the Taktsang in Kham where the Guru concealed Treasures in various places and caused the Treasure lords to pledge themselves as protectors. He then made predictions about the Treasures and left behind a list of their locations.

"This is a sacred place of my Speech," he said. "Those who practice here will enjoy wide renown and receive great blessings. But those without samaya will meet with much hindrance. Both supreme and worldly accomplishments may be gained here. When I was turning the wheel of the Doctrine at the Diamond Throne and other places, subjugating demons and those of misguided views, these three images spontaneously appeared here, together with the six-syllable mantra, the three-syllable and the twelve-syllable mantra, and so forth, as well as the supports of the Mind." And so saying, he blessed and prayed over them.

Those who wish to know of the travels of the Guru and the Lady Tsogyal to other destinations should search in the life stories of the Guru.

Then, once again, the Guru and his Consort dwelt in the central sanctuary, acting as spiritual guides to Tibet's great king. After bestowing liberally and in detail the oral instructions and predictions concerning the discovery of the Dharma Treasures, and after giving counsel to the king, ministers, queens, courtiers, and translators, on the tenth day of the monkey month of the monkey year, the Guru departed, riding on a sunbeam, for the continent of Ngayab in the southwest. Tsogyal remained behind for the benefit of the king and others, especially the three twin communities, thus accomplishing the benefit of beings and filling the earth with the Treasures of the Guru's teaching.

The Dharma king and his retinue escorted the Precious Guru to the pass of Gungthang. There they asked him for many predictions and instructions, and then they turned back, with sorrow in their hearts.

"But I, Tsogyal," the Lady recalled, "riding on a sunbeam, accompanied the Guru as far as the ravine of Tsashö on the frontier between Tibet and Nepal. Going down to the secret cave of Tsashö, we stayed there for three weeks. There the Guru opened the mandala of the *Dzogchen Ati Khyabdel* and gave me the empowerment. But the auspicious moment was spoiled through the doubts and overfamiliar attitude of Chönema.[77] The Guru said, 'Though the teachings of the Secret

Mantra will spread in Tibet, the Ati teachings, which are the summit of the Mahayana, will be a matter of contention, and those who gain liberation through them will be few, whether in the oral or the Treasure lineage. They will be of small benefit to beings. On account of this karmic circumstance, even the general teachings of the Secret Mantra will have little power and will be quick to rise and fall.'

"And he withheld the empowerment from Chönema. To me, Tsogyal, however, he granted it in full, leaving nothing out.

" 'This is the perfect time,' the Guru said, 'to give you this instruction. It belongs to that extraordinary vehicle that causes analytical intellection to subside. To have given you this teaching too early, at the improper moment, would have been to harvest the crop at once. The fruit would have been picked, and there would be no way for you to stay longer in this world. For one who practices this teaching, there is no such thing as good or bad karma, high station or low, youth or age, sharp faculties or dull. Its fruit is called the "total absorption in the space wherein all phenomena are extinguished." Had this instruction been given to you earlier, it would have been difficult for you to establish securely the benefit of living beings and the Buddha's Doctrine, and to conceal profound Treasures for the sake of others. For your material body would have been instantly consumed. Now you must practice without abandoning for an instant the direct recognition of ultimate reality. In this way you will swiftly attain Buddhahood while still in this body. Henceforth, practice in places such as Zabbu and Tidro, and within three years, the experiences of the recognition of ultimate nature will increase. Within six years, awareness will attain its ultimate reach. When that time comes, conceal all the remaining Treasures and, by means of the essential pith instructions, perfectly accomplish the benefit of others.

" 'Afterward, continue your practice in Lhodrak Kharchu, displaying supernatural wonders, sometimes visible, sometimes invisible. The fortunate will be benefited thereby. After about two hundred years, your body will fade away, and in the state of great primordial Wisdom, you will meet me in Ngayab, the realm of dakinis. There, inseparable, we will be Buddhas for the sake of beings.' So saying, the Guru made as if to set out, riding on a sunbeam. But I prostrated, imploring him desperately with tears. I cried out:

Sorrow and sadness! O my Lord of Orgyen!
Just now you have been with me, already you are leaving!
Is this not the meaning of 'to pass through birth and
  death'?
How might I arrest this tide of birth and death?

Sorrow and sadness! O my Lord of Orgyen!
Until this moment we were so inseparable,
And shall we in an instant now be parted?
Is this not the meaning of 'to join and to divide'?
How might I be with you, never separate?

Sorrow and sadness! O my Lord of Orgyen!
Lately in Tibet you were the Teacher going everywhere,
Only footprints of your presence now remain!
Is this not the meaning of 'impermanence'?
How might I reverse the wind of karma?

Sorrow and sadness! O my Lord of Orgyen!
Not long ago, Tibet was guarded by your teaching,
All is now just stories people listen to!
Is this not the meaning of 'to change and to become'?
How might I subject them to my mastery?

Sorrow and sadness! O my Lord of Orgyen!
Till now I was the friend who never left you,
But now, my Guru, you are leaving for the heights,
Forsaking me, a woman with bad karma.
Whom now shall I ask for blessing and empowerment?

Sorrow and sadness! O my Lord of Orgyen!
Deep were the instructions you bestowed on me,
But now you rise into the deathless skies,
Forsaking me, a woman caught in fleshliness.
Whom now shall I ask to bring me progress and dispel
my obstacles?

Sorrow and sadness! O Compassionate Lord!
I beg you, grant me still some words of teaching,
Look on me with eyes of unforsaking mercy,
Look upon Tibet with prayers and well-wishing!

"With terrible lamentation, I scattered thirteen handfuls of gold dust over the Guru's body. And he, riding on a sunbeam at a distance of a few yards, said:

Kyema!
Hear me, maiden, sea of qualities!
I, the Lotus-Born, now leave to discipline the ogres!
One who, through perfection of the Triple Kaya, is
powerful in his deeds,
Is not to be compared with beings who dissolve like
bubbles.
If birth and death alarm you, give yourself to sacred
Dharma.
Mastering Creation and Perfection,[78] the channels and the
winds:
This alone is how to vanquish birth and death.

Kyema!
Hear me, Lady, virtuous and faithful!
I, the Lotus-Born, now leave for others' benefit.
My compassion is impartial, all-regarding;
I cannot be compared to beings blinded by delusion.
Practice Guru yoga if you would be with me constantly.
With pure perception, all arises as the Teacher:
There is no other teaching for inseparability.

Kyema!
Hear me, Lady, lovely to behold!
I, the Lotus-Born, now go to teach for others' good.
My form, immaculate, supreme, whence all impurities have vanished,
Is not to be compared with that of beings driven by their evil karma.
The country of Tibet I filled with siddhas, the children of my teaching.
When you see impermanence, meditate on Mahamudra.
Freeing, as they stand, perceptions of samsara and nirvana,
There is no better way to check the wind of karma.

Kyema!
Hear me, young and faithful girl!
I, the Lotus-Born, will preach the Dharma in the land of ogres.
My flawless adamantine form, surpassing change,
Is not to be compared with that of beings racked by ills.
The country of Tibet I filled with Dharma, within the earth and on it.
If you are strong in practice and instruction,
No shortage of the Dharma will there be.
Hearing, study, meditation: if thus you hold the Buddha's teaching,
And naturally achieve your own and others' good,
There is no deeper way to overthrow "becoming."

Kyema!
Hear me, princess, maid of Kharchen!
I, the Lotus-Born, will go now to the realm of Lotus Light.
Summoned by the wisdom of the Buddhas past, present, and to come,
I cannot be compared with beings driven by the Lord of Death.
In the supreme body of a woman you have gained accomplishment;

Your mind itself is Lord; request him for empowerment
and blessing.
There is no other regent of the Lotus Guru.

Kyema!
Hear me, mistress Yeshe Tsogyal!
I, the Lotus-Born, will go now to the realm of Great
Felicity.
Sublime and deathless, dwelling in the sphere of
emptiness,
I cannot be compared with those whose minds forsake
their bodies.
Through profound instructions, Tsogyal is now free;
Meditate upon the Great Perfection, which extinguishes
the form of flesh.
Pray and meditate to banish obstacles and bring
advancement;
Only by compassion of the Guru will your hindrances be
scattered.

Kyema!
Hear me, Blue Light Blazing, dakini in truth!
Much counsel in the past and much instruction have I
granted you.
All is gathered in this key point: practice Guru yoga.

Above your crown, a cubit's length,
Upon a lotus and a moon, enfolded in the light of
rainbows,
I, the Lotus-Born, reside, the teacher of all beings.
I have one face, my two hands hold a vajra and a skull
cup.
I wear an underrobe, a brocade coat,
A tunic and the Dharma robe, a patched shawl and a
cape:
Signs of all the vehicles of practice.
The vulture-feathered lotus hat is on my head,

And earrings and a precious collar are my ornaments.
I sit in vajra posture, radiating light,
And bear the great and minor marks of Buddhahood.
Encircled by a five-hued rainbow light, the shimmering of dakinis,
Limpidly and clearly I appear, the brilliant radiance of the mind itself.

When you see me clearly, take empowerments,
And rest abiding in the View.
Until you see me so, persist in meditation.
Recite the quintessential Guru Siddhi mantra,
And in conclusion, let your body, speech, and mind
Be mingled with the Guru.
Call on me with prayers and dedication,
And stay within the Great Perfection,
The essential sphere beyond all action.

Nothing will surpass this, Mistress Tsogyal!
Padmasambhava's compassion neither ebbs nor flows;
The rays of my compassion for Tibet cannot be severed.
There I am in front of anyone who prays to me—
Never will I separate from those with faith.
From those with erring views I am concealed,
Though yet I stand before them.
My predicted children are forever guarded by my love.

In future, henceforth, on the tenth day of the moon,
I, the Lotus-Born, will come astride the lordly daystar.
In forms of peace, enrichment, attractiveness, and wrath,[79]
At four times I will show myself,
And thus will grant attainments to my children.
On the tenth day of the falling moon, my exploits will be likewise,
Though mostly in the aspects of attractiveness and wrath.
On the fifteenth I will come upon the moonbeams
And churn with prayers of mercy the abysses of samsara,

Wholly emptying the states of sorrow.
My works of power will be perfect for the sake of beings.
On the eighth, at dawn and dusk, at rising and at setting of the sun,
Astride my steed, who knows my every wish,
Through all the places of the world I'll ride
Accomplishments to grant.
The wheel of Doctrine I will turn in lands of fierce ogresses.
To pacify, enrich, enthrall, and subjugate
The dwellers in the one and twenty wild and lesser lands
And in thirty regions even more remote,
I'll show myself as fire or water,
Wind, space, rainbows,
Earthquakes, sounds—
Sending millions of magic forms to guide them all to bliss.
Never will my work for beings cease.

You, O maiden, for a century henceforth,
Will be the joy of beings in Tibet.
A hundred years and one will pass, and then you'll come to Ngayab,
To be the guardian of beings, with me, the Lotus-Born,
O Vidyadhara, Blue Light Blazing!
Your Body, Speech, and Mind will be the equal of my own.
The stream of birth and death will cease; the karmic wind will stop.
You will send forth emanations for the sake of future beings,
And in the regions of Tibet your stream of incarnations will not cease.
And you will never weary in your work for beings.

And so now, Tsogyal, keep the View,
And you and I are never for a single instant parted.
But, in the manner of the world, farewell!

By virtue of my loving prayers,
May all Tibet be happy!

"As he finished speaking, the whole sky was filled with dakas and dakinis playing music and singing, carrying ceremonial umbrellas, victory banners, pennants, tassels, canopies, tapestries, cymbals, drums, conches, horns, thighbone trumpets, drums, lutes, mandolins, bells, pipes, and a whole orchestra of instruments. In the heart of this immense cloud of offerings, a brilliant light shone out, as if beckoning to the Guru, and he stepped into it. This I could not bear, and cried out:

Guru Rinpoche!
You are alone the teaching of the Buddha,
Alone the father of beings,
Alone the eye of Tibet,
You are my heart itself!
Small is your compassion,
And your actions cruel!
Woe and sorrow! Alas! Alas!

"In this way I begged him to return, prostrating and striking my body on the ground. He turned his face to me and gave his first testament. Then, turning his gaze to the southwest, he left in a burst of flashing rays and pulsating lights. Yet again I struck my body on the ground, tearing my hair, clawing at my face, rolling on the earth. And I begged him:

Woe and sorrow! Lord of Orgyen!
Will you leave Tibet an empty land?
Are you taking back your light of love?
Do you cast aside the Buddha's teaching?
Will you throw away the people of Tibet so heedlessly?
Are you leaving Tsogyal with no refuge?
O look on me with pity!
Now, now, look at me!

"And that is how I was, weeping and lamenting bitterly. This time he did not reappear, but I heard his voice, vivid and clear, as he gave me his second testament. Then the whole sky was once more filled with radiance, and all the earth shot through with beams of light. Within this dazzling, luminescent fabric, dakinis could be seen darting to and fro, gradually becoming less and less distinct until everything had disappeared. Again I battered my entire body against the rocks. Pieces of my flesh came away and I offered them with my blood, as a ganachakra, calling on the Guru from afar in intense distress:

Alas! O Vastness of Compassion!
Stretching to the limits of the sky—
Such are the actions of my Guru.
But today his work is over in Tibet.
All nations have their different destinies,
And now today Tibet has met its fate.
All beings have by turn their joys and sorrows,
And now today it is my turn to suffer.
Sorrow! Alas! Look swiftly on me in your love!

"Although there was no one to be seen, there came a voice. 'Tsogyal,' it said, 'look here!' And as I looked, there fell from the sky before me a ball of light, the size of a human head. Inside it was the Guru's first legacy. Thereupon, all the lights, with which the entire regions of Tibet had been illuminated, were gathered together and shone towards the southwest in the direction the Guru had taken, and disappeared. Once again, it was completely beyond my powers of endurance, and I cried out, 'O revered one of Orgyen, do not lay aside your mercy! Look upon me! Is it possible that you could leave me?'

"There came a voice, just as before, and at that very moment, a casket of light, no bigger than a fist, fell down before me. Inside was the second legacy. Then the lights and rays, and the sun as well, were gathered together and set in the southwest, leaving behind the darkness of the night. The Guru and the dakinis were no longer there. It was like waking in the morning from a dream. Distraught and tearful, I thought of the Guru, and, weeping once again, I sang this song of grief:

Kyema!
Revered and Precious One of Orgyen,
Only father who protects Tibet,
You have gone away to realms of dakinis,
Tibet has now become an empty land.
Quintessential jewel, where have you gone?
For you, in truth, there is no "going" or "remaining,"
Yet on this day, away you go to Orgyen.
For all the dwellers in Tibet, both gods and men,
Behind each head the sun has set.
Who will warm them, naked and unclothed?
The eyes have fallen from the people's brow,
Who will lead them now, the staring blind?
From the people's breasts their hearts are torn,
Who will lead them, now, the living dead?
You came here for the good of beings,
How then that you do not stay forever?
Kyehü! Precious One of Orgyen,
For Tibet a time of inky darkness has arrived,
A time when hermitages lie untenanted,
When thrones of Dharma are unoccupied,
When the empowering vase is dry and left unfilled,
When the introduction to the Mind is done by boasters,
When people hope instruction can be found in books,
When the Teacher has to be recalled and visualized,
When one must have his image and his picture,
When one puts one's hopes in dreams and visions.
An evil time like this indeed has come to us.
Sorrow and grief, revered Lord of Orgyen,
Look on us with pity, Dharma Lord of Orgyen.

"So I spoke. And from the southwest there came a sudden cluster of light rays bearing at their extremity a casket of light, no bigger than my thumb. It floated down to me, and inside it was the third legacy. Thereupon I gained a fearless confidence: the nest of hope and fears fell to nothing, and the torment of defiled emotions was cleared away. I experienced directly that the Teacher was inseparable from myself, and with much devotion I opened the mandala of the *Lama Sangwa Düpa*. This I practiced for three months, during which time I beheld the Guru in each of the six periods of the day and night, receiving from him many predictions, counsels, and pith instructions of the ear-whispered lineage."

Then, in order to restore Chönema's samaya with the Guru, Yeshe Tsogyal, with the Master's permission, first practiced and then taught to her, as well as to many other faithful followers, the sadhana known as *Yang Phur Drakma—Vishuddha* and *Kila* conjoined. This has an "upper activity," containing a confession section, related to the root text of *Vishuddha*, as well as a "lower activity," consisting of a banishment of obstacles associated with Vajrakumara. This sadhana was transmitted by the Lady Tsogyal in both oral and Treasure lineages.

Afterward, the Lady made her way to Mangyul, where the monks, disciples, and the faithful Lodrö (whom she had left there previously) received her with great joy, celebrating a ganachakra feast and requesting her to stay there permanently. But she remained only for a month, bestowing on them many final instructions, advice on the elimination of obstacles, the development of meditation, and so on. Then she went to Tsang, where all the people of the province exclaimed that, whereas the Guru had departed for the land of fierce cannibals, the Lady had, to their delight, come back to them! And having the same devotion for her as for the Guru, they pressed around her so thickly that she could hardly walk. She gave empowerments and instructions and wrought the benefit of countless beings, before going on to Zurpa, where she stayed for a year. There, Nyen Pelyang, Bé Yeshe Nyingpo, Lasum Gyalwa

Changchub, Odren Pelgyi Zhönnu the younger, Langlab Changchub Dorje, and Dacha Rupa Dorje (who was but a child of seven years) were found ready to receive the teachings. Accepting them as her disciples, the Lady brought them to spiritual maturity and freedom. After this, she made her way to Shang where for three years she lived in the caves of Pama Gang, striving mightily for the benefit of beings. Later she went to Zabbu, where she remained in the effortless view of Ati, peak of the Mahayana. After one year, her experiences intensified. She was filled with an immense joy and progressed greatly in the practice. It was at Zabbu also that she concealed thirteen great Treasures. Leaving there, she went to Tidro in Zho, where she lived for six years. There her awareness reached its ultimate extent, and the realization of the Great Perfection penetrated her inmost being. The story is also told that she secured the welfare of many dakinis, traveling through sixty-two pure lands. But that tale is concealed elsewhere.

It was at that time that the Lady Tsogyal performed her last series of austerities, sacrificing herself for others.

As she herself recalled:

"The demonic minister Shantipa, who had caused me so much suffering in the past, had been reborn in the hell called Intense Heat, but with strength and vigor, born from my compassion, I drew him out. The detailed account of how I did so, and how I churned the depths of the abyss, making links between myself and all the beings born in hell, must be looked for elsewhere. In addition, I gave my body to the savage beasts, food to those who were hungry, clothing to those who were cold, medicine to those who were ill, wealth to the needy, refuge to the weak, and my lower limbs to the lustful.[80] In sum, for the sake of others, I gave away my body and my life. It was then, while I was engaged in the virtuous acts of generosity totally beyond self-attachment (even to the point of sacrificing the organs of my body), that both the god Indra and Nanda the naga came and put me to the test.[81]

"One day when I was at Tidro, a cripple came to me accompanied by three men, each one taking turns to carry him.

"'Where are you from?' I asked, 'and what brings you here?'

"'We are from Onbu in Tibet,' they replied. 'This man, though innocent, has been punished by the king and has had his kneecaps torn out. The learned physicians of Tibet all declare that there exists a way of transplanting kneecaps from a woman to a man. There is no other remedy. We have heard, Lady, that you give in charity whatever people need. And so we come a-begging. Is it possible that you might give him your knees?' And so saying, they heaved a great sigh.

"Compassion came welling up from deep within me, and I said, 'I will give you whatever you need. Come, take them. I made a promise to my Guru that I would help beings with my body, speech, and mind.'

"'In order to take them out,' said they, taking out their knives, 'we will have to inflict deep wounds. You might suffer greatly.'

"'No matter what happens,' I answered, 'take them out.'

"They made cross-shaped incisions on my knees and prized away the caps, which came away with a loud snapping sound. Round and red, they laid them down in front of me. I became slightly faint but, recovering myself, I said, 'Take your kneecaps,' and they went cheerfully away.

"Later, when my knees had healed, there came a leper, much worse than others. Blood and pus were dripping from the whole of his body, and his nose had rotted away, leaving behind a gaping wound. From his mouth the stench of decay spread for a mile around, and all he could do was weep.

"'What help is there in weeping?' I said to him. 'This is the outcome of your past actions. Crying is to no avail. Of far greater benefit would be to visualize the deity and recite the mantra.'

"'To be stricken by disease,' said he, 'is part and parcel of living in the world. But something worse than this has happened to me.'

"'But what,' I asked, 'could be more terrible than what you have?'

"'This illness came upon me suddenly and with great strength,' he answered. 'I had a wife. She was like you, a daughter of the gods! But she does not want me any more; she took up with another man and threw me out of the house. And I thought that since you live only for the benefit of others, you might be able . . . perhaps . . . to be a wife to me.' And once more he began to weep. With compassion welling up within me I said, 'Do not cry! I will serve you in whatever way you wish.' And so I lived with him and did his bidding.

"And thus I went through many trials. For instance, seven Bönpos came to me and in order to make a ritual bag for Yang, the god of prosperity, they asked me for my skin. I peeled it off and gave it to them. Many other people came asking for my eyes, my head, my limbs, my legs, my tongue, and so forth. I gave them everything with joyful prayers.

"But after a while, Indra himself appeared and offered me many things delightful to the gods: the five great robes of the celestial ones, the vase of amrita, the seven heavenly riches. And he praised me thus:

O human girl, O marvelous, supreme!
The deeds of Bodhisattvas of the past are yours.
Caring not for life or limb,
You give yourself away to others.
O Mother, glory of compassion,
To you I come.
Great and wondrously sublime, to you my praise!
From this day forth and while this age endures,
This, O Queen, will always be my prayer:
That you might always turn the wheel of Dharma.

"So saying, he disappeared, and my body was made whole just as before. The leper also changed and transformed into the naga Nanda, who heaped up in front of me the inconceivable wealth of the nagas. Folding his hands in devotion and with tears in his eyes, he sang to me:

> *Kyema!*
> Guru, mother, Yeshe Tsogyal,
> Key to the mysteries of Padmasambhava,
> With mercy taking up the pains of others.
>
> Free from concepts,
> "Clean" and "unclean" have no hold on you.
> Eager for the benefit of others,
> You bury underground all love of self,
> Mistress holder of the Teachings,
> Mother of Victorious Ones, I bow to you.
>
> Padma Thödreng is my guru,
> And you yourself my Dharma sister.
> Therefore look on me with loving eyes!
>
> All the ocean of the Doctrine, Secret Mantras,
> And Padma's deep transmissions,
> Oral and in Treasure,
> You propagate and keep from all decline.
> As long as I am in this world,
> Your shadow I will be, your shield and guard,
> Your servant, routing all adversity!

"He fell silent and vanished into the ground."

When King Mutri Tsenpo heard that the Lady was staying at Tidro, he sent her an invitation, and so she went to Samye and resided at Chimphu for six years. The religious king, with his retinue of translators, ministers, courtiers, and queens, offered her service and honor. From all the meditation communities established previously in Chimphu and elsewhere, the mahasiddhas who had achieved their own benefit had departed to work for the welfare of beings, while others, growing old, had passed beyond suffering. Thus these communities were somewhat reduced in numbers. At the king's command, one thousand five hundred new monks were ordained at a single ceremony by the Indian abbot Kamalashila. The Lady gave them instruction and set them to meditate in Chimphu itself. The practice of all of them was without exception fruitful, and there were many who gained accomplishment and were able to demonstrate signs of their realization.

Now, at that time, there occurred a controversy between two philosophical theories known as Tönmin and Tsemin.[82] A certain Hashang had propounded a mistaken teaching, which had been opposed and was being suppressed. Because of this, the religious community of Samye was divided. The master Kamalashila had established himself in the temple of Hayagriva, while Hashang had taken up his position in the temple of Maitreya. And for a short time there was controversy.

"At this point," the Lady recalled, "I, Tsogyal, together with an entourage of a hundred disciples, came down from Chimphu in order to make the peace. But as they did not listen to me, I displayed many miracles with the result that both the Tönmin and Tsemin factions began to have faith in me and were reconciled. Thenceforward a new religious law was proclaimed enjoining practice according to the tradition of Master Kamalashila. Master Hashang and his followers were loaded with gold and sent back to China, their native country. The great religious king expanded all the religious communities at Lhasa, Samye, Trandruk, and so on, causing thirteen thousand to enter the monastic order.

"And I, Tsogyal, while living at Chimphu, became a wellspring of teachings and instructions for the original disciples of the Guru, the new monks, my own disciples, and all who had faith in Guru Rinpoche—from Ngari, Mangyul, Purang, Mön,

Tsang, Jar, Loro, Kongpo, the four provinces of Central Tibet, the four northern provinces, Dokham Gangdruk, from China, Jang, Hor, Menyak, and other lands. Thus my work for the sake of beings became as boundless as the sky, and the lineages of my disciples, the disciples of the Lady, have covered and filled the world."

The Hiding of the Treasures

The third general section of this chapter briefly describes how, in order to attend to the Dharma Treasures and to achieve the benefit of infinite beings, the Lady went on foot to all the major and minor sacred places, hidden lands, and important sites.

Lady Tsogyal reflected to herself: "I have brought about the benefit of beings and of the Doctrine. Of the lifespan predicted for me by the Guru, half has now gone by. My awareness has reached its widest compass, and my activities likewise. I will therefore go to all the places blessed by the precious Master. There I shall conceal the Treasures, make prayers of good auspices, and engage in meditation."

First she went to Tidro, where she stayed for one year and seven months. She concealed ten Treasures, praying and wishing that all connections with them might be significant. Then she set off for the Crystal Cave in Yarlung where she lived for thirteen months, and with many prayers of aspiration concealed five Treasures. In Yangdzong she lived for a year and hid thirteen Treasures there. She stayed one month in Yerpa and concealed ten Treasures. Afterward she gradually made her way south to Tsari Gang, where she stayed for one year and four months concealing thirty great Treasures, then to Kongpo where she hid in all one hundred and fifty Treasures. Afterward in the south, in the snowy ranges of Nepal, she tarried for thirteen months and hid thirty-five Treasures. Then she went to the west, to the snowy ramparts of Lapchi, where she resided for four months and seven days, concealing eight Treasures. Then on to the north, to the snow range of Nöjin, where she stayed for three months and five days and hid three Treasures. Afterward she journeyed to the southeast, to Kembalung in Gyal, where she lived for one year and half a month, concealing ten Treasures. From there she went southwest to Drapulung, where she stayed for five months and ten days, hiding seven Treasures. Then in the northwest, in Jakmalung, she remained for one year and five months, concealing nine great Treasures. Then on to Dromalung in the northeast, where she stayed for eleven months and hid five Treasures. In the snowy range of Yarbu she lived for one month and ten days and hid there three Treasures. Likewise, in the snow mountains of Selje she remained for one year and hid there ten Treasures. In the snow range of Yulung she lived for three months and hid three Treasures. She visited the snow mountains of Drongje for ten days and concealed three Treasures. Again in the Yulung snow mountains she lingered for three months and hid four Treasures. In the snowy range of Jomo she resided for five months and concealed ten Treasures. In the snow mountains of Nyewo she stayed for five months and concealed four Treasures. She visited the snow mountains of Dzayul for twenty-one days, concealing one Treasure. She went to the Nanam snow range for seven days and hid five Treasures there. In the snow mountains of Lhorong she lingered for three months and seven days, concealing thirteen Treasures. In the snow range of Rongtsen she lived for seven months and concealed fifteen Treasures. In the snow mountains of Shelzang she stayed for two months and ten days and hid five Treasures. She resided in the snowy range of Gampo for one year, one month, and a day, concealing twenty Treasures. In the snowy mountains of Chephu she stayed for one month and hid fourteen Treasures. In the Pubol snowy range she stayed for twenty-one days, concealing three Treasures. She visited the Sengtrom snowy range for seven days, concealing two Treasures and going to the Tsonak snowy range for nine days and half a month and hid one Treasure there also. Likewise in the east, in Makunglung, she remained for one month and hid thirteen Treasures, while in the south, in Bachak Shri, she lived for a year and concealed seven Treasures there. In the west, in Drangmenlung, she stayed for one month and hid three Treasures, and in the north, in Semodo, she lingered for three months and hid four Treasures. Also, in the upper Tsari Dzong, the middle Kharak Dzong, the lower Gere Dzong, in Phakri Dzong in Mön, in Puchu Dzong in Kongpo, in Pakyul Dzong in Puwo, in Dorje Dzong in Den, in Nabun Dzong in Cham, in Nering Senge Dzong, in Yari Drakmar Dzong, in Kaling Sinpo Dzong, in Lhari Yuru Dzong, in Tolai Pelbar Dzong, in Pumo Dzong in Rekha, in Drakmar Dzong in Ling, in Lhadrak Dzong in Dri, in Drakar Dzong of lower Kongpo, and in other places she stayed for some months and days, making connections with those places and concealing there Treasures. In the same way she lingered for a few years in the eight great hidden lands, hiding many Treasures there appropriate to the place: namely, Dremo Shong in Nepal, Pemakö in Loyul, Zabbulung in Shang, Gowojong in Me, Mudojong in Gyalmo, Lhamo Ngulkhang Jong, Gyalung Jokpolung, Pudumlung in Mön.

All in all, Yeshe Tsogyal visited twenty-five ranges of snow mountains, the four places of benediction, the eighteen important places, and the hundred and eight places where the Precious Guru had himself practiced. There she meditated for years, months, or days, hiding Treasures and making prayers of good augury. Especially in the region of Dokham, she blessed the eight places hallowed by the eight manifestations of Guru Rinpoche, the five places of the five aspects of Thödrengtsel, the twelve places of his wondrous activity, the three places blessed by prophecy, and so on. She concealed Treasures there, just as it is specified in the extensive prophetic guides for discovery.

In general, taking the whole of Tibet, one hundred and five

great sacred sites might be mentioned, together with one thousand and seventy lesser holy places, and also millions of other locations where the Lady stayed and concealed the Treasures. But they have not been enumerated by name for fear of the length of such a list. Notwithstanding, accounts of how the Treasures were concealed all over Tibet, at Samye, Lhasa, Trandruk, and so on, may be found in the prophetic guides and in the detailed biographies of the Guru.

SAMAYA GYA GYA GYA

ITHI GUHYA KHATHAM MANDA ZABGYA

Eight
Buddhahood

When Tsogyal had blessed the great sacred places of Tibet and concealed Treasures there, she returned to Chimphu in the center of the country as the king's spiritual guide. There for a time she remained, laboring ever more strenuously for the welfare of beings. In the temple of Kharchung Dorying,[83] to seven worthy disciples, including the religious king Mutri Tsenpo, the prince Murum Tsenpo, and the queen Ngangchung Pel, she granted many unsurpassable teachings, profound and vast, which ripen and liberate. In particular, she opened for them the mandalas of *Lama Kasang Düpa*, *Yidam Gongpa Düpa*, and *Dzogchen Ati Düpa* and conferred the empowerments that placed them in the state of maturity and liberation. When the mandala of *Lama Sangdü* had been opened, they all practiced it. Before dawn on the seventh day, they began the sadhana and, at the moment of invocation, they recited:

> On the northwest border of the land of Orgyen,
> Arisen in a lotus flower's heart,
> With wondrous siddhi perfectly endowed,
> And celebrated as the Lotus-Born,
> You are encircled by a throng of dakinis.
> We follow in your footsteps practicing.
> Come, we pray, and grant your blessings![84]

"When we had finished the recitation of this prayer," Lady Tsogyal recalls, "the Guru himself appeared, enfolded in a halo of brilliant light. Approaching from the southwest in the midst of his retinue, he was accompanied by the sound of music, the fragrance of incense, sweet melody, elegant dance, and songs of realization. He took his place in the center of the mandala. I asked the king to prepare a throne for the Guru to sit on. But, overcome by the intensity of his faith, he had fainted away, so that the throne was not prepared.

"The Guru said, 'In the near future, not long from now, an unworthy nephew will be born to this royal house. The great king's descendants will no longer inherit the throne of his ancestors. As for this religious king himself, however, he will no longer be obliged to take a karmic body; such is the strength of his devotion. He will be able to assist others by means of emanations; his realization and liberation will occur simultaneously.'

"Thereupon, the prince Murum prepared many cushions and begged the Guru to be seated. Mutri Tsenpo, the king, offered a hundred mandalas of gold and turquoise to the Precious Guru and with prostrations made the following request:

> *Emaho!*
> Lotus Buddha, Holy One of Orgyen,
> Of all who live in the Tibetan land
> You are the one true father.
> Weighted by the heavy burden of my evil deeds,
> Drifting on the mire of my wandering mind,
> That is how I am!
> But in your goodness guard me. Never cast me off!
> Appearing here today: how great your kindness!
> Bestow your pledge that you will stay forever
> And turn the wheel of Dharma once again!

"To these words of the king, the Guru replied:

> Hear my words, O lordly, pious king,
> In your great faith a fertile field of merit,

Come to ripeness now; receive your Guru's blessing.
Be free; the Lady's secret door will open.
Realize, now, your mind, the Mahamudra.
And be accomplished in the vast expanse
Of Body, Speech, and Mind!

"As he spoke these words, the Guru placed his hand upon the head of the young monarch, who in that very instant became equally possessed of realization and freedom. Then the prince Murum Tsenpo made prostration and circumambulation, heaping up a mountain of offerings—with skin bags filled with gold and thirteen copper trays heavy with turquoises, of which the centerpiece was the great turquoise known as the Abyss of Space. When he had done this, he said, 'A typical prince, that is what I am! Arrogant and proud! I am indolent and given to distraction. I delight in sinfulness and take joy in soldiering and inflicting punishments. All I do is evil. So I beg you for instruction that is profound but concise; easy to understand and simple to perform; great in blessing, swift to bring accomplishment; a teaching that will swallow up my sins and repair my weakened samaya!'

"To this, Guru Rinpoche replied:

Son of the Conqueror, you have spoken well!
Your prayer is stainless and your actions also,
Faithful, samaya-holding Senalek.[85]
From now, when seven of your lives have passed,
No longer with a karmic body, you will teach
Disciples through your emanations,
Your mind the equal of the minds of all the Buddhas.
One kalpa then will take its course,
And you will then become the Buddha "Light of Stars."

"Having spoken thus, the Guru opened the mandala of Vishuddha, the deity swift to grant accomplishment, and bestowed on the prince a profound teaching—a special instruction called *Zhitro Gongpa Rangdrol*, thereby bringing him to spiritual maturity and freedom.

" 'Conceal this doctrine,' said the Guru, 'on the mountain peak of Dakpo Dar. In the future, it will be of great benefit to beings.' He further granted him an extraordinary method to accomplish the Guru, called *Lama Norbu Pemai Trengwa*, telling him to conceal it in the cliff of Ramoche. The precious Guru afterwards consecrated the temple of Kharchung and stayed for seven days. Then, just before dawn, as he was departing for the land of Orgyen, I, the Lady Tsogyal, requested him as follows:

> *Kyema!*
> You who dry the quicksand of defiled emotion,
> Loving Master, swift to liberate
> Even sinners who but see or hear,
> Remember you or touch you,
> Envoy of the Conquerors, O Lotus-Born!
> Now and always look upon the country of Tibet with pity!
> I have taught now all whom I might teach
> And hasten after you, Compassionate Lord,
> Praying never to be parted from you for a single instant.

"In reply, the Guru sang:

> *Kyema!*
> Mistress, Maid of Kharchen, listen!
>
> Stirred by the energy of wind,
> The fiery crystal of the Sun gives rise
> To day and night,
> The seasons' dance.
> The sky itself knows neither preference nor wanting.
> The harvest ripened to perfection
> Delights the husbandman
> But cannot stay.
>
> Yeshe Tsogyal,
> Through increase of wisdom,

Is now free
From fetters of defilements.
The seal has fallen from her body,
Whence all stain has been removed.

Impure minds still will cling to her,
And yet she cannot stay.
Such is the power of the perfect fruit
Arising from Creation, Perfection, and the
  Great Perfection.
Beings long for her,
And yet she cannot stay.
Now her karma is exhausted,
Phenomena worn out,
Her work is now complete,
Her body all consumed.
Five elements, five colors—all has ceased.
Now suffering is outrun,
And great the wonder of it!

When fifty years have run their course
And when the eighth day of the bird month dawns,
O Tsogyal, you will journey to the land of Lotus Light.
A throng of dakinis and dakas will come out to meet you.
But till that time comes round,
Labor for the good of beings.

"And with these words, he vanished from our sight. Whereupon I, Tsogyal, made my way to the great cavern of Lhodrak Kharchu, where I caused Namkhai Nyingpo to progress in the meditation on the subtle channels and energies. I granted the attainment of immortality, so that the bhikshu gained accomplishment, both supreme and ordinary.

"Afterwards, I abided evenly in the view of the Great Perfection beyond all action, and as the experience dawned on me wherein all phenomena are extinguished in the nature of reality, I was perceived in various forms according to the needs of beings.

To the hungry I was heaps of food and all good things,
and thus I brought them joy.
To the cold and freezing I was fire and sun-warmth,
thus their joy.
To the poor and needy I was wealth and riches, thus
their joy.
To the naked I was every kind of raiment, thus their joy.
To the childless I was sons and daughters, thus their joy.
To those who craved a woman, I became a lovely girl and
thus their joy.
To those who sought a lover, I was a handsome youth and
thus their joy.
To those who wanted magic powers, I gave prowess in the
eight great siddhis, and thus I brought them joy.
To the sick I was their remedy and thus their joy.
To the anguished I was all their mind desired, and thus
I was their joy.
To those hard pressed by punishments of kings, I was the
loving friend to lead them to the land of peace, and I
was thus their joy.
To those in fear of savage beasts, I was a haven, thus their
joy.
To those who fell into the depths, I was their drawing out
and thus their joy.
To those tormented in the fire, I was a quenching stream
and thus their joy.
To those in prey to any of the elements, I was their
medicine and thus their joy.

For those who could not see, I was their eyes and brought
them joy.
And for the halt and crippled I was feet and thus their
joy.
I was a tongue for those who could not speak, and thus
I brought them joy.

To those in fear of death I granted immortality, and thus
I was their joy.
I led the dying on the path of transference and brought
them joy.
To those who wandered in the bardo state, I was their
yidam, bringing them to joy.
I cooled the burning heat and warmed the cold of those
lost in the realms of hell.
Howsoever they were tortured, I changed myself to shield
them, being thus their joy.
To those who lingered in the land of hungry ghosts, I
was their food and drink and thus their joy.
I was freedom from stupidity and servitude for those
caught in the wordless state of beasts—and thus
I brought them joy.
Those beings born in savage lands—I turned them from
barbarity and brought them joy.
I was a truce from war and strife for the asuras and was
thus their joy.
The gods I guarded from their bitter fall and I was thus
their joy.
I shielded all from everything that tortured them and was
their every joy.

Wherever there is space, five elements pervade,
Wherever the five elements, the homes of living beings,
Wherever living beings, karma and defilements,
Wherever is defilement, my compassion also.
Wherever is the need of beings, there I am to help them.

"And thus I remained for twenty years in the great cavern of Lhodrak Kharchu, sometimes visible, sometimes invisible."

Now at that time, a former consort of the Precious Guru arrived from India, appearing from the sky together with her six disciples. She was a wisdom dakini and a queen of siddhas, the vidyadhara Dungmen Gyalmo, otherwise known as the princess Mandarava. She met with Tsogyal and remained with her for the space of thirty-nine days by human reckoning. Together they studied the oral teachings, endlessly discussing the Dharma. Mandarava requested the twenty-seven pith instructions, a special teaching of the Guru, unknown in India. And Tsogyal offered them to her. Now Mandarava was a dakini of longevity, a Lady of Immortal Life, and so Tsogyal asked her for the seven pith instructions of long life, as well as the thirteen pith instructions on Hayagriva and other deities, all of which teachings she concealed as Treasures. It was at that time that Tsogyal spoke these verses in offering to her guest:

Om Ah Hung!
Dakini who won the diamond state of deathlessness,
Whose body, like a rainbow, rides upon the sky,
You pass with mastery through things unhindered,
And crush the Demon Lord of Death,
And overthrow the Demon of the Aggregates.
Freed from shackles of the Demon of Defiled Emotion,
You humbled and brought low the Demon Son of Gods:
Dakini and mistress of longevity,
Is this not yourself?

From highest Akanishta down,
Throughout the three dimensions of existence,
Of every high and noble one you are the mistress.
The body of Great Bliss is yours,
Mandarava, sublime patterning of voidness,
Mother of wanderers, to you I bow!

For beings in the endless karmic stream of birth
  and death,
Caught on the mill-wheel driven
By the torrent of impure delusion,
You close the door to their descent and fall.
May my prayer to be as you are be fulfilled.

When karma is exhausted and the thought of pleasure vanished,
When the mire of delusion has dried up,
When the three worlds, all samsara, are exhausted
And every thought extinguished—
In the sphere of Great Bliss blissfully enclosed,
May I be never separate from Samantabhadri of Great Bliss.

Thus she prayed and requested many pith instructions that had never been heard of in Tibet. Then the queen of siddhas, Princess Mandarava, answered:

Kyeho!
Accomplished in the Secret Mantra,
Dancer in the sky,
Wonder-worker who dissolved her impure form
Into the sphere of purity,
You drank the nectar of the teachings
Of the Lotus-Born
And gathered all their essence—
Great Mother, Wisdom that has gone beyond,
Is this not yourself?

Entering the path wherein the truth
Of all phenomena is seen,
You utterly forsook the eight preoccupations[86] of this life
And, practicing austerities, lived upon essential substance,
Overcoming all phenomenal existence.
Tsogyal, ever-young, immaculate, to you I bow!

Sinful beings in the endless cycle of samsara,
Blown by the hurricane of karma—
These you tame and guide most skillfully.
Establishing the Dharma, you undid
The devilish perversity of Bön.
Mistress, sovereign strength, may I be one with you!

Hereafter in the purity of infinite pure space,
Which is the pure expanse of Lotus Light,
Bathed in the beams of Pema Thödreng's love,
May you and I together send out emanated forms
To work enlightened actions,
Churning thus the three worlds of samsara!

And with this prayer, she disappeared into space.

Then Tsogyal made her way to the valley of Zabbu in Shang, accompanied by her eleven root disciples: Bé Yeshe Nyingpo, Ma Rinchen Chok, Odren Pelgyi Zhönnu, Langlab Gyalwa Changchub Dorje, Dacha Dorje Pawo, Surya Thangwa of Ü, Trashi Chidren of Mön, the Nepali Kalasiddhi, Changchub Drölma from Li, Shelkar Dorje Tsomo, Kharchen Zhönnu Drölma, and also seventy-nine other faithful followers. She remained there for ten years altogether, greatly assisting her disciples. Then she rested in the concentration in which all phenomena are exhausted. Six of her disciples, excellent in their karma, led by Bé Yeshe Nyingpo and the faithful Khön, besought her not to pass away into nirvana but to stay and turn the wheel of the Doctrine:

Kyema Ho!
O you, Great Mother, Wisdom gone beyond,
true Dharmakaya!
The brilliance of the sun and moon is melting into space;
On whom shall we, who walk the earth, rely?
Open still for us the mandala of perfect knowledge.

Enlightened Mistress, cloud of the Sambhogakaya rain,
Your nectar pith-instructions melt away in space;
On whom shall we, the green shoots on the ground, rely?
Still rain down on us the nectar of your teaching.

Tsogyal, place of refuge, Nirmanakaya teacher,
The great and lesser marks of your enlightenment dissolve
in space;

On whom shall your dependents, Dharma-less like us, rely?
Still ripen and set free, we pray, all those who might be taught.

Kyema Kyehu! Lady Tsogyal, true and realized teacher!

Thus they prayed, their voices choked with tears.

"My children," the Lady answered, "prepare an abundant ganachakra feast. I will still open for you the mandalas of many most profound tantras and give instructions. But after the eighth day of this month, only the memory of me will remain in this land of Tibet."

And so, with heavy hearts, they laid out an enormous ganachakra feast. The Lady took her place in the center while, with downcast faces, her disciples sat in front of her with all their Dharma kin. They gazed through their tears at the Lady's face. Then she spoke:

Kyema Ho!
Listen to me well, all you assembled here;
Turn your minds and ears to my voice!

Rejoice with me; there is no need for sadness.
Life is but a meeting of contingent elements,
It cannot last forever.
The objects of our senses, mere perception,
Have no being in themselves.
The path, too, is illusion;
It is not the truth.
The ground[87]
Is the intrinsic way of being,
It is not a thing.
The mind is only thoughts,
Having neither base nor root.
Something real and solid I have never seen!

Faithful brothers, faithful sisters, gathered here,
Pray steadily to me who am your mother.
Blessèd in the Great Bliss of the space of voidness,
You will never part from me at any time.
Those by karma linked to me
Will hence receive my guidance naturally.
Others, not excluded, will be guarded
By the emanations of my love.
Death's sorrow will not triumph over me, your mother.
Therefore, sisters, brothers,
No need is there for grieving.

No more are there, on earth, whom I might teach.
For as the Glorious Lord of Orgyen said,
My life for training beings would endure two centuries—
Two hundred years and more have now passed by,
My caring for Tibet has not been brief but long!

From my thirteenth year, I was consort of the king,
And in my sixteenth, I was taken, through compassion,
by the Guru.
At twenty, on receiving all empowerments,
I embraced ascetic practice, hard to do.
At thirty, I attained accomplishment,
And fostered beings' good.
At forty, I attained the level of my Guru's mind,
And at fifty vanquished demons, guarding thus the
Doctrine.
At sixty, I promoted learning, prospering the Sangha,
And at seventy I touched the Real.
When I reached the age of eighty,
The Guru went away to the southwest.
At the age of ninety, the nature of reality I saw, perceiving
it directly,
And when I reached my hundredth year,
My awareness touched its utmost reach.
Twenty years then passed and I became

Preceptress to the pious king,
And ten years after that I crossed
The length and breadth of this Tibetan land.
When my age attained one hundred years and fifty,
Treasures I concealed, ensuring thus the benefit of beings.
Ten years later Mutri Tsenpo died,
A hundred years and seventy was then my age.
I labored for the rest of my disciples.
While at Lhodrak, ten years afterwards,
I sent forth emanations,
And ten years after that I met
My sister, Queen of siddhas.
Highest pith instructions she bestowed on me
And I attained the siddhi of Immortal Life:
The "facts" of birth and death were dissipated then
and there.
Two hundred and eleven years now have passed,[88]
And long enough Tibet has been my care.
And so now, gods and humans,
Are your hearts not welling up with gratitude?
I was indeed your friend, in joy and grief!

It will seem, when I have gone, that we have parted.
But my dear companions, do not suffer,
Rather pray repeatedly with sharpened minds.
Adopt the practice of the Great Perfection, free of action:
There is no other way to outstrip suffering.
Indeed this heart's blood of the Orgyen Lotus-Guru:
As I was instructed, now to you I teach it.
Practice it and you will gain accomplishment.
Pass it on to those of true capacity,
Withholding it from those unfit for its reception.
And do not let it fall to those who are
Degenerate in their samaya.
From those whose views are false,
Conceal and hide it.

She placed the seal of secrecy on her teachings and proceeded to open for her eleven root disciples the mandala of *Dzogchen Ati*, giving them her last oral transmission: the hundred pith instructions, the heart of everything. And in that very instant, all her disciples attained liberation.

Lady Tsogyal then went to stay in the upper cave of Pama Gang, and there, on her two hundred and eleventh birthday, the third of the bird month, she announced that five days later, on the eighth, they would go to the summit of Zabbu Mountain. They would go to see a great wonder, she said. Zangdok Pelri itself was there, the Copper-Colored Mountain.

And so, with a retinue of eleven of her most fortunate disciples, and in the company of about fifty other followers, she made her way to the peak of Zabbu. On the seventh day of the month, she reached a cave shaped like the mudra of folded hands, situated about halfway up the mountain. There she stayed and gave to her followers all the pith instructions of the twenty-five sections of Dharma. This done, she made a vast ganachakra feast offering, according to the sadhana upon the Guru.

And then, with all her disciples gathered before her, the Lady spoke and said: "Impermanence is an essential characteristic of living beings." Thereupon, Trashi Chidren offered a mandala of gold and made this plea:

Mother, Lady, full of grace and love,
Alone the mother of all beings in the triple world,
If you no longer guard your children,
Only those who know to feed themselves will manage to survive.
How shall pink-mouthed, toothless babes not perish?

You, the great, the golden ornament of heaven,
If you no longer drive away the gloom of beings' minds,
Only those who have the wisdom eye will find their way,
While those with normal sight will fall into the depths.

Ah, true regent of the Buddha!
If you no longer nurture Hearers of the Doctrine,
Only noble Arhats will survive.
But who will be the shield of untaught shavelings?

Dakini melodious with Brahma's voice,
If you no longer guard us here before you,
Only scholars and translators—only the accomplished ones will manage.
But who will be the guide of countless beings?

Kyema,
Lady, mother of accomplishments,
Look still with pity on your followers.
Bestow, I pray, the nectar of your words
Upon us, kindred, gathered here together.

And speaking thus, she made many prostrations. The Lady replied and said:

Kyema!
Listen, girl of Mön, my faithful one!
I, your Lady Tsogyal, have without regret or weariness,
Labored for the benefit of beings.
All Tibet is now beneath the shield of Dharma.
Many years, two hundred and eleven, now have passed.
The sum of those who might be taught by me is now fulfilled;
No further means is there for my remaining.
And just as at the death of everyone, it's hard to stay!
But I will leave a few words for my testament.

Brothers, sisters, gathered here, listen!
Past counting are the members of the human race,
But those who have embraced the Doctrine may indeed be numbered.
Still fewer are the ones who practice truly,

And those who win attainment are like stars at daytime,
While Buddhahood lies scarcely in the realms of
possibility.

Thus, in few words, give yourselves to Dharma.
The ways to enter Dharma number four and eighty
thousand—
A boundless quantity, but all may yet be gathered
In the system of nine vehicles.
Their pinnacle is Ati, which, divided threefold,
Has a single sense, distilled in one supreme instruction:
View, Meditation, Action, these three and their Result.
View is freedom from the mind's analysis and fixing,
Meditation is the savoring of uncontrived simplicity,
Action is defined as undistracted ease:
As Fruit you will perfect the Triple Kayas' strength.

These then are the crucial points of Dharma:
Let your outward conduct be attuned to the Vinaya;
Impurities and faults will naturally decrease.
Let inner training be according to the Sutra;
Merit naturally will multiply, reflecting thus its cause.
Let philosophic tenets harmonize with Abhidharma;
Uncertainty and misconception will be settled naturally.
For these three principles comprise the ground of
Dharma;
The Doctrine cannot be upheld without them.

Purify yourselves in tune with Kriya scriptures;
The stains of ingrained habits will be thereby cleansed.
Train your minds according to Ubhaya texts
And of itself will skill in Dharma come to you.
Let your View be practiced in accord with Yoga texts;
The blessings of compassion will pervade you naturally.
With Mahayoga tread the stages of approach and of
accomplishment;
And naturally, View, Meditation, Action—all will dawn.

With Anuyoga, practice on the subtle veins and energy;
Power and attainment you will naturally achieve.
With Ati purify the essence-drop
And in a twinkling will Buddhahood be gained.
Aside from this, you need no other teaching.

All you who follow me who am your mother,
Rely on what, throughout her life, your mother practiced.
For this is how to gain the twofold goal.

Then with many prostrations and circumambulations, Kalasiddhi, the girl from Nepal, made this request:

Ah, Mother,
When you have withdrawn into the womb of space,
How shall they fare who practice the deep path
Of Mantrayana in Tibet?
Who will scatter obstacles and nurture progress?
Continue to protect Tibet with loving mercy!

The Lady Tsogyal answered:

Kyema!
Listen, daughter of the lineage!
Born for Mantra, youthful maid endowed with siddhi.
Revealing perfect Dharma to all wandering beings,
You, endowed with freedoms, are engraced with
  bodhichitta!
All those gathered here, and all in future time,
Who practice the profound and mantric way,
Must first select a true authentic teacher.
From this master who has every mark and quality,
Beseech empowerment, offering true commitment.
Train the subtle veins and winds till you have mastery.
Request the third initiation and train upon desire;
For six months practice the Four Joys, or till
The signs reveal themselves within your body.
Blend and mingle energies of male and female.

Rely upon the skillful merging of the winds, above, below—
Male assisting female, female helping male.
All should do according to their measure.
Progress, persisting in the virtuosity of bliss.

But if there is no mingling of bliss with voidness,
All is useless and the path of Mantra is forsaken.
Taste rather bliss and voidness, as they rise, united!
Guard samaya with your partner as you would your eyes.
Take your artful pleasure with the five samaya substances
And train to perfect skill, not squandering your essence.
Counter the dark forces that bring hindrances,
And, should faults occur, be swift to make amends.

Do not let your bodies stray, distracted, into mediocrity.
Distracted, you will be like common men and women.
Meditate with vigor
And with the perfect self-esteem of deities—
Know that in the chakras of the veins are deities and retinues.

As for speech, endeavor with the subtle energies of Secret Mantra.
Without control of energy, the sexual act is commonplace.
Strike the vital point through exercise of pulling up and spreading,
Transfix it with the nail and seal of voidness.

Your mind must mingle with the essence.
If essence of the secret center is discharged,
The killing of a Buddha is the karma you will generate.
Attain therefore to mastery by every means.

Concentrate upon the key point of this practice on desire,
Or else the Secret Mantra is devoid of meaning.
The Great Bliss is perfected as the fruit of passion;

Afterward preserve this state and do not alter it,
Guarding your samaya as you would your living body.
If you spoil it, there is none you can confess to.
Such, then, are my counsels for your meditation.

You who enter through the door of Secret Mantra,
Bury underground ambition and conceit,
Throw into the river pride and ostentation,
Burn your lust and craving in the fire,
Throw out fame and misbehavior on the wind,
And into space dissolve pretense and trickery!
Hide your secret practices from others' eyes.
Do not reveal the secret teachings; keep them close.
Conceal, and do not show, the signs of warmth.[89]
Hold firmly to the yidam, the Three Roots unified.
Do not halt the stream of sacred feast and torma offerings.
Always guard, for others' sake, your love and bodhichitta,
And always dedicate your merit, free of concepts.[90]

All this is but your general scope of practice.
Ah, Siddhi, let it sink into your heart!
You and I possess a single nature,
Our emanations will protect all future beings.

After this, Bé Yeshe Nyingpo spoke and asked:

Éma!
Mother, Yeshe Tsogyal,
For me and those like me who wander in samsara,
I pray you, speak some words of guidance.
Still through the blessings of your love
Protect us always. Do not leave!

The Lady answered:

Kyeho!
Yeshe Nyingpo, listen!

Ask the Lord, your Teacher, for his blessing;
Ask the yidam for accomplishment;
From the four clans of the dakinis, request activities.
In times of need show forth your signs of power;
This, in brief, is how you should behave.

Yeshe Nyingpo, hear me once again!
Foster your disciples through monastic rule;
Others will respect and have recourse to you.
In your practice, strive and persevere in Secret Mantra,
And quickly you will gain accomplishment.
Endeavor in the Dharma, following the Sutras,
And in the teachings' textual tradition you will be a scholar.
Practice on your yidam, combining into one
The stages of approach and of accomplishment,
And any siddhi you desire will come to you.
With the texts of Abhidharma, eradicate your errors;
Thus you will be free, there is no doubt!

In your practice, focus on the subtle veins, the energies and essence.
Signs of warmth will swiftly be perfected.
Purify yourself according to the Kriya,
And swift will be the cleansing of your stains.
Strike upon the key point in View, Meditation, Action,
And certainly your true good will be realized.
Meditate upon the fruit, the Great Perfection free from action,
And exhaustion of phenomena, the state beyond all intellect, will be attained.
Have impartial aspiration,
And the good of beings
You will thus complete.

Ma Rinchen Chok then made this request:

Mother Tsogyal, my Lady and my Guru!
When to the land of Orgyen you have gone away,

What should be our prayers and how should we behave—
The spiritual kindred gathered here?
Teach us the way that we might never part from you.

As he spoke he wept, and in reply the Lady said:

Kyeho!
Listen to me now, O yogic adept.
You have now attainment in the mantric way;
And well do you intend the good of beings.
Yeshe Tsogyal, I, a woman,
Through the blessing of the Guru's love,
Have now the fruit complete in all its strength.
Tomorrow I will go away to Orgyen.

All you kindred gathered here before me.
Pray, and blessings will arise,
Hold fast the sacred Dharma, your own good to attain,
And labor unconceited for the benefit of beings.
Liberate yourselves by View, by Meditation, and
by Action.
Accompany your prayers with tuneful melody,
Bringing forth devotion from the marrow of your bones.
Meditate upon the Teacher as the glow of your awareness;
When you melt and mingle mutually together,
Taste that vast expanse of nonduality.
There remain.

And if you know me, Yeshe Tsogyal,
Mistress of samsara and nirvana,
You will find me dwelling in the heart of every being.
The elements and senses are my emanations,
And emanated thence, I am the twelvefold chain of co-
production:[91]
Thus primordially we never separate.

I seem a separate entity
Because you do not know me.

Therefore find my source and root!
And from within, awareness will arise;
The great and primal Wisdom will be all-pervading.
Bliss of the natural state will gather like a lake,
And Higher Insight, fishes' eyes of gold, will grow and
spread.
Nurture this production of experience and bliss,
And on the wings of such perfected virtuosity,
You will make the crossing to the other shore.
In meadows of appearance, you will skip and run,
And fly and tilt in the immensity of space.
Within the vast abyss of great primordial Wisdom,
The essence of Great Bliss will well up like a lake,
And deities and drops of light in ravishing display,
And syllables and chains of light will shimmer and
pulsate.
With such experience of the Real thus strengthened,
You will seize the stronghold of awareness reaching to
its limit.
All dissolves, exhausted, in the primal space,
And thus it is that you will never stray from me.

Then Odren Zhönnu Pel made this request:

Kyema!
Alas, O mother, Yeshe Tsogyal!
When you leave, and go away to Orgyen,
How shall we, so humdrum, so impervious to teaching,[92]
Ever manage with this View, this Meditation, and this
Action?
Would you give us just a little teaching?

The Lady answered and said:

Emaho!
Listen to me, faithful Zhönnu Pel.
An eagle nesting on a crag I never saw

To soar with elegance and ease until
His sixfold skill in flight was gained.
But with mighty beating wings, his art well learned,
He cuts across the razor-sharpness of the gale,
Alighting in whatever place he wills.
So it was with me, this woman, Tsogyal.
I longed to be enlightened, but until I gained
Perfection in the practice, I was forced to bide my time.
Creation and Perfection and the Great Perfection,
All is mastered now,
And this, my form of flesh, is melting into light.
Now I pass into the presence of the Lord of Orgyen,
But yet will leave you with these words of legacy.

The View is just the nature of all things.
When you focus on its meaning, making it a part of you,
It is not empty, since awareness and great clarity are there;
It has no entity, no permanence, for emptiness inheres
in it.
This then is the nature that we call the View.
But what about this View in terms of practice?
In the stage of Generation, it is itself the deity.
When lights are radiated and absorbed, it is compassion.
When you practice the Perfection stage, it is the
Mahamudra.
This nature is beyond both nothingness and being.
The truth is this: that when you turn to look upon
yourself,
And see yourself,
There's nothing to be seen.
The very recognition of that "seeing"—
The name applied to it is simply "View."

So-called Meditation is the ground of all the teachings.
If you focus on its meaning, making it a part of you,
You grow accustomed, undistracted,

Mindful and without fixation,
To what was seen or recognized
To be the nature of the View:
And "Staying in the View," indeed, is what we call it.

How, then, should we undertake this Meditation?
Whether you engage in Generation or Perfection,
Various experiences will show the wordless truth.
Whether Generation or Perfection is your practice,
Unimpaired by sinking, languor, heaviness,
Sealed by centeredness and recollection,
If you stay abiding in this View,
That is Meditation.

"Action" is the teachings' exercise.
If you focus on its meaning, making it a part of you,
This is to possess the View with certainty—
Strengthened and supported by successful meditation—
Remaining undistracted, yet relaxed
In all the different works you undertake.

As to how these actions are performed—
Whatever type of action there may be,
All is based in uncontrived simplicity.
There'll be no conflict with the state of meditation
To which your every action will bring progress.
I mean that in whatever deeds you may perform,
Working, walking, sleeping, eating, sitting,
You will never wander from the meaning of the practice—
Generation or Perfection or the Great Perfection,
Thus your actions will attain their final reach.

These are just my words of counsel,
And though I go now to the land of Ngayab,
Tibet I leave replete with teaching and advice.
All who have devotion, let them pray to me.

Then the lady Dorje Tso of Shelkar spoke and asked:

Kyema!
Mother of this whole Tibetan kingdom,
Mistress specially of me, who trust in you.
No other will there be for me if you depart.
Have mercy on me, do not cast me off.
Take me with you to the land of Lotus Light!
But if, too laden with my heavy deeds,
I cannot follow in your footsteps,
Grant, I beg you, teachings and instructions in abundant measure.

Her voice was shaken with weeping and she fainted away in despair. When she had awakened from her swoon, the Lady said:

Emaho!
Faithful maid of Shelkar, listen,
Dakini of wisdom, Dorje Tso!
This body, formed of flesh and blood,
This lowly body, laden with the weight of matter,
The way for it to voyage through the sky
Is meditation on the subtle veins and energies.
If you win dominion over energy and mind—
"Accomplishment," so called, is nothing else than that.

Minds beset by five deceitful poisons
Give rise to personalities untamed and barbarous.
If you wish to cleanse the crassness of your thoughts,
If you wish to gain enlightenment,
Rest firmly in the View of Mahamudra.
Primal Wisdom, emptiness, unveiled and free—
So-called "Buddhahood" is nothing else than that.

This imperfect form so treacherous,
Is ground and basis of all good and ill.

If you wish that it be worn away, to gain the rainbow body,
Practice Ati, Great Perfection.
If you reach the level where phenomena
Exhaust themselves and wear away in suchness,
There is nothing but Self-Presence[93] free from action.

There is no other way to voyage through the sky.
Therefore, for a while, until your coarse flesh has been purified,
I am destitute of means to bring you to the land of Lotus Light.
Therefore give your ears to my teaching.
Supplicate and pray to your root guru,
With pure vision, faith, and strong devotion,
Never for an instant thinking
She's a friend on equal terms.
Request her blessing and the four empowerments.
Meditate upon her vivid presence,
Never parted from you in the center of your heart.
Mingle your three doors with hers, inseparable.
As you meditate, remain in Mahamudra,
Otherwise preserve your Higher Insight.

Diligently cultivate the union of bliss and emptiness,
That meditation might progress and grow.
Detached, bring objects of desire upon the path.
Pursue the Great Perfection full of confidence;
Attain the ground of Ati where phenomena exhaust themselves.

Henceforth and for eleven of your lives to come,
Your skillful means will train the beings of Tibet.
Thereafter you will go to Lotus Light,
Renowned as Dorje Dechen Pema Tso,
Thence to send out emanations.
With bhikshu Namkhai Nyingpo, Essence of the Sky,

You will be joined as means and wisdom.
And wild hordes scattered
Numberless in barbarous lands,
Will have you for their teachers, helped beyond all telling.
Namkhai Nyingpo will be known as Ching
(And Che Jing Mir Gen will in fact be called),
And you will be the consort of his body
And live for thirteen times ten thousand human years.
After this, upon the mount of Lotus Light,
You will never be divided from the lord your Guru.

Thus Yeshe Tsogyal finished her prophecy and instructed Dorje Tso at great length.

Then Lasum Gyalwa Changchub made many prostrations and circumambulations. He prepared a mandala of seven turquoises in which there was a spirit-gem[94] known as the "thousand brilliant lights." Then he spoke up and said:

Emaho!
Mistress of the secret word of Padma,
You with memory that never fails,
Highest wisdom, Sarasvati of Great Bliss,
Mother Tsogyal, only sun to rise above Tibet's dark land,
It is sure now that you will depart towards the south and west.
And so I pray you, grant me this great blessing—
Brief words that yet condense the meaning,
A practice swift and sharp with all profound key points complete,
A teaching bringing Buddhahood within a single life.

And then, how many more lives must I live
Before I come to you who dance upon the sky?
I pray you, in your mercy, keep me with you, never parted.

In reply, the Lady bestowed the transmission of the *Kachö Trulkui Nyingtik*, of which the outer section was in accordance with the Sutras and contained ten topics.[95] The inner section was according to the Secret Mantra and comprised eleven topics.[96] Finally, the secret section was according to the tradition of the essential pith instructions and consisted of twelve ultimate teachings.[97] At that moment, when all this was bestowed, the Lady foretold that Gyalwa Changchub and six other disciples would attain freedom in the Radiant Clarity, without leaving their bodies behind. And indeed it so befell. Thereupon, Lady Tsogyal bestowed the following discourse and prophecy:

Emaho!
Listen, Gyalwa Changchub, undistractedly,
Chölo Gönpo, hear me carefully!
You are Arya Salé, my hero in the skillful means.

Formerly, O Salé, when Atsara was how they called you,
You and I were joined as skillful means and wisdom.
Propitious were the many sacred links we formed
In Secret Mantra most profound.
Thus you have been blessed with freedom in this life.
Yet times there were when you considered me your ordinary friend,
Sometimes scoffing, sometimes chiding, sometimes doubting.
And so throughout your stream of future lives,
Obstacles will dog you, even though a siddha in the Secret Mantra.
Wicked gossip will beset you,
And much ill-speech by evil mouths of slanderers.
From time to time, adversity will mar your work for beings.

Whatever happens, know that it is through your former karma.
Pray to Padmasambhava and Tsogyal indivisible.

Now henceforth, for thirteen lives to come,
You will achieve the benefit of beings.
Your emanation will at last appear
To westward, in a wild and rugged place beyond this hill.
You will have the name of Namkha
And the bearing of a wrathful vajra hero.
Known for three lives thence as Taksham,
You will halt the karmic wind and come to Lotus Light.
Then, inseparable from me through means and wisdom,
And until the stream of wanderers runs dry,
You will send your emanations.

Then the strength of virtuous prayers will be fulfilled.
Then the essence of profound and Secret Mantra will burst
into flower.
Then the fruit of your profound experience will ripen.
Then the Generation and Perfection will attain their peak
in strength,
Then the karmic residue will yield its perfect crop.
Then profound will blow great clouds of blessing;
Deep compassion's firmament will shed its rain,
And you, O Arya Salé, will have gained accomplishment.

Gyalwa Changchub, thus the strength of truth will
manifest.
In the meantime, pray with zeal and practice!

When night fell on the eighth day, twelve nyul-le dakinis appeared from Orgyen, realm of dakinis, proclaiming that their species numbered twelve millions. When midnight came, the twelve kinds of man-devouring dakinis arrived: mistresses of life, breath-stealers, flesh-eaters, blood-drinkers, bone-chewers and more, saying that in all they numbered five million five thousand five hundred. And thus the earth and sky became full of these ferocious beings. After midnight, a multitude of worldly dakinis, and dakinis of the twelve divisions of time, appeared, declaring that in all they numbered twelve million, one hundred and twenty thousand. They were all riding on lions and other ferocious beasts, various species of bird such as garudas, different domestic animals such as elephants, and a variety of wild creatures like deer and rhinoceros. They themselves had different shapes, with human heads or the heads of animals, and the whole earth was filled with them. Then at dawn, other dakinis arrived declaring that they were the dakinis of the four directions of the land of Orgyen, and dakinis of the twelve continents. They were assembled in groups of different colors: white, red, green, blue, and yellow. The white group comprised those who were fully white, and who were half red, half green, blue, or yellow. And it was the same for the yellow group and the others. All held different kinds of weapons, indicative of their nature, and all were adorned with silk shawls, bone ornaments, diadems and robes to cover their upper and lower limbs. Tiny bells they carried, and thighbone trumpets, skull-drums and a variety of other musical instruments. There were millions and millions of them, impossible to count, though in all they said that they numbered five million, two hundred thousand. Then from daybreak to sunrise, the dakinis of the sixty-eight mandalas, together with their mistress, Pema Garwang Lhundze, appeared, declaring who they were. The sky was vibrant with rainbows; the earth breathed the scent of frankincense, and the air was alive with dakinis. Later, between midday and the evening, all the dakinis of the thirty-two sacred lands, the ten holy places of the herukas, the eight great charnel grounds, from Thung Chö and Tsen Do and their neighboring regions, arrived and announced their presence. Each of them had a different physical demeanor with different gestures. They played different musical instruments and sang all sorts of songs, danced their different steps and displayed a variety of skills, making offerings in different ways and with various embellishments. For this was how they all worshiped and praised the Lady, and there were so many of them that the ground was scarcely visible.

The Lady then celebrated an immense ganachakra feast, and with a single fragment of molasses, she miraculously fed and satisfied all the human beings present, giving even more to the dakinis. And everyone she regaled and entertained with a single skull-cup of beer. Afterward, she conferred the secret symbol empowerment of the dakini, and all those present experienced an intense oneness with the dakini and were ultimately established in the level of nonreturner.

On the ninth day at dusk, the Lady left the Heart Cave, which was halfway up Mount Zabbu, and climbed to the summit, which was indeed shaped like the Copper-Colored Mountain. Before dawn on the tenth day, she opened the mandala of the *Lama Thukdrup Druchik*. In that very instant an immeasurable host of rakshasas appeared. They were so many that they could not be counted. Some had three heads, some one head; others were headless. Some had five heads, some nine, some a hundred. And they had any number of arms and legs, ranging from one to hundreds and thousands. "The Guru Padma has sent us," they cried, "to invite the Queen of all the rakshasas, the dakini Blue Light Blazing." And there they all were, in a great throng.

At daybreak, after the celebration of a ganachakra, I, Gyalwa Changchub, and the eleven faithful children and others, together with all the different races of humans, dakas, dakinis, rakshasas, gods, and spirits, made devout prostration to the Lady. With tears of grief in our eyes, we made this request:

Kyema Kyehü, Dakini of Wisdom,
Guru of us all, O mistress Yeshe Tsogyal,
Only mother of Tibet, departing in the sky,
What shall we now do, bereaved and toothless babes?
Guard Tibet, we pray, both now and evermore!

If now you go, if now you really cannot stay,
We beg you, tell us and describe

The fortunes, good and bad, of Dharma in Tibet.
Tell us who will be the holders of the teaching;
Tell us how will come the evil demon-wraiths, the workers of destruction,
And what might be the means to drive them out,
The causal sequences by which they might be parried.
And indeed reveal to us the advent of your emanations.
What will be their names, their place, their work and doctrine?
Do not hide, or merely hint, but tell us openly.
Omniscient Queen, we pray you, speak to us!

Your three biographies, moreover, lengthy or abridged,
The two transmissions, earlier and later—
Mother and son—passed down from mouth to ear,
And especially the teachings of the *Khandro Trulkui Nyingtik*—
Should they be passed down by word of mouth,
Or hidden and concealed as Treasures?
To whom shall they be given, to whom so fortunate?
If as Treasures they should be concealed, where should they be hidden?
Who will come to show them forth, and what will then befall?
Please be generous with precise instructions and prophetic indications.

What shall we do now, the kindred gathered here?
In whom can we confide and place our trust?
Who will give us counsel at the moment of our dying,
Who will drive away all hindrances?
Kyema Kyehü! look on us with swift compassion!

The full account of Yeshe Tsogyal's answer is to be found in the "Extensive Prophetic Indications." But this, in brief, is what she said:

Emaho!
Tibetans, gods, and humankind, pay heed to me!
Listen to me well, my faithful ones, endowed with virtuous karma!
Now that I, your mother, the enlightened Yeshe Tsogyal,
Have nursed Tibet two hundred and eleven years,
The Dharma-guarding king Tri Ralpachen,
An emanation of great Vajrapani,
Will uphold the sutras and the tantras to the heights of heaven.
And yet his younger brother Lang,[98]
A demon's wraith,
Will plot with evil ministers
And, his elder kinsman slain,
Will seize the throne.
Places of religion, seats of sutra-learning,
He will ruin, blotting out their names.
Based upon the ten nonvirtues
And sins that bring immediate perdition,
He will frame laws against the Buddhadharma.
The greatest of the monkhood will be slain,
The lesser will be exiled and the least enslaved.
And yet the vajra kindred of the Secret Mantra,
Householders, will keep alive the teachings.
Lhasa, yes, and Samye will decline and fall to ruin.

Yet Pelgyi Dorje will recall the prophecy[99]
And slay the royal fiend, and flee to Mekham.
Mar and Yo will trim the flame of the Vinaya teachings;[100]
At Langthang Drölma ten monks will assemble,
And to every part of Ü and Tsang,
The bright lamp of the Doctrine will be carried,
To spread again throughout Tibet's religious land.
And thanks to able monks and scholars,
The earth will be encompassed by the Secret Mantra.

But aberrant practices and errors will arise,
And so the emanation of the Speech of Orgyen,

Shantarakshita's rebirth, by name Atisha,[101]
Will widely propagate the sutras and the tantras.
And at that time, I, Tsogyal, then called Jayakara,
Will be the close disciple of the translator in the clan of Drom.
When the prime of human life is seventy years,
Religion will increase and spread.
The sutras and the tantras will arise and fill the world with light.
Afterward, when sixty marks the peak of human life,
An emanation of the Dharma king, named Sa, will hold the Doctrine.
The royal line will fail, and Horpas will become religious patrons.
An emanation of the Body of the Lotus-Born, named Drogmi,
Will arise to propagate the Path and Fruit,
Establishing the learning of the sutras and the tantras.
His coming will be like the advent of the peerless Shakyamuni.
Later, when the Sakya line is scattered into fragments,
When age will start at fifty, Phagmo's teaching will arise;
The ancient system of religious law will be restored, just as today.

From the gorges in the south will come an emanation of the Guru's Mind.
Renowned as Marpa, he will propagate the teachings of the Secret Mantra,
And Tsogyal, I myself, will be his wife and consort.
One called Mila will appear and,
Practicing austerities, will gain accomplishment.
An emanation of the Lotus Guru's Qualities
Will appear in Dhakpo;
Dri, Tak, Kar and Druk will gush forth like the streams of Kailash:
An ocean of the Doctrine, bliss-bestowing, will pervade.

At the time when people start to age at forty,
The Doctrine will disperse and crumble, the Teachings will rely
Upon the mainstay of the Horpa and Mongolian hordes.
Tibet will be partitioned into bits and parcels,
Looking like an ulcerated skin.
The Lotus-Born's Activity will then appear as karma.
The Doctrine will be spread throughout Tibet,
Its life extended for a further thirty years.
The sacred sound of Mani will pervade the kingdom.

When thirty marks the stage when age begins to fall,
The doctrine of the Virtuous ones will come to birth.
A Suchness emanation of the Lotus-Born will take his birth in Ü,
And Tibet will be as happy as a heaven of the gods.
A descendant of the Zahor line and powerful lord of men,
Will propagate the teachings in Ü, Tsang and Kham.
This will pass away [illegible],[102]
Tibet will sink in misery; all will be undone;
Everyone will seek support from Horpas and from Mongols.

When old age comes when twenty years have passed,
An emanation of the Speech of Padmasambhava
Will come in Lhodrak, restoring happiness to beings.
And a Dharma king, a birthmark on his shoulder, will arise in Li.
Then, when life attains its fullness at the age of ten,[103]
The Doctrine, dwelling then in foreign lands, will fail.
The present cycle will have reached its trough,
And emanations will be only masks and shadows,
The essence of the earth will fail:
The black age Dudjom Nagpo Gyachu will be here.

After this will be the coming of Maitreya, and all will be revived.

A falling cycle then, and two to rise,
And yet a third, and four more spans of time.

These, then, are but simple generalities.
Consult the teachings of the Lotus-Born
For how to counteract the troubles of the periods
of transition.
For his word is true, unable to deceive.

And Yeshe Tsogyal, I indeed,
Will never leave Tibet untouched by my compassion.

My emanations, radiating rays of skillful means,
Will guide all future beings to their happiness.
My Body, Speech, and Mind, my Qualities and Action,
Each will body forth five emanations.
These twenty-five will be the constant guardians of Tibet.
Each of them will send five emanations and each of these
a further five,
And all of these yet five and five again—
They will come in millions,
Until there are no beings left unfreed,
Till all are gathered in the joyful space
Of Samantabhadri, Mother of Great Bliss.

Five hundred years from now, to tell it all in brief,
Tibet will seem a stronghold filled with weapons,
And forts will cover all the land, both hill and dale,
Demonesses will deceive the people with false doctrine,
An evil parody of Chö will fill the land.
Then an emanation of my Body's Speech, renowned
as Drölma, will appear;
An emanation of my Body's Body, Kunga Zangmo,
will arise;
An emanation of my Body's Mind, called Palmo, will
appear in Ü;
An emanation of my Body's Quality, called Pu, will come
to Yeru;

And an emanation of my Body's Action will arise
in Kham, in Tamyul.
Learning in profound and Secret Mantra will be
reasserted.
The deep sense of the Prajñaparamita,
Instructions on the Chö, will be expounded.
Four Lion-sons will teach and tame the people.

Then Tibet will be the charnel food for Zahor,
And Ü and Tsang be like the spots on dice;
The Teaching of the Buddhas will be like
A lamp that's overfilled—a struggling flame,
And evil obstacles will swirl like fierce dust storms.

Then the hundred Treasure Finders will appear,
Foretold by Padma,
And the Dharma Treasures of the Secret Mantra
Will bring joy into the world.
Evil treasures also will appear, unlike the findings
of the hundred[104]—
Corrupt and counterfeit, the deadly troves and substances
of sorcery.[105]

When these spread, a Body incarnation of the Speech
of Tsogyal
Will take birth in Ngari, by name of Nyendrak.
She will judge the Treasures, showing true from false.
An incarnation of my Speech's Speech will rise in Ü,
And she will be a nun, entitled Orgyen.
She will found a house of meditation.
Signs displayed by her will show her as a siddha of
the Secret Mantra.

An emanation of my Speech's Mind will come to Tashö.
Known as Padma, she will take out Treasures.
Meaningful will be all links with her,
For she will lead disciples to accomplishment.

My Speech's Quality will emanate in Kongpo.
She will have the name of Pu and be a comfort to the lowly,
Removing obstacles that hinder Treasure Finders.
An incarnation of Activity will rise in Tsang.
Known as Jomo, she will found a center for the practice of Varahi,
And rituals of Varahi will spread through the land.

Then foreign armies will invade Tibet,
Aggressive like the stormy waves of summer.
For Sa and Dri there will be disagreement,
Soured by troubles in the border regions.
Each will hold to his own side and tenet,
And bigotry and faction will begin between the Old and New.
Doctrines, true and false, will be confused and practiced.
Then a Body incarnation of my Mind will come to Nyaksa.
She will have the name of Orgyen, and will be
A mighty siddha rich in realization and experience.

My Mind's Speech will appear as one called Sonam Peldrön.
In the north she will be born and have the bearing of a common woman.
Yet all connections with her will be meaningful,
And her death will show her as accomplished.
To many, blessed with fortune, she will give
Accomplishment, though veiled and indirectly.

My Mind's Mind incarnation, known as É, will come to Ü,
And will lead those linked with her to realms of dakinis.
To many yogis she will teach the path of liberation
Through practice on the subtle veins and energies.

An incarnation of the Qualities of my Mind will come to Lhodrak.

Displaying different forms, she will conduct all linked to her to happiness.
In Nepal my Mind's Activity will manifest,
And many will she bring, by skillful means, to Dharma.

Then the pious king will come again in fivefold emanation.
The governor of Tsang will flicker like a firefly.
Palaces will be like phantom cities,
Good news like the far-off songs of Faërie.
The bad advice of experts will be honeyed poison,
And teachers of religion like a lamp that sputters and goes out.

When the seats of patrons, the Horpas and the Mongols,
Touch the cushions of their teachers,
A Body incarnation of my Quality will appear, a dakini, in Ü.
Drölma, incarnation of my Quality's Speech, will appear in Kham.
An incarnation of my Quality's Mind will rise in Nyemo.
A teacher will appear to the north, the Quality incarnation of my Quality,
And my Quality's Activity will emanate in Tsang Rong.
They will all take different forms, endowed with wondrous powers
And various clairvoyances, leading those connected to the land of Great Felicity.

When this is passed, Tibet, both high and low, will fall in fragments.
The passes, vales, and gorges will be claimed and parceled.
Families will be recorded, and all will say, "This land belongs to me."
All wealth will be within the Horpas' land
And all will don their clothing.
Religious folk will fight, with monks to lead them;

The clergy will take arms, with camels as their beasts of burden;
Nuns will do the mason's work, and laity will teach religion.
Evil deeds will be the lot of little children.
Lhasa will be overthrown by water;
And hurricanes will lay waste Samye;
Trandruk will not last, and ruin fall on all four provinces.

Then a Body emanation of Activity will arise in Chimphu.
My Activity's Speech will manifest in Ngari.
My Activity's Mind will come to Puwo.
The Quality of my Activity will rise in Dokham.
The Activity of my Activity will appear in Ü, a woman leader.
All these emanations will have various forms
And lead the endless myriads of beings to where samsara ends,
And take those linked with them to Great Felicity.
Various of my incarnations will appear in hidden lands,
Bestowing help on those endowed with fortune, and dispelling hindrances.

And so, from now until the scouring of samsara,
My stream of emanations, primary and secondary,
Will flow unceasing.
Especially to those who in the future meditate
Upon the subtle veins and energies,
I'll show myself—at best directly,
Else in visions, or at least in dreams,
Appearing as a common person, or as the secret consort.
I shall clear the obstacles of those who keep samaya,
Bringing progress to their practice,
Helping to attain with speed the blissful warmth and thence accomplishment.

The three biographies of me, your mother—extensive or abridged:

Hide the long one here, on Zabbu Peak;
The shortest one conceal at Lhodrak Namkhachen;
And this, of medium length, conceal in Lhorong Kham.

Concerning now the teachings of the *Khandro Nyingtik*,
And the two transmissions, earlier and later,
Passed down from mouth to ear,
Best it is to follow the instructions that I gave for each.
Changchub, Bé, and Ma, these three endowed with fortune,
Will, in the future, be the ones to find them.

This biography, indeed, has nine auspicious possibilities.
First, if one called Chöwang takes it out,
Its fame and benefit will spread throughout the kingdom,
Touching those who live as far away as China.
If this chance is missed, the Treasure staying hid,
One called Trashi will appear from Latö.
If he, his hair all braided, takes it out,
Ü, Tsang, Kham will be the sphere of its effectiveness and benefit,
And its influence will reach the confines of Nepal.
If this chance is missed, the Treasure staying hid,
One called Dorje, but renowned as Pawo,[106]
Will appear to south of Lhorong's snowy mountains.

If he takes it, it will be renowned in Dokham,
Touching those, at last, as far away as Hor.
If the chance is missed once more, a yogi by the name of Radza
Will arrive from Shampo: he too will have power to take it.
Or else a certain Dorje, inhabitant of Puwo,
Or a man named Kunga from the east can take it.
The benefit, each time, will be decreased by half.
If even they do not discover it, a final opportunity remains.

Three women will unearth it, or it will appear of itself.
If so it is, the region of its finding will be all its field of influence.
Then in future, when the nine predicted children
Will gather at a single time, the teachings will unfold and spread.

Then in time to come,
Five hundred periods multiplied by five,[107]
There will be a place called Kathog,[108] to the east of here,
The place of teaching of the Guru Senge Dradok
And hallowed by the Lotus-Born by thirteen consecrations.
The mountain there, formed like a haughty lion,
Has Treasures hidden in its "throat" of great profundity.
In time to come, when circumstance is ripe,
The Lotus Guru and his consort's work for beings will pervade this region.
There, I, Tsogyal, will arise as Dampa Gyaltsen,
And the Ati teaching of the Secret Mantra will abide there till the end.
Though it will decline from time to time,
The karmically endowed will step by step arise.
Tsogyal's last disciples will appear and dwell there.
All this counsel and instruction have I now bequeathed to you,
No further means is there for Tsogyal to remain.
So hasten now to prayer and meditation.
Disciples gathered here and all in time to come,
Take to your hearts my words of prophecy and teaching!

Then, with her right hand, Tsogyal touched Trashi Chidren, the girl from Mön. She was transformed into a blue utpala lotus with eight petals marked with the syllables *Hung* and *Phat*, and dissolved into the right side of the Lady's heart. Then with her left hand, Tsogyal touched Kalasiddhi of Nepal, who changed into a red lotus of sixteen petals marked with the sixteen vowels and *Hri* and dissolved into the left side of her heart.

As night was falling on the ninth day, there appeared the four Guardian Kings at the head of a host of spirits, the inner and secret oath-bound ones belonging to the eight and twelve classes. They were coming to meet her. "Now," they cried, "all the entreaties and messages of invitation from Ngayab, the abode of dakinis, have been made. Therefore come, O knowledge holder, Blue Light Blazing!"

Nine times over, the gods and people of Tibet beseeched the Lady Tsogyal to delay her leaving, as has been described elsewhere. There then appeared all the great and powerful deities of the whole country, each accompanied by a special retinue: Dorje Lekpa from Tsang, Machen Pomra from the east, Rongtsen Mebar from the south, Tsomen Gyalmo from the north, Gangzang Hao from the west, Lijin Harlek from Ü, Thanglha Gangtsen from Nyen, and so on. Especially in favor of the twelve Tenma, Yeshe Tsogyal answered many questions and gave prophecies and so forth to the gods and spirits. But on account of their length, they have not been set down here.

At last, on the tenth day of the month, when the first light of dawn appeared in the sky, a palanquin of light in the form of an eight-petaled lotus, and borne by four dakinis, appeared in front of Tsogyal. The Lady stood, and, with a damaru in her right hand, and a skull-cup in her left, she stepped into it.

As she did so, a great wail of lamentation arose from all who had gathered there. "Alas, what shall we do?" they cried. "What shall we say to the people of Tibet?"

In reply, the Lady Tsogyal said:

Kyema!
Listen, faithful people of Tibet!
I am melting now into the space of universal ground;
My body is afflicted by no illness.
Impure Tsogyal now has blossomed into purity;

No longer is there place for impure pain and groaning.
This mirage-form of flesh now melts away;
No need is there for ritual, virtue, arts of healing.
The nature of all beings is now manifest;
There is nothing that is real and permanent.
This form of light, which through the Sacred Dharma
I have wrought,
Will be no blackened corpse, no bag of liquid mess.
Your mother Tsogyal is dissolving into *A*,[109]
So this is not the time for cries of "Oh!" and "Ah!"

The outer elements and inner, the mother and the son,
now mingle,
And for me there is no more of matter—earth and stones.
The Guru's love has never left me:
His emanations fill the world, and here they are inviting
me.

Your so-called "Lady," wild and fit for any deed,
To whom so many things befell, is now no more!
The wench who could not even keep her man
Is now the queen of Dharmakaya Kuntuzangpo!
That sluttish creature, brazen with conceit,
Pretension takes her now away to the southwest!
That whining vixen, fit for any intrigue,
Has tricked her way to dissolution in the Dharmadhatu!
That dejected widow no Tibetan wanted
Inherits now the endless sovereignty of Buddhahood!
Therefore pray to me and do not be despairing;
Those with faith I, Tsogyal, never leave.
For when you pray to me, I will be with you certainly.
Therefore pray, my friends, and go back to your homes,
May bliss and fortune, health and happiness, increasingly
be yours!

When she had finished speaking, Tsogyal became radiant with beams of five-colored brilliance difficult to look upon. She dissolved into a sphere of deep blue light, resembling a sesame pod in shape, and disappeared. The four dakinis took the lotus by its petals and raised the shimmering light higher and higher into the air until it vanished. At that moment, all the people cried out with a single voice:

Kyema Kyehü!
Ah, mother, Yeshe Tsogyal!
Oh the wicked deed! So small is your compassion!
If now you cease from guarding this Tibetan land,
In whom will guilty sinners place their trust?
Mother, you have gone into a field of purity;
Who will now protect Tibet, this land so stained?
Mother, you have gone into the space of utter purity;
Who will be the guide of those with evil karma ripening?
Mother, you have journeyed to the sphere of
Great Felicity;
Who will guide the ones who wander in samsaric sorrow?
Mother, you have gone away to Lotus Light;
Who will guide the beings in the steep abysses of Tibet?
Mother, you have gone into the presence of the
Lotus-Born;
Who will now protect the lost, defenseless
in the wilderness?

Kyema Kyehü!
Oh look upon us still with tender mercy!
We beg you, pray a little for our country's happiness.
We beg you, give brief words of testament for our Tibetan
land.
How can we escape our sorrow, we assembled here?
Lady and our mother, have pity on us still;
We beg you, lead us to the paradise of Lotus Light.

Thus, with tears and great sorrow, they called upon her from afar, striking their bodies on the ground, weeping and wailing.

And the Lady answered, not appearing physically, but speaking from a cloud of brilliant light:

Kyema Ho!
Kyema! Hear me, faithful people of Tibet.
Yeshe Tsogyal, I the great enlightened one,
Have withdrawn my impure form into unsullied space.
I am now a Buddha in the utter sphere of Lotus Light.
Therefore do not grieve; be filled with joy!

Tibetan people, sunk in endless sorrows,
Through your faults, the many evils that you do,
You are the authors of your own unhappiness.
Understand! And take the Triple Gem as refuge from all pain.
Pray to them, your only hope and surety.
I, the Buddha Yeshe Tsogyal,
Purged the elements' uncleanness and have gone into the sky.
Through wondrous emanations I will tend the good of beings.
Therefore do not grieve; be filled with joy!

This heavy form of flesh, result of evil action,
Is basis of defiled emotion, cause of evil karmas.
Understand! The Dharma is the means to win the wholesome fruit.
Therefore strive to implement the teaching on the tenfold virtue.
I, the Buddha Yeshe Tsogyal,
Brought the fruit to ripeness, and I have gone into the pure expanse.
My perfect actions for the sake of Dharma I bequeath to you.
Therefore do not grieve; be filled with joy!

Evil karma wrought by so much different action
Is a cause that ripens in the realms of hell.

Understand! The way to purify the lower realms
Is virtue practiced in your speech and body.
Bind your three doors into one, upon the path of virtue.
I, the Buddha Yeshe Tsogyal,
Have gone to Great Felicity's unsullied land.
To all those linked with me I taught the means of
  nonreturn,
Therefore do not grieve but sing for joy!

This endless ocean of samsaric pain,
See and understand its frightful nature!
A holy teacher is the sole means to escape from it.
Seek out one that's true, without mistake, and follow
  his instructions.
I, your mother, the enlightened Yeshe Tsogyal,
Have entered the abyss of space, the land of Lotus Light
And will be born within the hollow of a spotless lotus.
Therefore do not grieve; have faith in me.

Wild Tibet, this land of strife and sorrow!
When you crave its vales and crags no longer,
Give up useless business, stay in solitude.
Practice on the subtle veins, the energy and essence,
Apply yourselves to Dzogchen and the Mahamudra.
I, your mother, the enlightened Yeshe Tsogyal,
Perfectly accomplished through my pure devotion,
Held in the Teacher's loving mercy,
Have gone to him, my Master Padmasambhava.
Therefore do not grieve, but offer prayers.

This karmic body, like an unprotected bubble,
Liable to die at any time—
When you see its nature of impermanence,
Don't behave as if you'll live forever,
Make your practice equal with your life.
Practice what will lead to Ati, to phenomena's exhaustion.

Kyé Ho!
Listen to me; stop your wailing!

My love for you is totally unchanging.
You're acting just like those who cling to permanence!
I have not died, I have not left you, nor departed
anywhere.
Pray to me and you will truly see my face.
To those with unalloyed devotion, I will give the siddhi
that they wish,
From now until the final future generation.

Tibet, this land, this pure sphere of the
Great Compassionate,
Ripened as the field of teaching of the Lotus Guru,
With great Mañjushri as the master of the Doctrine,
And the powerful majesty of Vajrapani, Lord of Secrets,
The ocean of the Teachings will abide forever here,
Free from foreign unbelievers, free from harm.
When demons and demonic forces have been tamed,
May holders of the sutra teachings gain in strength
Through their attainment in the Secret Mantrayana.
May the kingdom all be filled with practicing
communities.
May all the people of Tibet, this central land,
Henceforth in this and future lives,
Adopt the Triple Gem as witness to their joy
and sorrow—
Ten virtues may they cultivate, ten vices cast aside.

For every act of thought or deed, consult the
noble Teachings.
As to wrong and right, obey the word of Padma.
In secular and social matters,
Let the customs of the pious king be followed.
Let the statutes of the land be based on Dharma.
Let foes on the four borders be subdued by strength
of Dharma,
Defeated by the yidam and the Triple Gem's compassion.

Monks and nuns should keep their practice
Following the teachings of the scriptures.
Layfolk, men and women, should maintain a pure perception.
Let all have boundless reverence for those above them,
And give with open hands to those below.
Let all recite, for their own good, the mantra of six syllables,
And confidently pray to Padmasambhava, their Lord.

With devotion take the four empowerments—you, all gathered here.
Raise your voices, call on Tsogyal—call me by my name!
Request the four empowerments,
Mingling your minds with mine inseparably.
And in your sessions practice thought-free meditation.

In general terms, and for the people of Tibet in times to come,
The Lotus-Born is your predestined teacher.
To accomplish the Guru you should strive,
Perceiving your own teacher in the form of Padma.
Thus the blessings of compassion will flow the more abundantly.
Practice on the Teacher's Mind in sadhanas both long and short,
And Buddhahood, I pledge, in one life will be yours.
Recite the quintessential Guru Siddhi mantra.
On the tenth day of the waxing and the waning moon,
And on the eighth day and the fifteenth of the month,
Keep the ganachakra feast with offerings.
A single ganachakra, and the door is closed to birth in lower realms!
I promise, it will lead you to the state of no returning.

This is certain truth. This know and understand!
The essence of the teacher is this Guru Siddhi mantra:

HUNG: the life force of all the Buddhas, past, present, and to come;
DHI: accomplishment of all victorious yidams;
SID: the perfect action of the oath-bound and the dakinis;
MA: this cuts delusion from our mothers, wandering beings;
PAD: the supreme land of Buddhas of the triple time;
RU: this shuts the door to karmic energy;
GU: confers empowerment of compassion as the aspect of primordial Wisdom;
JRA: this is Mahamudra, the void, the indestructible;
VA: the symbol of the Wisdom-space;
HUNG: Nirmanakaya, emanated form to teach all beings;
AH: the supreme Dharma, Sambhogakaya;
OM: Kuntuzangpo, Dharmakaya, Primal Purity.

These twelve essential syllables of the Guru, Lotus-Born,
If spoken in reverse one hundred thousand times,
Will purify the faults of body, speech, and mind.
Two hundred thousand times consumes the negativities committed in the triple time;
Three hundred thousand times will place you on the level whence there's no returning.
Recite it seven hundred thousand times and in this life you meet the Lotus-Born;
A million recitations and the four enlightened actions will be done;
Six million churns samsara's deep abyss;
Ten million brings equality with Buddha Amitabha—
And any siddhi needed will be doubtless won.
Know, too, that other goods unnumbered will be yours.

The normal way of recitation repels suffering and leads beyond it.

OM: is the union in five Bodies of all Buddhas gone to bliss;

AH: distills the essence of the fivefold wisdom Speech;
HUNG: is the Suchness Body, Wisdom Mind's five aspects.
VA: is the sign and seal of indestructibility;
JRA: is deployment of the diamond-like compassion;
GU: the guru herukas of the triple time;
RU: the drop of essence that matures and liberates;
PAD: the threshold of the pure abode of bliss;
MA: is staying in the womb of bliss unmoving;
SID: is compassion in great strength and power;
DHI: is the accomplishment that satisfies all wants;
HUNG: the gaining of dominion in the primal ground.

This mantra has indeed the likeness of a wishing-jewel.
And further, since the twelve dependent links thereby are purified,
It is the nature of the ten perfections,
And therefore the Great Mother.
Of every aspiration it is the fulfillment.
Thus, all of you now here, and those in times to come,
Should zealously recite this mantra.

For a time now, while your dualistic minds persist,
It will seem that I have left you, but take heart.
When your dualistic minds subside, you will see that we were never parted.
May health and happiness embrace the very limits of the sky!

When she had finished speaking, an intense and powerful light shot away, darting, sparkling, dancing to the southwest. Finally it disappeared and was no more. All who were there prostrated themselves countless times and prayed. Their minds were numb with grief and their chests were tight with anguish. It seemed as if their hearts and stomachs had risen to their very throats. They could hardly see their way for tears. Staggering, their legs barely able to support their bodies, with laboring breath, they made their painful way back to the Heart Cave of Zabbu, arriving there just as night was falling.

The three disciples, Bé Yeshe Nyingpo, Lasum Gyalwa Changchub, and Ma Rinchen Chok, opened the mandala of the sadhana of the Guru and Dakini, and practiced it, remaining at Zabbu for seven months. They gained the realization of the inseparability of the Guru and Dakini and received many prophecies and permissions.

It was at that time that Tri Ralpachen, the king of Tibet and the defender of religion, promulgated his first decree and invited all translators to the court. It was there that certain people said that before their eyes, in the cave of Mutig Pama Gang, Tsogyal had displayed the signs of experiencing the state in which all phenomena are worn away in the nature of reality, and that she had left behind her nasal membrane, teeth, nails, and hair. These, they said, had transformed into pearl-like relics, becoming thus a support for the faith of the people. Apart from that, they said, her body had disappeared; she had attained Buddhahood. Again, it was said by others that, on the eighth day of the bird month in the bird year, the Lady Tsogyal bestowed teachings. On the tenth day, in the evening, she subdued demons. At midnight, she turned the wheel of the Dharma, and then remained in meditation until dawn, when she attained enlightenment. Then, as day was breaking, she sat with her body straight and passed beyond sorrow. Her physical remains transformed into a heap of tiny pearls, they said, and the king of Tibet, defender of religion, had had them brought to him and placed in a stupa. Yet, in truth, I, Gyalwa Changchub, together with Bé Yeshe Nyingpo, Ma Rinchen Chok, Odren Pelgyi Zhönnu, Dacha Rupa Dorje Pawo, Nyima of Ü, the Lady Changchub of Li, and the Lady Dorje Tso of Shelkar, together with no fewer than a hundred other fortunate persons, who where all present at the time, saw with our own eyes the events that are described here.

ITHI GUHYA EWAM MANDA

SAMAYA GYA GYA GYA

[illegible]

I, Gyalwa Changchub, to whom Tsogyal gave her blessing and who attained accomplishment in a single life, together with Namkhai Nyingpo of Lhodrak, indivisible from the Lotus-Born (the great Master whom neither birth nor death has ever touched), wrote down these, the Lady's words, on sheets of yellow paper, without addition or subtraction and without exaggeration or interpretation of her deeds. This text we then committed to the hand of Tongyuk, the Black Water Lord, adjuring him to give it to the spiritual heir prophesied by Tsogyal. Thus these words are sealed. In future time, may one with proper karma come upon them.

DHATHIM ITHI ZAB GYA TE GYA

The Tertön's Colophon

Such a one am I,
A southerling of southern stock,
Hailing from a land of steep defiles and chasms:
A cheerless waste, untouched by Padma's love,
The pinnacle of sin and wicked deeds,
Where eyes look to the dark, the light of Dharma fleeing;
An evil land, a hunters' land,
Where black folk clothe themselves in black,
Black food eating, black beer drinking;
A region where black actions keep samsara turning;
From an evil town of black-housed dwellers,
Thence am I!
An offspring of black-wedded, sinful parents:
Black-born through the strength of karma,
Pawo Taksham—that is my black name!

I took this from the hand of the Black Water Lord,
On sheets of paper with black ink I copied it.
The deed I perpetrated in a forest dense and black,
And finished on the black day, twenty-ninth.
May all black beings, leaving none aside,
Be Buddhas, all black deeds exhausted!
Though black they be, may all of them be freed!

And I, my sins and veils,
And black possessions,[110] cleansed—
May I, in blue-black Akanishta, highest of all realms,
O blue dakini, radiant Blue Light Blazing,

Be one with you in nonduality.
May here and now this prayer become the truth!

Hé Hé, here is marvelous wonder!
I wrote this as it sprang into my mind!

This is Pawo Taksham Dorje's Dharma Treasure.

MANGALAM EWAM BHATI SVASTI HRITE KHATHAM

Notes

1. See chapter 4, page 25.
2. See chapter 3, page 20.
3. See *The Words of My Perfect Teacher* (New York: HarperCollins, 1994. Reissue: Boston & London: Shambhala Publications, 1998).
4. See pages 137ff.
5. See page 21.
6. A general exposition of Vajrayana may be found in *The World of Tibetan Buddhism*, by His Holiness the Dalai Lama (Somerville, Mass.: Wisdom Publications, 1995).
7. See Yönten Gyatso, *yon tan rin po che'i mdzod kyi 'grel pa nyi ma'i od zer*, vol. 3, chap. 10, p.181.
8. I. B. Horner, *Women under Primitive Buddhism* (New Delhi: Motilal Banarsidass, 1930).
9. See chap. 4, pages 30 and 61.
10. See Tulku Thondup Rinpoche, *Hidden Teachings of Tibet* (Somerville, Mass.: Wisdom Publications, 1986).
11. A fascinating account of two Terma discoveries described by an eyewitness is found in the introduction to Namkhai Norbu Rinpoche, *The Crystal and the Way of Light: Sutra, Tantra, and Dzogchen* (New York: Viking Press, 1995).
12. The symbolic dayig (*brda' yig*) script usually appears at the beginning of each chapter; however, a few characters also occur in one of the prophecies in the eighth chapter.
13. See *Hidden Teachings of Tibet,* p. 67.
14. *snang ba mtha' yas*, Buddha Amitabha.
15. *spyan ras gzigs*, Avalokiteshvara. Name of the Bodhisattva who embodies the compassion of all the Buddhas. The Sambhogakaya emanation of the Buddha Amitabha.

16. Guru Padmasambhava, also referred to, some lines later, as the Lord of Orgyen.
17. *mkha' 'gro 'i thugs khrag*, traditional metaphor for the most precious quintessential teachings.
18. This and the other formulas occurring at the end of each chapter are the seal of secrecy. They are peculiar to the Treasure-texts and indicate the latter's unaltered purity and power. The seal of secrecy is one of the four kinds of seal that in the Terma tradition are linked to the transmission of the teachings. The others are the seal of samaya, the seal of the treasure, and the seal of the mind mandate.
19. *'dzam bu gling*, the continent of rose apples (Skt. *Jambudvipa*), the name of the region in the traditional Buddhist cosmology corresponding to our world.
20. An account of the life of Mandarava is found in the collected writings of the great tertön Orgyen Lingpa (1323–?)
21. *grangs med bskal pa*. The expression *unnumbered ages* does not in fact mean infinity, but a specific period of time defined by Vasubandhu in his *Abhidharmakosha* as 10^{59} kalpas. A kalpa is a time sequence comprising four phases: formation, duration, and dissolution of a universal system, together with the period of voidness preceding the formation of the subsequent system.
22. These details refer to the story of how Tara, the female Bodhisattva of compassion, first generated bodhichitta, the decision to attain Buddhahood for the sake of beings. See *The Words of My Perfect Teacher*, part 1, chap. 6, pp. 153–157.
23. *rdo rje lha mo*, vajra goddess, dakini, the enlightened principle in female form.
24. The instrument in question is the *piwang*, a two-stringed "viol," held upright on the knee and played with a bow.
25. A three-thousandfold universe is a cosmic system comprising a billion universes (sometimes referred to as a thousand million worlds), which is the field of action of one supreme Nirmanakaya Buddha. For the description of one universe, see glossary entry for *Mount Meru*.
26. This lake is at Drakda (*sbrags mda'*) about twenty-five miles south of Lhasa.
27. The eighteen features that characterize a precious human existence consist of eight freedoms and ten endowments. The eight freedoms

consist in not being born (1) in the realms of hell, (2) as a hungry ghost, (3) as an animal, (4) in the realms of the long-lived gods, (5) among barbarous people, ignorant of pure ethics, 6) as one with wrong views such as those of nihilism, (7) in a place where a Buddha has not appeared, and (8) as mentally handicapped. The ten endowments are subdivided into five that are considered as intrinsic, and five as extrinsic, to the personality. The five intrinsic endowments are (1) to be born as a human being, (2) to inhabit a land where the Dharma is proclaimed, (3) to be in possession of normal faculties, (4) to be someone not karmically inclined to great negativity and (5) to have faith in the Dharma. The five extrinsic endowments are the facts (1) that a Buddha has appeared in the world, (2) that he has expounded the Doctrine, (3) that his Doctrine still persists, (4) that it is practiced, and (5) that one is accepted as a disciple by a spiritual master.

28. Apparently a reference to an incident already mentioned at the beginning of chapter one.

29. The divine sphere of the formless world, the most exalted state possible in samsara.

30. In tantric Buddhism much use is made of meditational deities in the peaceful and wrathful forms that enlightened beings may assume in accordance to the mental dispositions of disciples and in order to lead beings on the path. Between such peaceful and wrathful expressions, there is essentially no difference and it is important to understand that wrath in this context has nothing to do with ordinary anger. Such ferocious manifestations are means to pacify, transform, and liberate beings who cannot be tamed peacefully. Similarly, when a practitioner meditates on a wrathful deity, this is not meant as an expression of his own anger and is not a reinforcement of a mere defilement. It is rather a powerful technique that works on negative emotion, transforming it into the pure energy of wisdom.

31. *shing bal*, literally "tree wool," a kind of lichen or moss that grows in long strands and hangs from the branches of certain trees.

32. The point of mentioning Mount Meru and the four continents here is that, aside from actually offering his whole empire to the Guru, the king was visualizing it as an entire universal system.

33. *bden pa bzhi*. The Four Noble Truths (of suffering, the causes of suffering, the cessation of suffering, and the path to this cessation)

constituted the subject of the Buddha's first teaching after his enlightenment.

34. Buddhist teaching speaks of five kinds of eye, representing the five faculties of Buddhahood: (1) the eye of flesh, referring to the ability to perceive all forms, gross or subtle, throughout a thousand million worlds; (2) the divine eye, the knowledge of the births and deaths of all beings; (3) the wisdom eye, the knowledge of the void nature of all phenomena; (4) the Dharma eye, the knowledge of all the eighty-four thousand sections of the Doctrine; (5) the Buddha eye, or omniscience.

35. The three ways of serving a spiritual master are to put into practice whatever he teaches; to render him practical service, physical and verbal; and to make material offerings.

36. The great variety of practices exists to cater to the different needs and disposition of disciples. They are all paths leading to enlightenment, though some may be swifter than others. It is only the perseverance with which a given path is pursued that ensures the attainment of the goal; it is not that some paths are better than others. In the case of most practitioners, it is not necessary to implement all sadhanas; one sadhana, practiced perfectly, is enough to actualize the fruit. However, in order for all these spiritual disciplines to continue, it is necessary for them to be "held" and transmitted. For this reason, Yeshe Tsogyal practiced each and every teaching that she received from Guru Rinpoche and achieved the respective result. She was therefore able to transmit them with perfect authority and power. This way of practicing has been continued down to the present age by all the great masters of the Nyingma lineage.

37. In the course of this book we have usually given the phonetic spelling of the Tibetan title of sadhanas and teachings without translation. It is in fact practically impossible to produce an adequate rendering of titles of texts without an intimate knowledge of their contents, and approximate translations would only add to the confusion. In the present case, the title refers to an important cycle of teachings that was concealed as a treasure and discovered by Orgyen Lingpa in the fourteenth century.

38. The eight great fears refer to the dangers of fire, water, earth, air, elephants, snakes, bandits, and tyrants.

39. See glossary entry for *demon*.

40. Commenting on this obscure expression, Dilgo Khyentse Rinpoche said that it is a reference to an act of extreme asceticism. The meaning is undoubtedly that Yeshe Tsogyal devoted herself unsparingly to her meditation and yogic practice.

41. A reference to the subtle energies, conditioned by karma and the emotions, that course though the channels of the subtle body and have an effect on both the mind and the ordinary physical body. When these energies are purified and brought under control, they become the pure energy of wisdom.

42. This chakra is normally said to have sixty-four petals, or channels, branching out of it. The tantras sometimes vary in the descriptions they give of the chakras and channels.

43. Skt. *bhaga*, the secret space of the woman, the womb. Very often in the context of the Mantrayana this refers to the Dharmadhatu, the space of absolute purity.

44. The two kinds of knowledge are the knowledge of the nature of phenomena (*ji lta ba'i mkhyen pa*) and the knowledge of individual phenomena in all their multiplicity (*ji snyed pa'i mkhyen pa*).

45. Traditionally, one speaks of four degrees of faith: vivid, yearning, confident, and irreversible. See *The Words of My Perfect Teacher*, part 2, chap. 1.

46. "Jarung Khashor" refers to the great stupa of Bodnath near Kathmandu in Nepal. The three young men of Mön were earlier incarnations of Guru Padmasambhava, Abbot Shantarakshita, and King Trisong Detsen.

47. The physical features described mark out Arya Salé as a daka, a spiritual "hero," the male counterpart of a dakini. Dakas are said to have a pronounced webbing of skin visible at the base of their fingers.

48. Another name of Guru Padmasambhava.

49. *A-shé* is a technical name for the vertical line in the Tibetan letter *A*. It is slightly splayed at the top and pointed at the bottom and, when written upside down, symbolizes a flame.

50. These details allude to the mandala of a wrathful deity.

51. A careful reading will show that in this song Guru Rinpoche gives step by step the entire program of Tsogyal's life and practice as these unfold in the rest of the book.

52. Often a poetic epithet for the sun.

53. *gos dkar mo* (Skt. Pandaravasini, lit. Lady of the White Robe). This is the female Buddha, consort of Amitabha, representing the intrinsically pure nature of the element of fire. According to the explanation given by Zenkar Rinpoche, *gos kar* is still the current word in the dialect of the nomads for the hearth or fireplace.
54. This refers to a rare but still existing practice called chulen (*bcud len*), in which the yogi forsakes ordinary food for a varying space of time and instead nourishes himself on the essence of the elements, using as a support various medicinal pills and concentration. This is a powerful practice that purifies the physical body and refines the wind-energy and essence. It is, however, extremely difficult to perform nowadays, when the essential elements of the universe are so much weakened by physical and mental pollutants. It has been said, however, that there are still hermits in the mountains of Tibet who live without any means of ordinary sustenance and who have never been discovered by the Chinese forces. This practice of chulen is still performed among the Tibetans in exile.
55. The expanse of Samantabhadri is the space of absolute reality or emptiness (Tib. *chos dbyings*, Skt. *dharmadhatu*).
56. The seven seas are regions of the universal ocean around Mount Meru. They are the pleasant abode of the naga kings.
57. A reference to the classification of diseases according to the four Medical Tantras.
58. A reference to the counteractive meditations as a means of overcoming defilement, as described, for example, in Shantideva's *Bodhicharyavatara*, "The Way of the Bodhisattva."
59. This prophecy is fulfilled by the end of the book.
60. A reference to the great yogini Machig Labdrön (1055–1145), the foremost Tibetan disciple of Phadampa Sangye, mentioned below. See *Women of Wisdom* (London: RKP, 1984), pp. 143–204.
61. Phadampa Sangye, the Indian master who introduced the doctrine and practice of chö (*gchod*) and pacification (*zhi byed*) to Tibet.
62. *sgrub chen*. During a group practice of Tantric ritual, the participants are identified and nominated to specific functions.
63. A lake in western Tibet near Mount Kailash, still an important place of pilgrimage.
64. *glang*. A reference to King Lang Darma, who assassinated his brother Ralpachen and usurped the throne, after which he tried to annihilate Buddhism in Tibet.

65. This is described at the beginning of chapter five.
66. Shenrab Miwo of Zhang was the founder of the Bön religion. According to some traditions, he was a contemporary of Buddha Shakyamuni, but other authorities assert that he lived much earlier.
67. The temple of Lhasa (i.e., the Jokhang), the temple of Ramoche and that of Trandruk are among the most sacred places in Tibet. King Songtsen Gampo had two wives, the Nepalese princess Bhrikuti and the Chinese princess Wen Chen. Both were Buddhists, and each brought to Tibet a precious image of Buddha Shakyamuni, for which each built a special temple: the Rasa Tsuklakhang and the Ramoche Tsuklakhang respectively. Since the image brought by the Chinese princess was said to have been blessed personally by Shakyamuni, it has always been an object of particular reverence, being known as the Jowo Rinpoche (Precious Lord). Later the images were exchanged so that the Jowo was eventually located in the Rasa Tsuklakhang, which is consequently known as the Jokhang and which is regarded as the main temple in Lhasa. The Border-taming (*mtha' 'dul*) and Further-Taming (*yang 'dul*) temples were built in the same period. They had a geomantic function and were placed at certain key positions in the country, their purpose being to subjugate forces hostile to the propagation of the Doctrine. More information can be found in Dudjom Rinpoche, *History of the Nyingma School*, book 2, p. 510, n.543 (Somerville, Mass.: Wisdom Publications, 1991).
68. Gyalpo, Gongpo, place gods, and earth lords belong to a complex classification of nonhuman entities, the latter two being peculiarly attached to specific regions and places. The worship of these spirit powers was a fundamental characteristic of Bön, the aboriginal tradition of Tibet. Since Buddhism precludes the taking of refuge in such beings and the adoration of them, its gradual propagation in Tibet eventually disrupted the link that had been created between the human inhabitants and the spirits of the country. This resulted in a profound disturbance in which the spirits played havoc and seriously prevented the progress of the teaching, specifically the building of the monastery of Samye. The main purpose of Guru Padmasambhava's journey to Tibet was to pacify these chthonic and elemental powers. He brought them under control and bound them under oath, thus harnessing their energies for the protection and service of the Dharma. As we have seen in chapter five, Yeshe Tsogyal did the same.

69. There seems to be a parallel here with the three levels of the formless realm of Buddhist cosmology, except that the Bön enumerate them in the reverse order.

70. The temple precinct of Samye constituted an enormous mandala representing the structure of an entire universal system.

71. *dran pa nam mkha'*. Although he is mentioned only in passing, Drenpa Namkha is a figure of particular interest. He was an important Bönpo priest who later became a disciple of Guru Padmasambhava. He is said to have offered many Bönpo teachings to Padmasambhava, who subsequently concealed them as Treasures. See Tulku Thondup, *Hidden Teachings of Tibet*, pp. 173 ff.

72. This is presumably a reference to the Jowo Rinpoche, one of the images of Shakyamuni Buddha brought to Tibet by the wives of Songtsen Gampo and which was, and still is, in the main temple of Lhasa. See note 67.

73. See the earlier mention of Bönmo in the account of the Samye debate on page 120.

74. In other words, they would never again revert to the samsaric state.

75. In other words, the secret empowerment. See glossary entry for *empowerment*.

76. *bsdu ba'i dngos po bzhi*, the four ways in which a Bodhisattva attracts disciples: generosity, pleasant speech, teaching in accordance with individuals' needs, and acting in accordance with what is taught.

77. See the incident described in chapter 5, page 96.

78. See glossary entry for *Creation and Perfection*.

79. See glossary entry for *four activities*.

80. This sentence, which is echoed by a great song of realization in chap. 8, page 161, may be compared with similar passages in the *Bodhicharyavatara* (chap. 3, verses 8–11, 18–22). See Shantideva, *The Way of the Bodhisattva: A Translation of the Bodhicharyavatara*, trans. by the Padmakara Translation Group (Boston & London: Shambhala Publications, 1997).

81. Indra and Nanda have already been mentioned, summoned in Tsogyal's song of accomplishment on page 80.

82. *Tönmin* and *Tsemin* are Tibetan forms of Chinese words. The first refers to the teachings of Hashang Mahayana, a Chinese master who propounded the theory of instantaneous enlightenment. The term *Tsemin* refers to the gradualist position of the master Kamala-

shila. These two masters confronted each other in the celebrated debate of Samye (792–794), in which Kamalashila was victorious. Subsequently, the teachings of Hashang disappeared from Tibet.

83. The temple of Kharchung had been built by Mutri Tsenpo, the second of Trisong Detsen's sons.

84. This is the famous "Seven-Line Prayer," the single most sacred and important invocation of Guru Rinpoche, originally recited by the dakinis. It appears almost without fail in every Terma Treasure. Its many levels of meaning, which contain the outer, inner, and innermost teachings of the tantra, have been explained in the *rnam bshad pad ma dkar po* of Mipham Rinpoche (1846–1912).

85. Here, the nickname Senalek refers to the prince Murum Tsenpo. In other sources, this name is given to his elder brother, Mutri Tsenpo.

86. Otherwise known as the "eight worldly dharmas," these are the normal preoccupations of ordinary people who lack a clear spiritual perspective. They are gain and loss, pleasure and pain, praise and criticism, fame and infamy. A spirit of indifference with regard to these eight situations is a mark of a true spiritual practitioner.

87. The ground: primordial purity, voidness.

88. According to Tsele Natsok Rangdrol (see *The Lotus-Born* [Boston & London: Shambhala 1993]), the ancient Tibetans calculated time using the Indian system of six-month "years." According to this reckoning, Yeshe Tsogyal left the world at the age of 106, which is more plausible than the figure given in the text. This is more or less corroborated by other historical calculations. Tibetan dates are notoriously difficult to pinpoint, but following the normally accepted dating, a period of ninety-five years separates the birth of Trisong Detsen and the death of Tri Ralpachen (who is recorded as being alive at the time of the Dakini's passing). In other words, assuming that Yeshe Tsogyal was exactly the same age as Trisong Detsen (though she was probably younger), she can reasonably be said to have lived for about a hundred years. This also fits well enough with the fact that one of her final songs is addressed to the incarnation of her former disciple and companion Arya Salé—given that the latter died young and Gyalwa Changchub was in his thirties, say, at the time of Yeshe Tsogyal's departure.

89. In other words the signs of progress on the path.

90. This means to dedicate one's merit in a way that is free from three

conceptions: the notions of a truly existent subject who dedicates, merit that is dedicated, and the aim of dedication.

91. See glossary entry for *twelve interdependent links*.

92. *chos dred*, impervious to teaching: in other words, one on whom the Dharma has no effect. A person may have an excellent intellectual understanding of the Doctrine, but if he fails to put what he knows into practice, his mind remains hard and coarse.

93. *lhun grub*, self-presence: clarity, the spontaneous presence of awareness.

94. *bla gyu*, spirit-gem: a stone, in this case a turquoise, closely connected with the life force of human beings.

95. These are: *mkha' 'gro sku gsum rkyang sgrub; spyod yul 'dul ba dkar po; thog 'beb drag spyod rnam gsum; bla ma sku gsum rkyang sgrub; byin brlabs dbang gi sgo mo; gzer 'joms lta ba cig chod; rtags tshad so pa dgu 'dres; gnad kyi me btsa' rnam gsum; rdzas sngags dmigs yul brgya rtsa; rjes gcod lcam bu gzer them*.

96. *bla ma mkha' 'gro zung 'jug tu sgrub thabs; bsgom pa sgyu ma 'phrul 'gros; rtsa rlung 'gag don bcu pa; man ngag gcig chog zab mo; bsgyur sbyang spel ba rnam gsum; mkha' 'gro'i bang mdzod mig gcig; mkha' 'gro'i dmar ba snying cig; mkha' 'gro gnyen po srog cig; man ngag sngags kha sum sbrel; 'od zer zhags pa rnam gsum; dpa' bo gyad stobs rnam gsum*.

97. *bla ma mkha' 'gro rang lus dbyer med du sgrub thabs; lta ba phyag rgya chen po; 'bras bu rdzogs chen cig chod; man ngag gtum mo gsum sbrel; gdams ngag thos chog rnam gsum; nyams len bsgom pa rnam gsum; gcig chog mun chos rnam gsum; las phran dgos pa rnam gsum; rten 'brel me long rnam gsum; rgyab chos dgos pa rnam gsum; bka' srung myur mgyogs rnam gsum; drag sngags gnad kha rnam gsum*.

98. See the incident of the wounded ox in chapter five. This is a reference to the king Lang Darma.

99. See chapter five, page 97.

100. A reference to the reestablishment of the monastic order after Lang Darma's persecution. Lower Kham, or Mekham, was one of the places where the monastic lineage was preserved and from where it began to spread again when the persecution was lifted.

101. This and the following three paragraphs contain references to the growth of the so-called New Translations Schools (*gsar ma*) of Tibetan Buddhism, which spread at the revival of the Dharma after the assassination of Lang Darma.

Atisha (982–1054) was a renowned teacher of the university of Vikramashila in India. He spent the last twelve years of his life in Tibet reviving the teachings and breathing new life into the monastic tradition of which he was a staunch upholder. Perhaps surprisingly, his closest disciple was the layman Drom Tönpa (1005–1064), who founded the monastery of Reting (*ra bsgrengs*) and inaugurated the renowned Kadampa tradition, which emphasized strict and earnest practice and a full understanding of the teaching. The traditional lineage of the Kadampas did not survive as a distinct entity but has had a pervasive influence on all four schools of Tibetan Buddhism.

The teachings of Path and Fruit (*lam 'bras*) propounded by the Sakya school were translated from the Sanskrit by Drogmi Yeshe (993–1050). The leaders of this school eventually assumed temporal power in Tibet, the first dynasty, so to speak, of lama kings, and exerted spiritual influence over the Chinese emperor.

The Kargyu schools base themselves on the teachings of the Kadampas and the tantras of the new translations. The founder of Dhakpo Kargyu was Marpa the Translator (1012–1099), himself a student of Drogmi Yeshe. He journeyed to India and Nepal several times and received the teachings of Mahamudra from numerous great Indian masters. His lineage passed to his celebrated disciple Milarepa and from him to Gampopa of Dhakpo.

The Phagtru Kargyud was founded by Phagmo Trupa Dorje Gyalpo (1110–?), who received the Mahamudra teachings from Gampopa.

The Karma Kagyu was founded by Karmapa Dusum Khyenpa (1110–1193), also a student of Gampopa. He was to become the teacher of the Chinese emperor, who bestowed on him the title Karma Pakshi.

Other Kagyu schools include Drigung, founded by Kyura Rinpoche (1143–1192), a disciple of Phagmo Trupa, as was also Taklung Trashi Pel (1142–?), who founded the Taklung Kargyud. Another great disciple of Phagmo Trupa was Lingje Repa (1128?–1188), who founded the Drukpa Kargyu lineage.

The lineage of the Virtuous Ones, or Gelugpas, was founded by the renowned scholar and monk Tsongkhapa Lobzang Drakpa (1357–1419). It was the Gelugpa order that grew to political dominance in Tibet, lasting until the present time.

102. This verse line, in which the symbolic script appears, remains a

mystery. It has been explained as a possible hidden reference to the catastrophe that has overwhelmed Tibet in the twentieth century.

103. This diminution of age follows the traditional cosmological teaching according to which the "abiding phase" in the history of a universal system comprises several so-called "intermediary" time cycles. In the course of each cycle, the span of human life gradually decreases and increases—going from the eighty thousand years to ten years and back again. Our present era is said to be located close to the lowest point of one such intermediary cycle.

104. The hundred: rather, the hundred and eight main authentic tertöns.

105. It is said (see Tulku Thondup, *Hidden Teachings of Tibet*) that sometimes false Termas are discovered, the product of evil-intentioned persons in the past who made powerful aspirations to corrupt the Terma teachings. It also happens that other people, without spiritual accomplishment but inspired by evil influences, produce apparently great and beneficial works, which nevertheless are incapable of leading to enlightenment. In Tibet, all newly discovered Treasures were for this reason verified and checked by acknowledged masters.

106. This is probably a reference to the Tertön Pawo Taksham Dorje, also referred to as Taksham Samten Lingpa, who did in fact discover the present Treasure.

107. Five hundred periods multiplied by five: This refers to the evolution of a Buddha's doctrine, passing through five stages, each comprising five hundred periods. These periods refer not to predetermined lapses of time, but to sequences of growth and decline in the life of the Dharma, varying in length according to causes and conditions.

108. A reference to one of the most important monasteries of the Nyingma tradition, located in Kham and founded by Kadampa Deshek (1122–1192).

109. *A* (pronounced *Ah*): the last letter in the Tibetan alphabet, symbolizing emptiness, the ultimate nature of all phenomena.

110. *dkor nag*, black possessions: This refers to the possessions of the Sangha and all objects dedicated to religion but wrongly appropriated and used for private purposes.

Glossary

ABHIDHARMA, Skt. (*mngon pa,* Tib.). The third part of the Tripitaka, the "three baskets." The Abhidharma is the corpus of texts expounding Buddhist metaphysical teaching.

ACCOMPLISHMENTS, SUPREME AND ORDINARY (*dngos grub,* Tib.; *siddhi,* Skt.). The supreme accomplishment is the attainment of Buddhahood. Ordinary accomplishments are miraculous powers acquired in the course of spiritual training. These powers, the reality of which is also recognized in spiritual traditions other than Buddhism, are not regarded as ends in themselves. They are, nevertheless, taken as signs of progress and are employed for the benefit of the teachings and disciples.

AGAMA, Skt. (*lung,* Tib.). A text elucidating the meaning of a tantra.

AKANISHTA, Skt. (*'og min,* Tib.). In general, this term indicates the highest of all Buddha-fields. Akanishta is in fact divided into six levels, ranging from the highest heaven of the form realm up to the absolute pure land of the Dharmakaya.

AMITABHA, Skt. (*'od dpag med* or *snang ba mtha' yas,* Tib.), lit. Boundless Light. The Buddha of the Lotus Family corresponding to *all-perceiving wisdom,* which is the pure nature of the aggregate of perception and the affliction of desire. It is associated with the enlightened activity of attraction or magnetizing. *See* five Families

AMITAYUS, Skt. (*tshe dpag med,* Tib.), lit. Boundless Life. An aspect of Buddha Amitabha, usually represented in Sambhogakaya form. Meditation on Amitayus prolongs life.

AMOGHASIDDHI, Skt. (*don yod grub pa,* Tib.), lit. Accomplishment of Purpose. The Buddha of the Activity Family, corresponding to *all-accomplishing wisdom,* which is the pure nature of the aggregate of conditioning factors and the affliction of jealousy. It is associated with the enlightened activity of forceful subjugation.

AMRITA, Skt. (*bdud rtsi,* Tib.), lit. nectar of immortality, sometimes translated as "ambrosia." A substance (liquid or solid) prepared with the help of tantric rituals. It symbolizes Wisdom.

ANUYOGA, Skt. In the system of nine vehicles used in the Nyingma tradition, the second of the inner sections of tantra. In Anuyoga, emphasis is placed on the perfection stage of tantric practice. This is characterized by the experience of emptiness and meditation on the subtle channels, energies, and essence of the physical body.

APPROACH AND ACCOMPLISHMENT (*bsnyen sgrub,* Tib.). Progressive stages in the generation stage of tantric practice, in the course of which yogis gradually identify themselves with the deity through visualization and the recitation of mantra.

ARHAT, Skt. (*dgra bcom pa*, Tib.), lit. Foe-Destroyer. One who has vanquished the enemies of afflictive emotion and is thus definitively liberated from the sufferings of samsara. Arhatship is the goal of the teachings of the root vehicle, the Shravakayana.

ARYA, Skt. (*'phags pa*, Tib.), lit. noble. A being who has transcended samsaric existence. There are four classes of Aryas: Arhats, Pratyekabuddhas, Bodhisattvas, and Buddhas.

ASURA, Skt. (*lha min*, Tib.). Demigods, one of six classes of beings in samsara.

ATI, ATIYOGA, Skt. The last and highest of the inner tantras, the summit of the system of nine vehicles according to the Nyingma classification. *See also* Great Perfection

ATSARA. Tibetan deformation of the Sanskrit word *acharya*, teacher. By extension, the Tibetan word indicates any Indian.

AVADHUTI, Skt. (*rtsa dbu ma*, Tib.). The subtle central channel of the body into which, by means of the practice of the perfection stage (*rdzogs rim*), the subtle wind-energies are gathered, a process that gives rise to nondual wisdom. By extension, the term *avadhuti* is often used loosely to indicate nondual wisdom.

AVALOKITESHVARA, Skt. (*spyan ras gzigs*, Tib.), the "Lord who Sees." Name of the Bodhisattva who embodies the compassion of all the Buddhas. Avalokiteshvara, sometimes called Avalokita, is the Sambhogakaya emanation of the Buddha Amitabha.

AWARENESS (*rig pa*, Tib.). The primordial state of the mind, clear, awake, free from grasping: the union of emptiness and clarity.

BARDO, Tib. (*bar do*). An intermediary state. This term most often refers to the state separating death and subsequent rebirth.

BHAGA, Skt. Womb. By extension, this term refers to the Dharmadhatu, emptiness.

BHIKSHU, Skt. (*dge slong*, Tib.). A fully ordained monk.

BODHICHITTA, Skt. (*byang chub kyi sems*, Tib.). On the relative level, this is the wish to attain Buddhahood for the sake of all sentient beings, together with the practice necessary to accomplish this. On the absolute level, it is nondual wisdom, the ultimate nature of the mind, and the true status of all phenomena. In certain tantric contexts, it refers to the essential physical substance that is the support of the mind.

BODHISATTVA, Skt. (*byang chub sems dpa'*, Tib.). One who through compassion strives to attain the full enlightenment of Buddhahood for the sake of all beings. Bodhisattvas may be "ordinary" or "noble" (sometimes referred to as mundane and transmundane respectively), depending on whether they have attained the Mahayana Path of Seeing and are residing on one of the ten Bodhisattva grounds.

BODY. *See* Trikaya

BÖN. The ancient native religion of Tibet, existing at the time of the introduction of Buddhism in the eighth century and surviving to this day. In this translation, the term *Bön* may refer to the tradition itself and also to its adherents, who are, however, sometimes referred to as Bönpo. The relationship between Buddhism and Bön is very complex. Usually a distinction is made between white Bön and black Bön, corresponding to the Inner Bön and the Gyu Bön of the story. The Inner Bön, which exists to this day and has been recognized by the Dalai Lama as the fifth religious tradition, has many teachings in common with the Buddhadharma, to which it is very close.

BRAHMA, Skt. (*tshang pa*, Tib.). A deity of the Hindu pantheon, belonging, in the Buddhist system, to the world of form.

BUDDHA, Skt. (*sangs rgyas,* Tib.). One who has awoken from the deep sleep of ignorance and whose mind has blossomed with the knowledge of all things. According to the Mahayana perspective, there are innumerable Buddhas, the historical Buddha, Shakyamuni, being a single example.

BUDDHA-FIELD (*zhing khams,* Tib.). A sphere or dimension manifested by a Buddha or great Bodhisattva, in which beings may abide and progress towards enlightenment without ever falling into lower states of existence. In fact, any place, viewed as the pure manifestation of spontaneous Wisdom, is a Buddha-field.

CANNIBALS. *See* orc

CAUSAL VEHICLE (*rgyu mtshan nyid kyi theg pa,* Tib.). The vehicle of teachings based on the sutras, according to which beings possess the potential of Buddhahood, which must be gradually developed in order to be fully actualized. By contrast, the Vajrayana or tantra teachings work on the understanding that this Buddha-nature is fully perfect already with no need of development (for this reason it is known as the result vehicle). The purpose of the practice is to dispel the defilements that obscure it.

CENTRAL CHANNEL. *See* avadhuti

CENTRAL LAND. (*yul dbus*, Tib.). A term indicating a country in which the Buddhadharma is proclaimed and practiced.

CHAKRA, Skt. (*'khor lo*, Tib.). Centers of subtle wind-energies situated on the central channel of the body, the avadhuti.

CHANNELS, ENERGIES, AND ESSENCE-DROPS. The subtle channels or veins (*nadi,* Skt.; *rtsa,* Tib.), the wind-energies (*prana; rlung*), and the bodily essences (*bindu; thig le*), which are manipulated and brought under control in the course of Anuyoga practice.

CHIMPHU (*mchims phu*). A mountainside above Samye monastery and the location of many cave hermitages.

CHÖ (*gcod*), lit. cutting, to cut. The name of a yogic practice based on the teaching of the Prajñaparamita, brought to Tibet by the Indian master Phadampa Sangye and propagated by the yogini Machig Lapdrön. The goal of chö is the destruction of ego-clinging.

CLAIRVOYANCE (*mngos shes*, Tib.). There are six kinds of clairvoyance or preternatural knowledge: for example, the knowledge of one's own and others' past existences. The sixth one is the knowledge of the exhaustion of karma and defilement. This is enjoyed by the Buddhas alone.

CONCENTRATION OF HEROIC FEARLESSNESS. *See* threefold concentration

CONTINENT (*gling*, Tib.). In this text, this term refers not to regions of modern geography, but to the regions located around the vast universal mountain that, according the Buddhist cosmology, forms the central axis of one universal world system.

COPPER-COLORED MOUNTAIN (*zangs mdog dpal ri*, Tib.). The Buddha-field of Guru Padmasambhava in Ngayab. *See* Ngayab

CREATION AND PERFECTION. The two principal phases of tantric practice. The creation (also referred to as "generation" and "development") stage (*bskyed rim*) involves meditation on appearances, sounds, and thoughts as deities, mantras, and wisdom, respectively. The perfection stage (*rdzogs rim*) refers to the dissolution of visualized forms into emptiness and the experience of this; it also indicates the meditation on the subtle channels, energies, and essence of the body.

DAKA, Skt. (*dpa' bo*, Tib.), sometimes translated as "hero." The tantric equivalent of a Buddha or Bodhisattva.

DAKINI, Skt. (*mkha' 'gro*, Tib.). Pronounced with the stress on the first syllable: dákini. A feminine personification of Wisdom. A distinction is made between wisdom dakinis who are fully enlightened, and "ordinary" or "worldly" dakinis, who, though not fully enlightened, nevertheless possess spiritual power. In Tibetan, the term is used as a title of respect for highly realized yoginis.

DAKINIS OF THE FOUR CLASSES. This refers to the four enlightened Families of Vajra, Jewel, Lotus, and Action, corresponding to the four types of activity.

DAMARU, Skt. A small ritual drum.

DEITIES AND THEIR CONSORTS (*yab yum*, Tib.). A way of representing the inseparable union of Wisdom and Method, Appearance and Emptiness.

DEITY. *See* god

DEMON (*bdud*, Tib.). When not being used in an obviously metaphorical sense, this term refers either to a spirit or, symbolically, to obstacles on the path. The Demon of the Aggregates refers to the five skandhas (body, sensation, perception, conditioning factors, and consciousness) as described in Buddhist teaching as the basis for the imputation of the notion of "I," the personal self, which constitutes the root cause of suffering in samsara. The Demon of the Afflictions refers to defiled emotions such as attachment, anger, ignorance, pride, and jealousy, which are productive of suffering. The Demon Lord of Death refers not only to actual death but to the momentary transience of all phenomena, the nature of which is suffering. The Demon Son of Gods refers to mental wandering and the attachment to phenomena apprehended as really existent.

DHARMA, Skt. (*chos*, Tib.). The Doctrine, or corpus of teachings given by the Buddha and other enlightened beings, which shows the path to Awakening. It has two aspects: the Dharma of transmission, namely the scriptures and teachings, and the Dharma of realization, the qualities resulting from the spiritual practice.

DHARMADHATU, Skt. (*chos dbyings*, Tib.). The expanse of ultimate reality, emptiness.

DHARMAKAYA, Skt. *See* Trikaya

DHARMAPALA, Skt. (*chos skyong,* Tib.). A protector of the teachings. These normally nonhuman entities are sometimes emanations of Buddhas and Bodhisattvas, and sometimes local spirits, gods, or demons who have been subjugated by a great spiritual master and bound under oath. The harnessing of their energy in the service of the Doctrine is considered to have played a decisive role in the preservation of the teachings from its beginnings in Tibet until the present time. In the form of oracles, such as that of Nechung, for example, the dharmapalas continue to exert a direct influence on Tibetan life.

DHARMATA, Skt. (*chos nyid*, Tib.). The ultimate nature of phenomena.

DIAMOND BODY or VAJRA BODY. *See* Trikaya; rainbow body

DIAMOND THRONE (*rdo rje gdan*, Tib.; Vajrasana, Skt.). Bodhgaya in India, where the Buddha Shakyamuni attained enlightenment beneath the Bodhi tree.

DORJE DROLÖ, Tib. (*rdo rje gro lod*). A wrathful manifestation of Guru Padmasambhava.

DRI, Tib. (*'bri*). A female yak.

DZO, Tib. (*mdzo*). A cross between a yak and a cow.

DZOGCHEN, Tib. (*rdzogs chen*). *See* Great Perfection

EIGHT GREAT HERUKAS (*sgrub pa bka' brgyad*, Tib.). The eight main yidam deities and sadhanas of the Mahayoga tantra. They are *gshin rje gshed* (*Yamantaka*—body), *rta mgrin* (Hayagriva—speech), *yang dag* (Vishuddha—mind), *che mchog* (Amrita—qualities), *phur pa* (Kila—activities), *ma mo rbod gtong* (or Lame Heruka), *dmod pa drag sngags* (or Tobden Nagpo), *'jig rten mchod bstod* (or Drekpa Kundul). The last three sadhanas are connected with three classes of worldly deities (*'jig rten pa'i sde gsum*).

EKADZATI, Tib. (Ekajati, Skt.). A female wisdom protector of the tantric teachings, an emanation of Samantabhadri. *See* dharmapala

ELEMENTS (*'byung ba*, Tib.). *See* five elements

EMAHO. *See* Kyeho

EMPOWERMENT (*dbang*, Tib.). In this text, the terms *empowerment* and *initiation* are treated as synonyms. Of these two, *initiation*, though in many ways unsatisfactory, has the advantage of indicating that it is the point of entry into tantric practice. On the other hand, *empowerment* is closer to the Tibetan term, which refers to the transference of wisdom power, from master to disciple, allowing and enabling them to engage in the practice and to reap its fruit. In general, there are four levels of tantric empowerment. The first is the Vase Empowerment, which purifies the defilements and obscurations associated with the body, grants the blessings of the Vajra Body, authorizes the disciple to practice the yogas of the generation stage, and enables him or her to attain the Nirmanakaya. The second is the Secret Empowerment. This purifies the defilements and obscurations of the speech faculty; grants the blessings of Vajra Speech; authorizes the disciple to practice the yogas of the perfection stage connected with the subtle channels, wind-energies, and essence of his own body; and enables the disciple to attain the Sambhogakaya. The third empowerment is the Wisdom Empowerment. This purifies the defilements and obscurations associated with the mind; grants the blessings of the Vajra Mind; authorizes the practice of yogas of the "Skillful Path," and enables the disciple to attain the Dharmakaya. The final empowerment, which is often simply referred to as "the Fourth Initiation," is the Precious Word Empowerment. This purifies the defilements of body, speech, and mind and all karmic and cognitive obscurations, grants the blessings of Primordial Wisdom, authorizes the disciple to engage in the practice of Dzogchen, and makes possible the attainment of the Svabhavikakaya.

This is a simplification of a highly complex subject. It is perhaps worth pointing out that these empowerments only truly occur when the transition of spiritual power from the master is actually experienced by the disciple, who is thereby completely transformed. Failing that, which is of course the case for most people, empowerment does not, strictly speaking, occur. Empowerment ceremonies are, in the vast majority of cases, symbolic; they are, so to speak, "sacramental blessings." These blessings are nevertheless important and in fact indispensable, in that they constitute an authorization for the practice and create auspicious links that prepare the disciple for the moment when real empowerment can take place. It goes without saying that in the case of Guru Rinpoche and Yeshe Tsogyal, the empowerments were truly transmitted and received.

ENERGIES, WIND-ENERGIES (*rlung*, Tib.). Subtle energies circulating in the subtle channels of the body and acting as the vehicle of the essence-drops, the support of the mind.

ESSENCE, ESSENCE-DROP (*thig le*, Tib.). On the external level, this is regarded as the quintessential element of the physical body. On the subtle level, the term is used to refer to the "absolute bodhichitta," in other words, the nature of the mind.

FELICITY, GREAT. *See* Great Bliss

FIELD OF MERIT (*tshogs zhing*, Tib.). The focus or object of a practitioner's devotion, offerings, and prayers, whereby merit and wisdom are accumulated on the path towards enlightenment.

FIVE AGGREGATES (*phung po lnga*, Tib.). Body, feeling, perception, conditioning factors, and consciousness. These are the constituting elements of the "personality." When they occur together, there arises the false impression of a self existing separately as an independent entity.

FIVE BODIES. *See* Trikaya

FIVE ELEMENTS (*'byung ba lnga*, Tib.). Earth, air, fire, water, and space, the principles of solidity, movement, heat, liquidity, and unobstructiveness.

FIVE FAMILIES (*rigs lnga*, Tib.). The five Buddha Families, namely: Tathagata, Vajra, Jewel, Lotus, and Action. These represent five aspects of Buddhahood. They are presided over by the Dhyani Buddhas, who are generally depicted in a mandala arrangement as follows: blue Vairochana in the center (Tathagata), white Vajrasattva in the east (Vajra), yellow Ratnasambhava in the south (Jewel), red Amitabha in the west (Lotus), and green Amoghasiddhi in the north (Action).

FIVE SCIENCES (*rig lnga*, Tib.). The five subjects traditionally mastered by a pandita, namely: art and handicrafts, medicine, philology, logic, and philosophy.

FIVE SUBSTANCES OF SAMAYA (*dam tshig gi rdzas lnga*, Tib.). Semen, blood, urine, excrement, and flesh. These substances, which are ordinarily regarded as repulsive, are transformed into the five nectars (and are so called) when their pure nature is realized.

FIVE WISDOMS (*ye shes lnga*, Tib.). Five aspects of Buddha's mind, correlated with the Dhyani Buddhas of the five Families: the wisdom of the absolute space (Vairochana), mirror-like wisdom (Vajrasattva), the wisdom of equality (Ratnasambhava), all-perceiving wisdom (Amitabha), and all-accomplishing wisdom (Amoghasiddhi).

FLEET-FOOT (*rkang mgyogs*, Tib.). One of the ordinary accomplishments. The yogic ability to travel great distances extremely quickly and without fatigue.

FOUR ACTIVITIES (*phrin las bzhi*, Tib.). Four types of activity performed by realized beings to help others and eliminate unfavorable circumstances: pacifying, increasing, attracting or magnetizing, and fierce subjugation.

FOUR GREAT KINGS (realm of). Four spiritual powers ruling over a celestial realm situated in the world of desire. They are associated with the four cardinal directions, of which they are considered to be the guardians.

FOUR IMMEASURABLE QUALITIES (*tsad med bzhi*, Tib.). Four thoughts directed to the entire aggregate of living beings, which are therefore described as incomensurable. They are boundless love, boundless compassion, boundless sympathetic joy, and boundless impartiality.

FOUR JOYS (*dga' ba bzhi*, Tib.). Four experiences, totally transcending ordinary pleasure, that are in essence wisdom. They form an aspect of the practices associated with the third initiation.

GANACHAKRA (Skt.; *tshogs*, Tib.) feast or sacred feast. A ritual offering in tantric Buddhism in which food and drink are blessed as the elixir of wisdom and offered to the yidam as well as to the deities of the mandala of one's own body.

GANDHARVA, Skt. (*dri za*, Tib.). A member of a class of nonhuman beings said to be nourished on smells. They are renowned for their beauty and generally associated with music.

GARUDA, Skt. (*khyung*, Tib.). A kind of bird, in Indian and Tibetan mythology, traditionally of great size, the chicks of which are said to emerge from the shell already equipped with feathers and able to fly immediately. It is a symbol of Primordial Wisdom.

GENERATION AND PERFECTION. *See* creation and perfection

GOD (*lha,* Tib.; *deva*, Skt.). A class of beings, superior to the human state, enjoying immense longevity, but not immortal. It is worth bearing in mind that in Sanskrit and Tibetan, *deva* and *lha* are technical terms commonly used to refer to the yidams and other deities in a mandala, the Buddha, the Guru, and any great figure such as a king. As Radhakrishnan points out, the term *deva* is associated with the act of giving, and there is no doubt a connection with this term and the words for giving in many Indo-European languages. The creator is termed *deva* because he "gives the universe," sun and moon are so called because they give light, the king because he gives protection, and the Buddha and the Guru because they give the Doctrine. The fact that gods or deities are often referred to in Tibetan Buddhism does not therefore imply that it is a species of polytheism.

GREAT AND LESSER MARKS OF ENLIGHTENMENT (*mtshan dang dpe byed*, Tib.). Thirty-two major marks and eighty minor physical marks characteristic of a Buddha. These include the wheels that mark his palms and soles, golden hue of his body, copper-colored fingernails, among others.

GREAT BLISS (*bde ba chen po*, Tib.). Bliss inherent in the nature of the mind but totally beyond the ordinary sensation of pleasure.

GREAT COMPASSIONATE ONE (*thugs rje chen po*, Tib.). A title of Avalokiteshvara, the Bodhisattva of compassion; the Sambhogakaya aspect of the Buddha Amitabha, of whom Guru Rinpoche is himself the Nirmanakaya aspect.

GREAT MOTHER (*yum chen mo*, Tib.). The Prajñaparamita, transcendent Wisdom, direct realization of emptiness, so called because such realization is the source or "mother" of Buddhahood.

GREAT PERFECTION (*rdzogs pa chen po*, Tib.; *mahasandhi*, Skt.). Dzogchen, the ultimate view of the Nyingma school—the union of voidness and awareness, of primordial purity (*ka dag*) and spontaneous presence (*lhun grub*).

GREAT VEHICLE. *See* Mahayana

GROUND (*sa*, Tib.; *bhumi*, Skt.). The ten levels of Bodhisattva realization in Mahayana Buddhism, covering the paths of Seeing and Meditation.

GURU SENGE DRADOK. One of the eight manifestations of Padmasambhava.

GURU YOGA, Skt. (*bla ma'i rnal 'byor*, Tib.). The most important practice in tantric Buddhism, consisting of the visualization of the Guru, prayers and requests for blessing, the reception of these blessings, and the merging of the mind with the Guru's enlightened wisdom mind.

HAYAGRIVA, Skt. (*rta mgrin*, Tib.). Wrathful yidam of the Lotus Family.

HEARER (*nyan thos*, Tib.). *See* Shravaka

HERUKA, Skt. Usually a generic term for a male yidam or meditational deity (generally wrathful or semiwrathful). In whatever form, a heruka is a representation of the ultimate nature of the mind.

HIDDEN LAND (*sbas yul,* Tib.). There are basically two kinds of hidden lands: those physically located on the earth's surface and those which exist in dimensions, so to speak, other than the present world, but which can be entered by certain individuals. Strictly speaking, the Tibetan word *sbas yul* or *béyul* refers only to the first kind, while the second kind are normally referred to as Khachö (*mkha' spyod*). Béyul are regions, secret valleys, etc., specially blessed and sealed by Guru Padmasambhava, and other beings of great spiritual attainment, as places of protection for the teachings in later times of decadence and peril. Except in the case of people with special karma and good fortune, they cannot be entered, or even perceived.

HIGHER INSIGHT (*lhag mthong*, Tib.; *vipashyana*, Skt.). The perception of the ultimate nature of phenomena.

HORPA. A central Asian race, probably the Uighurs, a nomadic people of Turkoman stock.

INDRA, Skt. (*brgya byin*, Tib.). Sovereign god of the Heaven of the Thirty-three, a celestial realm located in the world of desire.

INITIATION. *See* empowerment

KALPA, Skt. (*bskal pa*, Tib.). A time sequence comprising the four phases of formation, duration, and dissolution of a universal system, together with the period of voidness preceding the formation of the subsequent system.

KAMALASHILA. One of the principal disciples of Shantarakshita, continuing his master's synthesis of the Madhyamika and Yogachara (ninth century).

KANGYUR (*bka' 'gyur*, Tib.). The collection of 108 volumes containing the canon of Buddhist scriptures embodying the teachings of the Buddha Shakyamuni.

KAPALA, Skt. (*thod phor*, Tib.). A cup or bowl made from the top of a human skull. Kapalas are used in tantric ceremonies and symbolize nonattachment and the nonexistence of the ego.

KARMA, Skt. (*las*, Tib.). Action; the psychophysical principle of cause and effect (*las rgyu 'bras*), according to which all existential states arise as the result of previous action. Actions that result in the experience of happiness are defined as virtuous; actions that give rise to suffering are nonvirtuous.

KARMAMUDRA, Skt. (*las kyi phyag rgya*, Tib.). In this context, a name given to partner in the practice of skillful means (see definition of *third empowerment* in the entry for *empowerment*). The karmamudra is the source of the wisdom of bliss-voidness.

KATANGA, Skt. (*khatvanga*, Tib.). A special three-pronged trident carried by tantric yogis and specifically by Guru Padmasambhava. No doubt in connection with the story given here of Tsogyal's being hidden in the Guru's trident, in representations of Guru Rinpoche, the katanga is regarded as a symbol of the spiritual consort.

KAYA. *See* Trikaya

KRIYATANTRA, Skt. (*bya rgyud*, Tib.). The first of the three outer tantras, according to the Nyingma system of the nine vehicles, in which emphasis is placed on the purification of the body and speech.

KUNTUZANGPO. *See* Samantabhadra

KYEHO; KYEMA; etc. Tibetan poems, and various other forms of expostulation, are often preceded by exclamatory words or phrases indicative of the general tone and content of what is being said. For example, *Emaho* is an expression of wonder, *Ho* of courage and determination, while *Kyema* and *Kyehü* express grief.

LAMA (*bla ma*, Tib.; Guru, Skt.). Spiritual teacher, explained as the contraction of *bla na med pa*, "nothing superior." The title is sometimes used loosely as a general term to denote a Buddhist monk or even anyone claiming to be a teacher. In the traditional context, however, the title is exclusively attributed to masters with great knowledge and high realization.

LHATHOTHORI. King of Tibet (born ca. 173 CE) during whose reign the Buddhadharma first made its appearance in Tibet in the form of relics and Sanskrit texts of the Buddhist scriptures. While not understanding these writings, the king recognized their sacred character and respectfully preserved them. The first Buddhist king of Tibet, Songtsen Gampo, appeared four generations later.

LIGHT UNBOUNDED. *See* Amitabha

LORDS OF THE THREE FAMILIES. The Bodhisattvas Manjushri, Avalokita, and Vajrapani. In this context, the three Families are respectively those of the Buddha's Body, Speech, and Mind.

LOTUS LIGHT (*pad ma 'od*, Tib.). Name of the palace of Guru Padmasambhava in his pure land, the Glorious Copper-Colored Mountain of Ngayab.

MADHYAMIKA, Skt. (*dbu ma*, Tib.). The highest philosophical view of Mahayana Buddhism, propounded by Nagarjuna in the second century CE.

MAHAMUDRA, Skt. (*phyag rgya chen po*, Tib.). The Great Seal, i.e., the seal of emptiness on all phenomena. It refers both to the path (teaching and practice of the Mahamudra) and the result (accomplishment of Mahamudra). Mahamudra is comparable to the Nyingma teachings of Dzogchen, from which it is, however, subtly different.

MAHASIDDHA, Skt. (*grub thob chen po*, Tib.). *See* Siddha

MAHAYANA, Skt. (*theg pa chen po*, Tib.). The Great Vehicle, the tradition of Buddhism practiced mostly in the countries of northern Asia, China, Japan, Korea, Mongolia, Tibet, and the Himalayan regions. The characteristic of Mahayana is universal compassion and the desire to deliver all sentient beings from suffering and its causes. To this purpose, the goal of the Mahayana is the attainment of the supreme enlightenment of Buddhahood, and the path consists of the practice of the six paramitas. On the philosophical level, the Mahayana comprises two principal schools, Madhyamika and Chittamatra or Yogachara. The Vajrayana, the tantric teachings of Buddhism, is also a branch of the Mahayana.

MAHAYOGA, Skt. The first of the three inner tantras in the Nyingma system of nine vehicles. Here the emphasis is placed on the generation stage practices.

MAITREYA, Skt. (*byams pa*, Tib.). Lit. the Loving One. The Bodhisattva now dwelling in heaven of Tushita who will become the fifth Buddha of this age.

MALA, Skt. (*'phreng ba*, Tib.). A string of 108 beads used for counting during mantra recitation.

MAMO (*ma mo*, Tib.). A dakini, usually of wrathful aspect; a kind of flesh-eating demoness.

MANDALA, Skt. (*dkyil 'khor*, Tib.). This word has several levels of meaning. Most basically, it may be understood simply as a configuration, an intelligible unit of space. The mandala of the deity, for example, is the sacred space at the center of which a wisdom deity is located. A mandala can also be understood as the arrangement of an offering and a powerful means of accumulating merit. It can take several forms, beginning with the offering of desirable objects, including one's own body, and extending to a symbolic offering of the entire universe and even the three kayas. The term is also used honorifically, as when speaking, for instance, of the mandala of the Guru's body.

MANDARAVA. An Indian princess, the daughter of the king of Sahor, Mandarava became the disciple and spiritual consort of Guru Padmasambhava. Her father was outraged and condemned both of them to be burned to death. While they were on the blazing pyre, Guru Padmasambhava miraculously transformed it into a lotus pool (now renowned as the lake Tsopema at Rewalsar in India). This convinced the king of Padmasambhava's great wisdom and power, and he requested teachings and allowed his daughter the freedom to pursue her spiritual destiny. Mandarava went with Guru Padmasambhava as his consort to the great cave of Maratika (now in Nepalese territory) where they actualized the state of vidhyadhara of immortality. Mandarava remained in India but visited Tibet several times.

MANI. *See* mantra of six syllables

MAÑJUSHRI, Skt. (*'jam dpal dbyangs*, Tib.). Name of a Bodhisattva personifying the wisdom of all the Buddhas.

MANTRA, Skt. (*sngags*, Tib.). Syllables or formulas which, recited in the context of sadhanas, visualizations, etc., protect the mind of the practitioner from ordinary perceptions. Mantras are also invocations of, and manifestations of, the yidam in the form of sound. There are three kinds of mantra: (1) vidya-mantras (*rig sngags*), associated with the outer class of tantras, are the essence of skilful means; (2) dharani-mantras (*gzungs*) are the essence of transcendent wisdom and derive from the teachings of the Prajñaparamita; (3) secret mantras (*gsang sngags*) related to the Mahayoga, Anuyoga, and Atiyoga.

MANTRA OF SIX SYLLABLES. The "Mani," the mantra of Avalokiteshvara: *Om Mani Padme Hung*.

MERIT (*bsod nam*, Tib.). Good karma, the positive energy generated by wholesome actions of body, speech, and mind.

MIRAGE-LIKE CONCENTRATION. *See* threefold concentration

MÖN. A Himalayan region corresponding more or less to modern Bhutan with the addition of certain contiguous regions in Tibet itself.

MOTHER (*yum*, Tib.). The feminine principle, wisdom or emptiness. *See* Great Mother; Prajñaparamita

MOUNT MERU (*ri rab*, Tib.). The king of mountains and world-axis, according to the cosmology of ancient India. Around it are located the four continents and eight subcontinents, of which one universe is composed. All universes, of which there are an infinite number, are arranged in the same way.

MUDRA, Skt. (*phyag rgya*, Tib.). Lit., a ritual gesture, sign, seal. There are four types of mudra, which have numerous levels of meaning according to the context.

NAGA, Skt. (*klu*, Tib.). A magical and powerful creature frequently figuring in the Buddhist and Hindu worldview. Nagas are associated with serpents and are said to inhabit the watery element or regions below the surface of the earth.

NAMKHAI NYINGPO (*nam mkha'i snying po*). One of the foremost disciples of Guru Padmasambhava. A great translator, monk, and siddha of the Nub clan whose main seat was Lhodrak Kharchu.

NAMRI TSENPO (*gnam ri btsan po*). Tibetan king, father of the king Songtsen Gampo.

NGAYAB, Tib. (Chamara, Skt.). The name of the subcontinent lying to the south and west of the continent of Jambu (our world) according to Buddhist cosmology (*see* Mount Meru). It is here that the Buddha-field of Guru Rinpoche is located.

NIRMANAKAYA. *See* Trikaya

NIRVANA, Skt. (*myang 'das*, Tib.). Lit., the state beyond suffering. This term indicates the various levels of enlightenment as set forth in both the Shravakayana and Mahayana teachings.

NONRETURNER. A level of spiritual attainment after which it is impossible to fall again into the sufferings of samsara.

NYATRI TSENPO. According to Buddhist tradition, the first king of Tibet. He was of Indian origin and is credited with the construction of the first stone edifice in Tibet, the tower of Yumbulakhar.

NYINGMA (*rnying ma*, Tib.). The ancient tradition. The first and mother school of Tibetan Buddhism, so called in contrast with the subsequent schools founded at a later date.

NYINGTIK (*snying thig,* Tib.). The innermost teachings of the pith-instruction section of Dzogpa Chenpo, or Great Perfection.

OATH-BOUND. *See* dharmapala

ODDIYANA. *See* Orgyen

ORCS, OGRES, AND CANNIBALS (*srin po*, Tib.; *rakshasa*, Skt.). A class of dangerous, flesh-devouring nonhuman beings figuring in the Hindu and Buddhist worldview.

ORGYEN. Also called Oddiyana, a country to the northwest of ancient India, nowadays identified as the Swat Valley in Kashmir. It was here that Guru Padmasambhava was born.

ORGYEN SAMBHA. Another name of Guru Padmasambhava.

PADMA THÖDRENGTSEL (*pad ma thod 'phreng rtsal*, Tib.). Lit., Mighty Lotus Garlanded with Skulls. A name of Guru Padmasambhava.

PADMASAMBHAVA (*pad ma 'byung gnas,* Tib.). Lit., Lotus-Born. The Indian Master of the Mantras who is said to be been born miraculously, appearing in a lotus flower in the land of Orgyen. He was predicted by the Buddha Shakyamuni in several sutras and tantras. In the ninth century and at the invitation of King Trisong Detsen, he quelled the forces obstructing the spread of Buddhism in Tibet and introduced and nurtured there the teachings of the Vajrayana. Some of his other names mentioned in this text are Lotus Guru, Guru Rinpoche or Precious Guru, Precious Master, Guru Drakpo, Guru or Lord of Orgyen, Master of Orgyen, Orgyen Sambha, Guru Senge Dradok, Dorje Drolö, Padma Thödrengtsel. For the detailed story of his life, see *The Lotus-Born*: *The Life Story of Padmasambhava*, by Yeshe Tsogyal (Boston & London: Shambhala Publications, 1993).

PANDITA, Skt. A scholar, someone learned in the five traditional sciences. *See* five sciences

PARAMITA. *See* perfections

PATH (*lam*, Tib.). In both the Mahayana and Hinayana (though differently in each case), progress towards enlightenment is described in terms of five paths or degrees of attainment. The paths are called, progressively, Accumulation, Joining, Seeing, Meditation, and No More Learning. Bodhisattvas on the Mahayana paths of Accumulation and Joining are referred to as "ordinary" or "mundane" since their practice has not yet brought them beyond samsara. Those on the levels of the Mahayana Path of Seeing and Meditation (in which emptiness is directly perceived) are called "noble" or "superior," i.e., Aryas. *See also* grounds

PERFECTIONS (six or ten) (*pha rol tu phyin pa*, Tib.; paramita, Skt.). These represent the fundamental practices of the Mahayana path. The six are Generosity, Ethical Discipline, Patience, Diligence, Concentration, and Wisdom. The ten consist of the six just mentioned but with the last perfection of wisdom broken down into the aspects of Means (*thabs*), Strength (*stobs*), Aspiration (*smon lam*), and Primordial Wisdom (*ye shes*). They are called transcendent because, in conjunction with wisdom, they lead beyond samsara.

PHURBA (*phur ba*, Tib.). A ritual implement somewhat resembling a dagger or peg. Also the Tibetan name of the yidam Vajrakila or Vajrakumara.

PRAJÑAPARAMITA, Skt. (*shes rab kyi pha rol tu phyin pa*, Tib.). Transcendent knowledge, direct realization of emptiness, and thus the Mother of all the Buddhas. Referred to also as wisdom that has gone beyond.

PRETAS, Skt. (*yi dvags*, Tib.). Hungry ghosts, spirits tormented by lack of nourishment. The pretas constitute one of the six classes of beings in samsara.

PURE FIELD (*dag pa'i zhing*, Tib.). *See* Buddha-field

PURE LAND (*dag pa'i zhing*, Tib.). *See* Buddha-field

RAINBOW BODY (*'ja lus*, Tib.). The rainbow body, synonymous with the diamond body (*rdo rje sku*), is the name given to the attainment of Buddhahood according to the practices of the Great Perfection of the Nyingma school. There are three kinds of rainbow body: the rainbow body so called (*'ja lus*), the radiant body (*'od sku*), and the rainbow body of great transference (*'ja lus 'pho ba chen po*). The first is attained through the practice of Trekchö. When someone accomplished in this practice dies, his or her body will be seen to emit rainbow light and diminish (often very considerably) in size. After about a week, if left undisturbed, the body will disappear completely, leaving behind only hair and finger- and toenails. Yogis have demonstrated this attainment well into modern times, indeed the present day. The Radiant Body is accomplished through a Dzogchen practice called thögal, and at death the body is transformed directly into light, leaving behind no remainder whatever. In the case of the rainbow body of great transference (*'ja lus 'pho ba chen po*), the accomplished practitioner transforms his physical body into an indestructible form composed of rainbow light and continues to live for centuries, remaining visible for as much this is of benefit for sentient beings. When there is no further purpose for such a manifestation, the practitioner dissolves his or her body into a radiant body and merges into the Primordial Ground.

RAKSHASAS, Skt. (*srin po*, Tib.). *See* orcs, ogres, and cannibals

RATNASAMBHAVA, Skt. (*rin chen 'byung gnas*, Tib.). Lit., Source of Jewels. The Buddha of the Jewel Family, corresponding to the wisdom of equality, which is the pure nature of the aggregate of feeling and affliction of pride, and is linked with the enlightened activity of increase.

SACRED LANDS AND PLACES. The twenty-four countries, thirty-two locations, and eight charnel grounds inhabited by dakas and dakinis. They have a psychophysical significance and are correlated with certain points of the subtle body.

SADHANA, Skt. (*sgrub thabs*, Tib.). Method of accomplishment. A tantric meditation practice involving visualization of a deity and the recitation of the associated mantra.

SAMADHI, Skt. (*bsam gtan*, Tib.). Meditative absorption or concentration. There are four levels of samadhi corresponding to the form realm. *See also* threefold concentration

SAMANTABHADRA, Skt. (*kun tu bzang po*, Tib.). The utterly enlightened mind, pure, immutable, omnipresent, and unobstructed. It is symbolized in the form of a Buddha, naked and colored the deep blue of endless space. Samantabhadra is the origin of the tantric transmission of the Nyingma school.

SAMANTABHADRI, Skt. (*kun tu bzang mo*, Tib.). Consort of Samantabhadra, symbol of emptiness.

SAMAYA, Skt. (*dam tshig*, Tib.). The sacramental bond and commitment in the Vajrayana established between the master and the disciple to whom he or she gives empowerment. Samaya also refers to the sacred links between the disciples of the same master and between the disciples and their practice.

SAMBHOGAKAYA, Skt. *See* Trikaya

SAMSARA, Skt. (*'khor ba*, Tib.). The wheel or round of existence; the state of being unenlightened, in which the mind, enslaved by the three poisons of Desire, Anger, and Ignorance, moves uncontrolled from one state to another, passing through an endless stream of psychophysical experiences, all of which are characterized by suffering. *See* world of desire *and* six realms of samsara

SAMYE (*bsam yas,* Tib.). Lit., beyond imagination. The complex of temples built by the king Trisong Detsen beside the Tsangpo River near Hepori in Central Tibet.

SANGHA, Skt. (*dge 'dun*, Tib.). The community of all Dharma practitioners, from the ordinary beings up to the aryas, who have attained the path of Seeing and beyond.

SARASVATI (*dbyangs can ma*, Tib.). The female deity of art, science, music, and speech, traditionally regarded as the original teacher of the Sanskrit language.

SECRET MANTRA; SECRET MANTRAYANA (*gsang sngags*, Tib.). *See* Vajrayana

SHAKYAMUNI. Gautama, the historical Buddha of our age, the founder of Buddhism.

SHANTARAKSHITA. Also traditionally referred to as Khenpo Bodhisattva, the Bodhisattva Abbot. A great Indian master of Mahayana Buddhism, abbot of the university of Nalanda, invited to Tibet by King Trisong Detsen.

SHRAVAKA, Skt. (*nyan thos*, Tib.). One who hears the teachings of the Buddha, transmits them to others, and practices them. The characteristic goal of the Shravaka is Arhatship, a personal, individual liberation from samsara, rather than the perfect enlightenment of Buddhahood for the sake of all beings. Shravakas are practitioners of the Hinayana or Root Vehicle, hence Shravakayana.

SIDDHA, Skt. (*grub thob*, Tib.). One who has gained accomplishments through the practice of the Vajrayana.

SIDDHI, Skt. (*dngos grub*, Tib.). *See* accomplishments

SINS OF IMMEDIATE PERDITION (*mtshams med lnga*, Tib.). Five negative actions that are so grave that they provoke immediate descent into the lower realms after death. They are killing one's mother; killing one's father; killing an Arhat; with evil intention causing the blood of a Buddha to flow; and provoking a schism in the spiritual community. Whoever commits such an action is said to be reborn in the Hell of Torment Unsurpassed immediately after death, without even passing through the bardo state.

SIX REALMS OF SAMSARA (*rigs drug*, Tib.). The experience of beings in samsara is traditionally schematized into six general categories, referred to as realms or worlds. They are the result of previous action or karma. None of these states is satisfactory, through the degree of suffering in them varies. The three upper or fortunate realms, where suffering is alleviated by temporary pleasures or where pleasure predominates, are the heavens of the mundane gods, the realms of the asuras or demigods, and the world of human beings. The three lower realms, in which suffering predominates over all other experiences, are those of the animals, the hungry ghosts, and the hells.

SIXTY QUALITIES OF MELODIOUS SPEECH (*gsungs dbyangs yan lag drug bcu*, Tib.). Sixty qualities described differently in the sutras and tantras.

SKILLFUL MEANS AND WISDOM. An important pairing in Mahayana Buddhism. It refers to the wisdom (*shes rab*) of emptiness, and the voidness aspect of phenomena, together with the skillful means (*thabs*) of compassion, and the appearance aspect of phenomena. Skillful means and wisdom are indissociable.

SONGTSEN GAMPO (*srong btsan sgam po*). The first Buddhist king of Tibet, who flourished in the seventh century and is said to have been a manifestation of the Bodhisattva Avalokiteshvara, or Chenrezig. Four reigns separate him from Trisong Detsen (eighth and ninth centuries).

SOUTHWEST (*lho nub*, Tib.). *See* Ngayab

STUPA, Skt. (*mchod rten*, Tib.). Lit., support of offerings. Symbolic representation of the Buddha's mind. The most typical Buddhist monument, frequently containing the relics of enlightened beings and varying in size. It often has a square base, a rounded midsection, and a tall conical upper section topped by a sun and moon.

SUGATA, Skt. (*bde bar gshegs pa*, Tib.). Lit., One Who Has Gone to, and Proceeds in, Bliss. An epithet of the Buddhas.

SUMERU, Skt. *See* Mount Meru

SUTRA, Skt. (*mdo*, Tib.). Buddhist scripture, a transcribed discourse of the Buddha. There are Mahayana sutras and Hinayana or Shravakayana sutras.

SVABHAVIKAKAYA. *See* Trikaya

SWASTIKA, Skt. (*gyung drung*, Tib.). Throughout this text the swastika appears as the symbol of the Bön. It is also used, however, in the context of Vajrayana Buddhism and represents immutability and indestructibility.

TANTRA, Skt. (*rgyud*, Tib.). A term with many levels of meaning. Here it mainly refers to the esoteric texts of Vajrayana Buddhism expounding the natural purity of the mind.

TARA, Skt. (*sgrol ma*, Tib.). According to the level of the teaching, a female Sambhogakaya or Bodhisattva, manifestation of great compassion, displaying peaceful and wrathful forms. The most well known and practiced are green and white Tara. "Tara of the Seven Eyes," mentioned in the first chapter, is a reference to White Tara, who is always depicted with a third eye in her forehead and eyes on the palms of her hands and feet, symbolic of her all-seeing compassion.

TATHAGATA, Skt. (*de bzhin gshegs pa*, Tib.). Lit., One Who Has Gone Thus. An epithet of the Buddhas.

TEN DIRECTIONS (*phyogs bcu*, Tib.). The four cardinal directions together with the four intermediate directions, the zenith, and the nadir.

TEN TRANSCENDENT VIRTUES. *See* Perfections

TEN VIRTUES (*dge ba bcu*, Tib.). In the Buddhist teachings, virtuous behavior is systematized into ten wholesome activities. Three concern the body and consist of the abstention from killing, stealing, and sexual misconduct; four concern the speech faculty and are to refrain from lying, divisive speech, violent and aggressive speech, and worthless chatter; three concern the mind and are to refrain from covetousness, ill-will, and wrong views.

TENMA GODDESSES (*brten ma bcu gnyis*, Tib.). Twelve spirits, associated with mountain ranges in Tibet, who in the presence of Guru Padmasambhava vowed to protect the religion and the people of Tibet.

TERMA. *See* Treasure

THÖNMI SAMBHOTA. A minister of the king Songtsen Gampo. After studying in India, he composed the grammar of the Tibetan language and devised the alphabet.

THREE DIMENSIONS OF EXISTENCE (*sa gsum*, Tib.). The world of humans and animals inhabiting the earth's surface, the realm of the gods and spirits in the heavens above or the upper airs, and the kingdom of the nagas, etc., in the subterranean regions. Translated also as "three levels of the world."

THREE DOORS. Body, speech, and mind.

THREE FAMILIES. *See* Lords of the three Families

THREE JEWELS (*dkon mchog gsum*, Tib.). The Buddha, the Dharma, and the Spiritual Community (Sangha), in which a Buddhist takes refuge.

THREE LEVELS OF THE WORLD (*sa gsum*, Tib.). *See* three dimensions of existence

THREE ROOTS (*rtsa gsum*, Tib.). The three objects of refuge as expressed in the tantric teachings. These are the Guru, who is the root of blessings; the Yidam, the root of accomplishment; and the Dakinis, the root of activities.

THREE WORLDS (*khams gsum*, Tib.). A categorization of samsaric existence: (1) the world of desire, consisting of the six realms, from the hells up to the first six spheres of the god realm, (2) the divine realm of form, and (3) the divine realm of nonform.

THREEFOLD CONCENTRATION. The three highest forms of concentration cultivated by Bodhisattvas and begun on the path of Seeing. Mirage-Like concentration (*sgyu ma lta bu'i ting nge 'dzin*) is an absorption in which the Bodhisattvas on the seven impure grounds perceive all phenomena as illusory. The concentration of heroic fearlessness (*dpa' bar 'gro ba'i ting nge 'dzin*), which is possessed by Bodhisattvas on the pure grounds, eliminates all obstructions to enlightened activity. The vajra-like concentration (*rdo rje lta bu'i ting nge 'dzin*) eliminates the most subtle obscurations veiling the perfect state of Buddhahood. It is virtually synonymous with the enlightenment itself, for only the Boddhisattvas who are at the very end of the tenth ground possess it.

TORMA (*gtor ma*, Tib.). "That which eliminates the dualistic clinging of hope and fear (*gtor*) and unites one with the absolute nature of phenomena (*ma*)." A ritual object of varying shapes and composed of a variety of substances. Depending on the context, the torma is considered as an offering, a symbolic representation of a deity, a source of blessings, or even as a weapon for dispelling obstacles.

TORMENT UNSURPASSED (*mnar med*, Tib.; Avici, Skt.). The lowest of the hot hells, according to Buddhist teaching, characterized by the most intense and protracted form of suffering.

TRANDRUK. (*Khra 'brug*). One of the most important sacred sites of Tibet, a temple built by the king Songtsan Gampo to the south of Lhasa.

TREASURE (*gter ma*, Tib.). Teachings and sacred objects concealed by Guru Rinpoche and other enlightened beings, to be revealed later, at a time when they would be most beneficial. The Terma teachings are composed in the symbolic letters of the dakinis, or other writing, and consist sometimes of a few words, sometimes of an entire text. The Treasures were concealed in the nature of the elements—water, rocks, etc.—or in the minds of the disciples. When they were with Guru Rinpoche, these disciples fully realized the meaning of these teachings and are for this reason the only ones who can rediscover them in the course of subsequent incarnations. The purpose of the symbolic script is in fact to awaken in the tertön's mind the memory of the teaching entrusted to him or her by Guru Rinpoche.

TRI RALPACHEN (*khri ral pa can*, Tib.). The third major Buddhist king of Tibet. He lived in the eleventh century and instigated the systematization of Tibetan grammar and vocabulary for the purposes of translation of texts from Sanskrit. He was assassinated by his brother Lang Darma. He is said to have been a manifestation of the Bodhisattva Vajrapani.

TRIKAYA, Skt. (*sku gsum*, Tib.). According to the teachings of the Mahayana, the transcendent reality of perfect Buddhahood is described in terms of two, three, four, or five bodies or kayas. The two bodies, in the first case, are the Dharmakaya, the Body of Truth, and the Rupakaya, the Body of Form. The Dharmakaya is the absolute, "emptiness" aspect of Buddhahood. The Rupakaya is subdivided (thus giving rise to the three bodies mentioned above) into the Sambhogakaya, the Body of Perfect Enjoyment, and the Nirmanakaya, the Body of Manifestation. The Sambhogakaya, the spontaneous clarity aspect of Buddhahood, is perceptible only to highly realized beings. The Nirmanakaya, compassion aspect, is perceptible to ordinary beings and appears in our world most often, though not necessarily, in human form. The system of four bodies consists of the three just referred to, together with the Svabhavikakaya, the Body of Suchness, which refers to the union of the previous three. Occasionally there is mention of five bodies—the three kayas together with the immutable diamond or vajra body (the indestructible aspect of Buddhahood) and the Body of Complete Enlightenment (aspect of qualities).

TRIPLE GEM. *See* Three Jewels

TRISONG DETSEN (*khri srong sde'u btsan*, 790–844). Thirty-eighth king of Tibet, second of the three great religous kings, said to be a manifestation of the Bodhisattva Mañjushri.

TSEN (*btsan*, Tib.). A powerful, wrathful spirit.

TUMMO (*gtum mo*, Tib.). Inner heat generated in the course of a certain yogic practice of the same name, belonging to the level of Anuyoga.

TWELVE INTERDEPENDENT LINKS (*rten 'brel*, Tib.; *pratityasamutpada*, Skt.). The twelvefold chain of interdependent arising, which defines the whole round of samsaric experience. These are (1) ignorance (*ma rig pa*), (2) conditioning factors (*'du byed*), (3) consciousness (*rnam shes*), (4) form and mind (*ming dang gzugs*), (5) the six senses (*skye mched*), (6) contact (*reg pa*), (7) feeling (*tshor ba*), (8) desire (*sred pa*), (9) craving (*len pa*), (10) becoming (*srid pa*), (11) birth (*skye ba*), (12) aging and death (*rga shi*).

TWOFOLD GOAL (*don gnyis*, Tib.). Enlightenment for oneself and the immediate and ultimate benefit of others.

UDUMBARA, Skt. A mythical lotus, extremely large and rare. It is said to flower only once in a single kalpa.

UNFAILING MEMORY (*gzungs*, Tib.). Grounded in the realization of emptiness, and cultivated on the Path of Seeing and above, unfailing memory is one of the characteristics of the highest attainment. Generally speaking, one can distinguish eight (in this text seven) different powers of unfailing memory, such as the power to give an explanation of and teaching on one word for an infinite length of time.

UPADESHA, Skt. (*man ngag*, Tib.). An essential instruction for the practice of tantra.

UPATANTRA, Skt. (*spyod rgyud*, Tib.). Known also as Ubhaya or Charyatantra. It exposes the philosophical view of the Yogatantra and the discipline of the Kriyatantra.

USHNISHA, Skt. (*gtsug tor*, Tib.). The crown protuberance that is a mark of Buddhahood and is to be seen on all traditional representations of the Buddha in more or less realistic or stylized form.

VAIROCHANA, Skt. (*rnam par snang mdzad*, Tib.). The Dhyani Buddha of the Tathagata Family, corresponding to the wisdom of all-embracing space, which is the pure nature of the aggregate of form and affliction of bewilderment, and is linked with the spontaneous accomplishment of the four enlightened activities. *See* five Families

VAJRA, Skt. (*rdo rje*, Tib.). Diamond or vajra weapon. The symbol of indestructibility and of compassion. A vajra is also a small implement used in conjunction with a bell (*dril bu*, the symbol of the wisdom of emptiness) during tantric rituals.

VAJRA CONCENTRATION. *See* threefold concentration

VAJRA KINDRED (*rdo rje mched grogs*, Tib.). Practitioners linked together by tantric samaya.

VAJRA POSTURE (*rdo rje dkyil krung*, Tib.). A way of sitting, with legs crossed and feet placed on thighs, in which the body is placed in a state of equilibrium especially favorable to the practice of meditation.

VAJRADHARA, Skt. (*rdo rje 'chang*, Tib.). A Sambhogakaya form of Buddha representing the union of the five Buddha Families. Also used as a title of respect for the lama, the spiritual master.

VAJRAKILA, Skt. (*rdo rje phur ba*, Tib.). The principal yidam of the Nyingma school. Vajrakila or Vajrakilaya is a wrathful manifestion of Vajrasattva.

VAJRAKUMARA, Skt. *See* Vajrakila

VAJRAPANI, Skt. (*phyag na rdo rje*, Tib.). The Bodhisattva who personifies the Mind of all the Buddhas.

VAJRASANA, Skt. Vajra Seat. *See* Diamond Throne

VAJRASATTVA, Skt. (*rdo rje sems dpa',* Tib.). Lit., Indestructible Being. The Buddha of the Vajra Family, corresponding to the mirror-like wisdom that is the pure nature of the aggregate of consciousness and affliction of aversion, and is linked with the enlightened activity of pacifying.

VAJRAVARAHI, Skt. (*rdo rje phag mo*, Tib.). Female yidam deity, usually depicted with a sow's head protruding from the crown of her head. She is the Sambhogakaya form of Samantabhadri.

VAJRAYANA, Skt. (*rdo rje theg pa*, Tib.). Diamond Vehicle. Corpus of teachings and practices based on the tantras, scriptures that discourse upon the primordial purity of the mind. It is the vehicle of result, as opposed to the causal vehicle of Shravakas and Bodhisattvas. Synonym of *Mantrayana*.

VAJRAYOGINI, Skt. (*rdo rje rnal 'byor ma*, Tib.). Female Sambhogakaya form of Buddha.

VARAHI. Synonym of *Vajravarahi*.

VEHICLES, SIX AND NINE (*theg pa*, Tib.). According to the teachings of the Nyingma school, the teachings of the Buddha are classified into nine sections or vehicles. These are the three vehicles of sutric teachings, Shravakayana, Pratyekabuddhayana, and Bodhisattvayana; the three outer tantric vehicles of Kriya, Upa, and Yoga; and the three inner tantric vehicles of Maha, Anu, and Ati. The six vehicles refer to the three sutric vehicles and to the three outer tantras.

VIDYADHARA, Skt. (*rig 'dzin*, Tib.). Lit., Knowledge-Holder. A being of high spiritual attainment. According to the Nyingma tradition, there are four levels of Vidyadhara, corresponding to the ten levels of realization of the Sutrayana and the state of Buddhahood. They are (1) the Vidyadhara with residues, (2) the Vidyadhara with power over life, (3) the Mahamudra Vidyadhara, (4) the Spontaneous Vidyadhara.

VIMALAMITRA (*dri med bshes gnyen*, Tib.). One of the greatest masters and panditas of Indian Buddhism who brought the Dzogchen teachings to Tibet.

VINAYA, Skt. (*'dul ba*, Tib.). The ethical teachings of Buddhism, particularly in relation to the code of monastic discipline.

VISHUDDHA, Skt. (*yang dag*, Tib.). A heruka of the Vajra Family, representing the mind aspect; one the main yidams of the Mahayoga tantra.

VOICE OF BRAHMA (*tshangs pa'i dbyangs kyi yan lag drug bcu,* Tib.). Sixty aspects of melodious speech, differently described in both sutra and tantra.

WISDOM, PRIMAL (*ye shes*, Tib.). Pure awareness, spontaneously present in the minds of beings from beginningless time.

WORLD OF DESIRE (*'dod khams*, Tib.). A general term referring to the six samsaric realms: hells, world of hungry ghosts, animals, humans, asuras, and the first six levels of the divine abodes of the gods.

YIDAM DEITY (*yi dam*, Tib.). A form of a Buddha used as a support in meditation in the Mantrayana. Such deities may be masculine or feminine, peaceful or wrathful, and are regarded as being inseparable from the mind of the meditator.

YOGATANTRA, Skt. (*rnal 'byor rgyud*, Tib.). The third of the outer sections of tantra. It emphasizes meditation, the importance of the mind, in order to realize emptiness, without neglecting, however the external discipline of the body and speech.

ZHANG ZHUNG. A region in the west of Tibet, the traditional birthplace of the Bön religion.

Index

About the Padmakara Translation Group

PADMAKARA is a team of translators and editors of various nationalities specializing in the rendering of Tibetan texts and teachings mainly into English, French, German, and Spanish. Since 1987, under the guidance of Pema Wangyal Rinpoche and Jigme Khyentse Rinpoche and other Tibetan scholars and lamas, they have been translating and publishing classical and contemporary Tibetan literature, thus opening up a vast treasure of sacred knowledge for a Western readership. (Educated in Western languages and culture, the translators are themselves committed Buddhists who, in the environment of long meditation retreats, have had the opportunity to train in the experiential side of Buddhist practice and receive extensive instructions from accomplished spiritual teachers.) Padmakara has a reputation for accurate, clear, and accessible translations that are faithful to the spirit and style of the tradition.

Translations into English

The Excellent Path of Enlightenment by Dilgo Khyentse, (Editions Padmakara, 1987)

The Wish-Fulfilling Jewel by Dilgo Khyentse (Shambhala Publications, 1988)

Dilgo Khyentse Rinpoche (Editions Padmakara, 1990)

Enlightened Courage by Dilgo Khyentse (Editions Padmakara, 1992; North American ed.: Snow Lion Publications, 1994)

The Heart Treasure of the Enlightened Ones by Dilgo Khyentse and Patrul Rinpoche (Shambhala Publications, 1992)

A Flash of Lightning in the Dark of Night by the Dalai Lama (Shambhala Publications, 1993)

Wisdom: Two Buddhist Commentaries by Khenchen Kunzang Palden and Minyak Kunzang Sönam (Editions Padmakara, 1993)

The Words of My Perfect Teacher by Patrul Rinpoche (HarperCollins, 1994; Sage Altamira, 1998; Shambhala Publications, 1998)

The Life of Shabkar: Autobiography of a Tibetan Yogi (S.U.N.Y. Press, 1994)

Journey to Enlightenment by Matthieu Ricard (Aperture, 1996)

The Way of the Bodhisattva: A Translation of the Bodhicharyavatara, by Shantideva (Shambhala Publications, 1997)

For further information on Padmakara translations and publications, please contact:

Editions Padmakara
24290 St. Léon Sur Vézère
France

Padmakara
109 Mowbray Drive
Kew Gardens, NY 11415